The Promise of POWER

THE EMERGENCE OF

CONTRIBUTIONS IN LEGAL STUDIES
Series Editor: Paul Murphy

Stability, Security, and Continuity: Mr. Justice Burton and Decision-Making in the Supreme Court, 1945-1958
Mary Frances Berry

Philosophical Law: Authority, Equality, Adjudication, Privacy
Richard Bronaugh, editor

Law, Soldiers, and Combat
Peter Karsten

Appellate Courts and Lawyers: Information Gathering in the Adversary System
Thomas B. Marvell

Charting the Future: The Supreme Court Responds to a Changing Society, 1890-1920
John E. Semonche

The Promise of POWER

THE LEGAL PROFESSION IN MASSACHUSETTS 1760-1840

Gerard W. Gawalt

Contributions in Legal Studies, Number 6

Greenwood Press

Westport, Connecticut • London, England

Library of Congress Cataloging in Publication Data

Gawalt, Gerard W
The promise of power.

(Contributions in legal studies ; no. 6
ISSN 0147-1074)
Bibliography: p.
Includes index.
1. Lawyers—Massachusetts—History.
2. Practice of law—Massachusetts—History.
I. Title. II. Series.
KFM2478'.G38 340'.09744 78-57764
ISBN 0-313-20612-0

Library of Congress Catalog Card Number: 78-57764
ISBN: 0-313-20612-0
ISSN: 0147-1074

First published in 1979

Greenwood Press, Inc.
51 Riverside Avenue, Westport, Connecticut 06880

Printed in the United States of America

10 9 8 7 6 5 4 3 2 1

With thanks
to
my wife Jane Cavanaugh
and
our children
Susan, Ann, and Ellen

Contents

Tables

Acknowledgments

I happily acknowledge the guiding influence of my professional adviser, George A. Billias of Clark University, whose encouraging spirit was as important as his expert advice. I especially want to thank Eugene Sheridan, Maxwell Bloomfield, and Paul H. Smith for commenting on several drafts of this book. I also benefited from the help of Milton J. Klein, John Cushing, Stanley Katz, George L. Haskins, and David Flaherty, who read and commented on various sections. I would also like to thank the staffs of the American Antiquarian Society, Worcester, Massachusetts, and the Massachusetts Historical Society, Boston, for their unstinting service. The court clerks of Worcester County, Suffolk County, and Essex County, Massachusetts and Kennebec County and Lincoln County, Maine, went beyond the call of duty in aiding my work. My thanks also go to Sylvia Sheridan for typing two final drafts. I would like to thank the editors of the *American Journal of Legal History* for permission to reprint parts of two articles that appear throughout this work. My deepest gratitude goes to my wife, Jane, who helped me struggle through all of the drafts of this book, and my parents, John and Regina Gawalt, for their life-long encouragement and support.

The Promise of POWER

Introduction

Two men rode unsurely through the unbroken wilderness, halting periodically to search for the blaze-marked trail. When they emerged at the frontier shiretown of Pownalboro, Massachusetts, they rode swiftly ahead to the rudimentary courthouse. These were not backwoodsmen reporting from a scouting mission but men of the law—Boston lawyers riding the circuit of the superior court of judicature. In the 1760s, both their province and profession were roughly shaped. Eight decades later both had undergone a remarkable transformation.

If John Adams and his companion had surveyed their situation in 1765, they would have found fewer than fifty trained lawyers laboring in a British colonial population of 244,149. Commerce and cosmopolitanism had yet to emerge from the coastal shipping centers of this basically agricultural, homogeneous society. British law was argued in a court system conferred by royal charter in 1691 and dominated by the province's merchant elite. The practice of law was barely a profession—politically, economically, socially, and numerically weak. These unorganized lawyers with their uneven training and unstable incomes seemed an unlikely group to dominate society.

Eighty years later, more than six hundred lawyers operated in an independent state of 737,699 people, comprising one of the most cosmopolitan, commercial, and industrial sections of an increasingly pluralistic American society. Although agriculture and village life remained important, they were becoming islands in the rising tide of industrialization in Massachusetts. American law dominated arguments in courts that were staffed and controlled by trained lawyers. Politically powerful, economically and socially secure, the legal profession performed vital roles in the state's economy and government, despite episodic attacks of antielitist and entrepreneurial reformers.

This book analyzes the growth of a weak, corporate guild into a powerful, individualistic profession. It details lawyers' pioneering use of a voluntary, self-help organization—the bar association. It explains their reliance on education for achieving technical training, internal control, and external recognition of their authority. It documents how lawyers co-opted the leadership of radical reform movements, blunted their cutting edge, and ultimately used them to strengthen the role of lawyers, judges, and law in society. It demonstrates their political coup d'état during the revolutionary and early national periods.

Certainly lawyers were not alone. A general movement toward occupational specialization and professionalization was one of the dominant themes of the period from 1760 to 1840. Not only lawyers but doctors, scientists, and college instructors insisted upon definite requirements for entrance into their professions. By these means they could eliminate untrained practitioners, create monopolies controlled by educated specialists, and establish authority for their profession in society at large. The rising concern for education, for example, resulted in plans by reformers for professional training of public school teachers. Art and architecture began to reflect the impact of rigid professional training. Along with the learned professions, farmers and craftsmen also turned to occupational organizations to strengthen their sense of group identification, as well as to share technical information. Agricultural societies served as vehicles for farmers; labor unions performed much the same function for workingmen; doctors had medical societies; and lawyers clustered in bar associations.

In the eighteenth century lawyers sought service as agents of the agrarian-merchant elite. At the same time, they put much effort into molding themselves into a profession of "gentlemen practisers of the law," based on an idealized and slightly out-of-focus view of the English legal profession. Emphasizing the need for a liberal education, training as a legal expert, and graduated initiation into full membership in a mutually supportive fraternity or societal subgroup, they achieved only moderate gains toward their stated goals. Political, economic, and social changes stemming from the revolutionary era changed many lawyers' concept of the ideal lawyer and legal profession. Many urban-cosmopolitan lawyers formed a mutually beneficial alliance with emerging industrialists and radically aggressive commercial leaders. Besides boosting the profession's economic power, this tie gave added impetus to the movement for a centralized classroom or "factory system" of legal education. It also may have tipped the scales against the powers of bar associations when workingmen stigmatized these associations in the eyes of industrialists and their allies by claiming the same exclusionary control over the right to work, wages, and training procedures through unions. Moreover lawyers undoubtedly imbibed the competitive spirit that commercial law began encouraging after 1800, leading some to oppose bar association restrictions on professional competition.

Ultimately it was the lawyers' burgeoning political power in the postrevolutionary era that had a crucial effect on the legal profession. Men began to study law, not to practice it, but as a first step into the political arena. These men were not interested in technical intricacies or local institutional autonomy. Politics involved them in statewide, regional, and national issues. When these men became bar leaders, they could visualize the need for statewide regulations. They realized the possible fruits of law school education, which emphasized broad principles and theories of law. Such men did not fear centralized, institutional power. They sought it.

Rather than the collapse of the legal profession, the Jacksonian years marked the emergence of the modern legal profession in Massachusetts. Its traditional institutions and regulations may have been discredited and disorganized, but control of a judicial system that recognized law as an instrument for social and economic change gave it a vastly expanding role. With the simultaneous breakdown of traditional religious institutional power in the Bay State, as symbolized by the disestablishment of the Congregational church and the end of legally required church tithes in 1833, a fundamental shift had occurred in Massachusetts society. Law was replacing religion as the dominant force in Massachusetts, and lawyers were its high priests.

Because lawyers had replaced clerics as the controlling force at Harvard College by the War of 1812, innovative lawyers were able to establish professional training there. As a result, when the vestiges of bar association control over admission and apprenticeship training standards were eliminated in the 1830s, "enlightened" and scientifically minded lawyers had already transferred their hopes for maintaining professional excellence to the university law school.

The solidification of lawyers' economic and social status buttressed their power in government and education. Statistical studies of marriage patterns, paternal occupations, education, and both occupational and geographic mobility combined with analyses of professional caseloads, income, and taxable wealth provide a distinct professional profile. By the early nineteenth century, lawyers had become part of an exclusive, prosperous, and expanding professional elite, part of the upper-middle class. At the same time that institutional barriers were collapsing, entrance into the profession was increasingly restricted by the invisible barriers of family connection, the cost of education, and the expenses of beginning a professional practice, making law another occupation providing more horizontal than vertical mobility.

These broad conclusions might easily lead to visions of a unified occupational group, composed of standardized members with nearly identical plans and goals. This was far from reality. Within these general developments, lawyers bitterly battled over legal education, the system of law, the purposes and use of bar associations, and even the nature of the profession. They were divided geographically, politically, economically, and along lines of occupational specialization. These divisions contributed to new professional developments, but the ability to exercise power as a corporate group was undermined and eventually lost.

The individualism that marks the American legal profession today can be traced to the triumph of competition over the corporate spirit that had motivated eighteenth-century organizers of the professional bar in Massachusetts. When the bar associations proved to be too limiting and narrowly focused, many lawyers willingly abandoned the guild system. And to the discerning minds of the 1830s, the protective myth of a unitary profession had evaporated, and economic, ideological, geographical, and political divisions within the profession stood undisguised. The Massachusetts legal profession had been transformed from a small, occupational group on the periphery of British governing circles to a major profession with a powerful impact on the mainstream of the American political, economic, and social systems.

1

The Profession Emerges

In mid-eighteenth-century Massachusetts, trained lawyers drew up plans to create a highly trained, self-regulated, corporate profession modeled on the rigidly structured occupation of law in England. They expected this Anglicization and professionalization to elevate their social and economic status, winning recognition for themselves as legal experts and "gentlemen of the bar."[1] Colonial lawyers, however, faced far different cultural, political, and economic realities than their British counterparts did.

In England a mature society recognized the need for legal specialists. In Massachusetts Bay, the environment had been hostile to professional men of law. Leaders and a majority of the people had prided themselves on being ruled first by the law of God and only second by the law of the civil courts. They had lived in a rural, underdeveloped society that had seldom needed the few trained lawyers who had practiced in their courts. By the end of the seventeenth century, the province's economy had just begun to demand experts in commercial and land law. The commercial class that generally utilizes legal technicians did not expand throughout the colony until well into the eighteenth century. The rural and noncommercial people usually lacked the financial ability or never perceived the need to retain a professional lawyer.

Court records and studies of the law in Massachusetts reveal the laymen's skilled uses of the judicial process.[2] Attempts to eliminate or severely restrict the operation of a fee-collecting legal group were not meant to eliminate reliance on law. Trained lawyers did not bring more dedication to the law than laymen, but they did have a greater technical knowledge of the law and legal procedures. Intellectual achievement and procedural skills became the lawyer's justification for demanding an occupational monopoly and professional autonomy.

A long tradition of antilawyer prejudice in both Britain and its colonies opposed the acceptance of lawyers. Puritans carried a distrust of the "king's attornies" from England to Massachusetts Bay, adding the religious view that the administration of justice in a "Godly community" should be based on individual conscience and the word of God more than on legal precedents. Questions of law that were theological as well as legal did not require the counsel of common-law lawyers.[3]

Puritan leaders tried to prevent lawyers from practicing. In part this reflected their concerns that the advocacy role of lawyers might conflict with morality, because an attorney would be obliged to defend his client regardless of guilt or innocence. On a more personal level, John Winthrop's experience of being forced out of legal practice in England because of his religious beliefs may have led the provincial leader to question the judicious nature of English law and legal practice. Moreover governing officers in several colonies feared the dissension that open court litigation might produce. During times of insecurity and unrest, Virginia and Maryland, as well as Massachusetts, banned the practice of law by professional pleaders.[4]

Early residents of Massachusetts quickly reacted to possible irregularities in legal practice. When Thomas Lechford, the colony's only practicing trained lawyer and a religious opponent of the ruling officials, stood accused of attempting to influence a jury out of court in 1639, the court not only disbarred and censured him but ultimately forced him to return to England. Much of the opposition stemmed from his criticism of the ruling elite's church polity, but Lechford's occupation offered a popular justification for his ostracism.[5]

During the next forty years, lawyers received the narrowest recognition through efforts to restrict the practice of law. The Body of Liberties, the colony's first written law code, for example, forbade the payment of fees to legal practitioners. This was repealed in 1648, and a slight basis for a legitimate advocacy role for lawyers appeared the next year in a law that prohibited magistrates from offering legal advice to plaintiffs or defendants in cases before them. A 1656 statute that proposed to fine "attornies" who argued their causes for more than an hour reflected the courts' begrudging tolerance of lawyers. Then in 1673 the general court acknowledged the role of lawyers by authorizing any plaintiff or defendant to appoint an attorney "under his hand and seale."[6]

Some of these early lawyers of Massachusetts consistently reappeared in court records, indicating that they were regular practitioners. But most tended to be a kinsman or friend of the client. In occasional Suffolk County cases, a woman argued her own cause in the 1670s, particularly in the absence or death of her husband. These men had mixed qualifications. Training for the law was highly uneven and was left to personal discretion, with no prescribed educational standards. Nor did any organization or government institution attempt to prejudge potential practitioners. All corrective measures apparently were remedial. None of the men acting as counsel during the 1670s in Suffolk County, for example, were found to have any legal training and only one, Elisha Cooke, had a college education or the equivalent training in the liberal arts. Magistrates, however, did exercise their right to control attorneys in court and, on at least two separate occasions, forbade men to appear as attorneys because of past activities in doctoring writs, fomenting litigation, or buying debts to bring into court.[7] Despite the absence of a legal profession, court findings represented an intelligent view of English local law with complex pleadings.[8]

A reorganization of the Massachusetts government as a royal colony in 1691 dramatically altered conditions for legal practice. The new court system created more formal demands for legal experts. And increased political connections with England, in conjunction with burgeoning commercial relations, stimulated the use of common law and men trained in the complexities of both local and English law.[9]

Subsequently government increased both its recognition and regulation of lawyers and legal practice, establishing lawyers' dual public and private roles. In 1701 legislation brought lawyers into the courts' official family and established an oath of office for attorneys. Maximum fee schedules were instituted and courts were allowed to tax fees for only one attorney. The scarcity of capable lawyers led to laws in 1708 and 1714 forbidding any party in a suit from hiring more than two lawyers so that the opposing party "may have liberty to retain others of them to assist him, upon his tender of the established fee, which they may not refuse."[10]

As more legally sophisticated court officials in the eighteenth century emphasized the technicalities of the law and pleading, the abilities of superficially trained lawyers were severely tested. Occasionally they failed to provide adequate professional services under the stress. As early as 1720, the general court sought to protect clients from lawyers' errors by a law ordering attorneys to draw a new writ without a fee if a cause was nonsuited due to an error in the writ.[11] Sometimes courts did inquire about an aspirant's moral character as a prior qualification for legal practice; and when character references were sought, the man most able to judge a person, the local minister, was called upon. Daniel Rogers, for example, was admitted to the practice of law early in the eighteenth century upon presentation of certificates of approbation to the Ipswich Court from three local ministers—one his brother.[12] Still there is no evidence that courts or lawyers made organized efforts to determine a prospective lawyer's expertise before allowing him to practice and plead.

In other colonies, regulations controlling the admission of attorneys varied widely. In Virginia, for example, no laws regulated attorneys between 1682 and 1715, when the governor and council banned lawyers who were not licensed by them. In 1732 the House of Burgesses ordered licensing of lawyers for the county courts, requiring men "learned in the law" to judge individual petitions. By 1730 in New York, lawyers were already calling for a seven-year clerkship.[13]

Other efforts to improve legal services in Massachusetts continued to emphasize the advocacy role of lawyers. In 1728, a court of common pleas ruling prohibited nonresidents from taking the attorney's oath and forbade anyone not sworn as an attorney to charge legal fees. Less than a decade later, Timothy Ruggles, a young lawyer and member of an elite colonial family, steered a bill through the general court that prohibited sheriffs and their deputies from drawing and filing writs. A companion measure in 1742 extended the prohibition to the giving of legal advice.[14] All these measures aided the business interests of sworn attorneys while protecting laymen from potentially unskilled or unscrupulous practitioners and avoiding potential conflicts of interest among law enforcement personnel.

Perceptive lawyers could see that these measures only slightly altered the status of lawyers in the province. In principle the practice of law had been accepted into the judicial process, and lawyers had been institutionalized as members of the court. Yet they knew their occupation was in its infancy and that they had to find the proper goals and methods to nurture and strengthen it.

Like other colonials, lawyers naturally looked to England for ideas and the means to improve their prestige and quality, but they did not try wholesale imitation of the complex English legal profession. In England the division was along occupational lines, and practitioners were permanently placed in one category, such as conveyancer, attorney, solicitor, or barrister who specialized in case preparation or pleading and practiced before only one court system—ecclesiastical, equity, or common law. Although they eventually established a graded profession headed by barristers, who alone could argue points of fact and law in the high courts as in England, the Massachusetts legal profession never did transfer the English design of stratification in toto—in part because of the absence of the complex English judicial system and the scarcity of lawyers during these formative years. And there is little evidence that many colonial lawyers wanted this development to occur. Colonial lawyers, even barristers, for example, usually prepared their own cases and then argued them in all courts; they also functioned as accountants, land agents, business agents, and clerks.[15] To install occupational specialization to the degree found in England would have eliminated too many opportunities.

Neither did they pattern their educational requirements and regulatory institution on the Inns of Court, where elite barristers were trained in England. Rather the newly founded English society for attorneys and solicitors seems to have become their institutional model. The Society of Gentlemen Practisers in the Courts of Law and Equity was founded in 1739 by London attorneys, who practiced in the lower common law courts, and solicitors, who handled cases for the courts of equity. The society's founders sought to control the professional conduct of practitioners, to stiffen requirements for admission, to exclude irregular attorneys—lawyers who were informally trained or self-taught and not approved by the lawyers' society—from the courts, and to enforce the comprehensive rules for attorneys and solicitors passed by Parliament in 1729. They emphasized three legal regulations: candidates for admission must have studied five years as an articled clerk in the office of an attorney or solicitor; attorneys or solicitors could have no more than two students in their offices at one time; and irregular practitioners would be fined £50 for conducting a suit. The lawyers also fought court actions that restricted their practice, while pressuring the judiciary to control admission to their profession. In 1742 and again in 1743, for example, they opposed the courts' recognition of clerks of court as solicitors for the purpose of accepting law clerks. Drives were mounted in 1745 and in 1746 to disbar attorneys who had failed to fulfill their clerkships.[16] In short they wanted a strong professional organization to solidify their privileged position within the court system.

No testimony has been found that directly links Massachusetts lawyers with the English law society, but the province's bar associations strongly resembled its form and actions. Massachusetts men acquired a knowledge of English affairs through correspondence, books, newspapers, travel, visiting English officials and immigrants. Surely they were aware of professional developments in England at least through legally trained government officials. Moreover Paul Dudley, the chief justice of the Massachusetts Superior Court from 1745 to 1752, had studied law in London, and two eighteenth-century governors were English lawyers, although few local lawyers had ever been trained at the Inns of Court.[17] The Society of Gentlemen Practisers better served the need for a self-generated organization requiring neither the authority of tradition nor the rule of law. It granted power to itself and exercised authority through its own efforts.

Other colonial regulatory associations of a voluntary nature undoubtedly served as models for Massachusetts lawyers. Even at this early date, they could look to ministerial associations in Massachusetts, Connecticut, and New Hampshire. More directly applicable was a New York regulatory bar association, founded in 1748. In neighboring Rhode Island lawyers had signed a "Bar Compact" in 1745 that regulated practice and fixed fees. And in Boston Dr.

William Douglas had temporarily organized a medical society in the 1730s.[18]

Lawyers combined the voluntary organization with the traditional guild system to form a corporate society designed to improve their professional training and status. Brought together in part by group consciousness or a sense of common interest and by societal hostility, lawyers unintentionally formed a prototype for professionalization through group voluntarism, a phenomenon that would become endemic to American society by the nineteenth century.

John Adams asserted that the Suffolk County Bar Association was formed in 1758 upon his recommendation because "the practice of the Law was grasped into the hands of Deputy Sheriffs, Pettyfoggers and even Constables."[19] But some informal organization had existed before then. As early as 1754, Robert Treat Paine implied the need to seek the "bar's" approval before beginning court practice.[20] And Jeremiah Gridley told John Adams in 1758 that before recommending him for admission as an attorney, he would have to consult the "Bar, because the Court always inquires if it be with the Consent of the Bar." Perhaps only sporadic and ad hoc consultations among lawyers constituted "bar association" functions until 1763, but surviving records indicate that the Suffolk County lawyers formally organized in that year.[21]

Increasing numbers, technical expertise, and sympathetic judges made conditions auspicious for eastern, cosmopolitan lawyers in the mid-eighteenth century to organize. Geographic and commercial expansion placed a premium on legal exactness and discipline, as laymen found it difficult to handle the complexities of the common-law system without professional training. These growing financial opportunities attracted men of greater abilities and broader education, who in turn sought to make law a career of higher social and financial rewards.[22] Trained lawyers' numerical strength increased steadily from 15 in 1740 to 640 in 1840, dramatically lowering the ratio of lawyers to the general population from one in 10,108 to one in 1,153 (table 1). Organization-minded lawyers such as Adams, Gridley, Benjamin Kent, and Robert Auchmuty seized the opportunity to form a bar society that would strengthen the practice of law. In 1760 these lawyers resided almost exclusively in the eastern, maritime counties and extended legal services throughout the

TABLE 1 NUMERICAL STRENGTH OF LAWYERS, 1740–1840

YEAR	NUMBER	RATIO OF LAWYERS TO TOTAL POPULATION
1740	15	1:10,108
1775	71	—
1780	34[a]	1:9,349
1785	92	—
1790	112	1:4,244
1800	200	1:2,872
1810	492	1:1,424
1820	710	1:1,159
1830	582[b]	1:1,049
1840	640	1:1,153

Source: Numerical strength is based on a study of court records, local histories, and the *Massachusetts Register*; U.S. Bureau of the Census, *Historical Statistics of the United States, Colonial Times to 1957* (Washington, D.C., 1960), pp. 13, 756.

a. Decline due to twenty-nine lawyers remaining loyalists.

b. Decline due to loss of nine counties with the formation of the state of Maine.

province by riding the circuit with the judges of the superior court.

One pressing problem for lawyers was the prevalence of irregular practitioners. The soundness of the legal advice handed out by tavern advocates, educated laymen, judges, and clerics was not the only issue. Justice and the provincial courts had operated well without trained lawyers for over a century. But from the lawyers' perspective, the solution to the problem of irregular practitioners would determine the future reputation of the legal profession, the ability of the activist lawyers to control members of the profession, and, some lawyers believed, the existence of a legal profession in the colony. Organizers saw restricted entrance as the key to the creation and control of the profession.

Despite legislation that prohibited sheriffs from practicing law and curbed the charging of fees by unsworn practitioners, trained lawyers daily faced competition from men whom they considered incompetent pettifoggers—menaces to their professional ambitions and society at large. Yet the courts often supported sheriffs and laymen who engaged in legal practice, and even judges were not above offering pretrial legal advice contrary to contemporary legal standards. A Plymouth County Court of Common Pleas judge, Thomas Clapp, for example, faced misconduct charges after receiving a fee for arranging bail in 1751 for a local farmer, Abiezar Turner. Clapp claimed that because the farmer had not needed to retain a lawyer, the farmer could afford to share his savings with him. Judges of the Worcester County Inferior Court in 1757 recognized the right of unsworn laymen to appear in court as long as they possessed signed and sealed powers of attorney. Not even all lawyers accepted the exclusion of untrained pleaders. James Otis, Jr., a skilled Boston attorney, openly opposed the Suffolk Bar's request in 1763 to the Suffolk County Inferior Court to limit practice to regularly sworn attorneys. The judiciary chose to side with Otis to the chagrin of the trained lawyers in general and Auchmuty and Adams in particular.[23]

Lawyers also favored a stratified division of labor permitting advancement from court to court under lawyers' direct supervision. They hoped that this process would screen out undesirable attorneys or limit their practice to the least lucrative and prestigious courts. A semigraded profession based on admission to the inferior court of common pleas and the superior court of judicature already existed, based on a 1701 statute that authorized courts at both levels to admit attorneys within their jurisdiction and to make necessary rules for orderly practice in each court. This system produced geographic and institutional divisions within the profession: those who could practice on a province-wide basis in the superior court, and those who could argue cases only within a county's inferior court of common pleas.[24] Because the more important cases and more lucrative fees usually came in the superior court, admittance to it meant higher status within the profession and greater opportunities for practice. No regulatory agency, either voluntary or governmental, exercised the authority to determine qualifications for proceeding from advocacy in the lower courts to the superior court. Furthermore unlike in England where barristers had the exclusive privilege of arguing causes in the high courts while attorneys could only prepare the cases, attorneys as well as barristers could also plead in the Massachusetts Superior Court. In 1762 the newly appointed chief justice of the superior court, Thomas Hutchinson, moved the profession into formal occupational divisions by instituting the rank of barrister.

Political circumstances surrounding Hutchinson's appointment probably contributed as much to the introduction of the "long gown" or the rank of barrister as lawyers' desires for enhanced stature. A leading lawyer and a bitter political opponent of Hutchinson, James Otis, Sr., had expected the appointment. Hutchinson's lack of legal training was seized upon as a vehicle for opposition by leaders of the profession, such as Otis and his son James, Gridley, Benjamin Prat, and Oxenbridge Thacher. Some lawyers had independently begun to demand that judicial appointment be based on legal training. Thacher believed that judges should be given sufficient time to study law and be freed from political pursuits and obligations if they could not be trained lawyers. As early as 1760, John Adams thought that superior court judges should be trained lawyers. In the turmoil, political leaders of both factions tried to capitalize on the issue. It may be that Hutchinson hoped to placate trained lawyers by aiding their efforts to create a stratified profession.[25]

The desire to pacify lawyers in large measure stemmed from a fear of their nascent political power. Lawyers had played an insignificant role in Massachusetts politics until the eighteenth century. Merchants and prosperous farmers had controlled provincial and local politics. Until 1691, in fact, statutes excluded practicing attorneys from the legislature on the grounds that a conflict of interest might arise when it acted as a court of appeals. Professional lawyers first appeared in the general court in the early 1700s. John Reed became the first practicing lawyer elected to the general court from Boston in 1738. Other lawyers, such as Otis, Sr., Ruggles, Joseph Dwight, Joseph Hawley, and Benjamin Prat, played important roles in colonial politics before 1760.[26]

Lawyers' access to political office before the revolutionary era, however, appears to have been independent of their training and profession. Wealth, power, family status, and kinship ruled together. Recent studies indicate that political leadership belonged to a small group of social notables, who inherited, in large measure, their social prestige and wealth. These two prerequisites combined with initiative and skill brought political power.[27] After 1760 shifting balances of political power, the enhanced value of legal knowledge in a sensitive governmental situation, and an increasing tendency of sons of notables to enter the legal profession enabled lawyers to achieve many positions of political and judicial influence.

A turning point for Boston lawyers' political fortunes was their alliance with moderate merchants, which grew out of the case of the Writs of Assistance, twice argued before Hutchinson in 1761. Thacher and Otis, Jr., had represented the merchants in this heated political and legal case. Gridley, who ironically had argued for the government, and Otis subsequently became influential members of the politically powerful Merchants Club in Boston. Three other lawyers—Adams, Kent, and Perez Morton—entered the merchant-dominated North End Caucus, and Adams also attended meetings of the South End Caucus. The 1763 selection of the younger Otis and Thacher for representatives by the Boston Caucus and South End Caucus can be said to symbolize an alliance of merchants, lawyers, and the artisan-oriented South End Caucus.[28]

Hutchinson, no less than some lawyers, probably also believed that barristers added dignity and prestige to English courtroom procedure, as well as providing a new patronage source. When twenty-five attorneys achieved the rank of barrister at the Suffolk term of the superior court in August 1762, Massachusetts lawyers had taken another step closer to a graded legal profession.[29]

Hoping to capitalize on their new recognition, lawyers sought to push province-wide regulations to raise the profession's technical competence. Two years later a summons by the Suffolk Bar for a mass meeting of all barristers produced a number of suggestions for a regular program of training and advancement within the profession, but nothing more. An efficient means to control the number of untrained lawyers, who, according to Adams, "swarm and multiply,"[30] continued to elude them, despite the superior court's acceptance of the Suffolk Bar's recommendation at the 1765 Suffolk County session that blank writs not be issued to anyone except "a regularly admitted" attorney of the court.[31] But most avenues of practice—those in the courts of common pleas and general sessions—stayed open to untrained attorneys, making it clear that the courts would not readily ban laymen from the practice of law.

Forced back on their own voluntary organization, members of the Suffolk County Bar Association instituted a seven-year program of professional advancement based on education and seniority. In order to secure the association's approval, candidates for admission to the inferior courts had to serve as a trained lawyer's apprentice for three years; promotion to superior court attorney required a probationary period of two years of practice in the court of common pleas; and to be admitted to the rank of barrister, two years of experience as an attorney at the superior court were necessary.[32] Lawyers hoped that progress through their graded system would be long enough to ensure adequate legal preparation and slow enough to blunt the spiraling competition.

These standards compared favorably to those prevailing in other provinces. New York modified its rules in 1764 to demand two years of college and a five-year clerkship before admittance to practice. Virginia, in contrast, had no regulations for clerkship, but the average period for apprenticeship appears to have been about four years without an education requirement.[33]

Despite this relatively selective admission policy, the Suffolk lawyers' goal of gentlemanly status could not be fulfilled by any eighteenth-century English definition until they obtained the proper liberal education and broke the direct tie between work and income. As long as lawyers depended on their own labors for their money and used the same training as traders or artisans, they could not escape their middle-class association. Eventually lawyers upgraded their educational standards to conform to current thoughts on scientific training and the need for a liberal education.[34] Yet only when lawyers, like other Americans, accepted the rapidly developing commercial and industrial society and redefined "gentleman" to encompass those directly involved in a trade or profession could they gain the coveted status and escape their frustrations. Massachusetts lawyers in the 1760s, however, did not envision changing status definitions and therefore concluded that a strong program of liberal education would secure recognition by society that they had become a "learned profession" rather than a "skilled trade."

Lawyers looked to the local intellectual elite, the ministerial profession, for educational standards. In an attempt to curb lay preachers and sects such as Baptists and Quakers, religious leaders anxiously sought legal confirmation of the traditional requirement of college-educated ministers. The Massachusetts Religious Act of 1760 authorized the assessment of taxes only for the support of a minister who had a formal college education or the testimony of the majority of the clergy in his county that his learning was sufficient. A Worcester barrister, James Putnam, stoutly defended this statute in a 1769 court appearance, claiming that "learning is necessary" for a stable and beneficial profession. Ministers in neighboring New Hampshire expected "Piety & Learning particularly a good Acquaintance with the Scriptures & a Conversation as becomes the Gospel" as qualifications for preaching candidates. In a society that honored education and a learned clergy, but where most men lacked even a grammar school education, a college or liberal education increased a person's status and often served as a springboard to fame and fortune.[35]

Early in the profession's development, some lawyers set out to broaden their professional educational experience beyond the technical expertise gained from office work, limited libraries, and attendance at courts. One effort came in 1765 when two Boston lawyers, Gridley and Samuel Fitch, formed the Sodalitas, a law club, for the informal study of law and political philosophy. Its members, who included Gridley, Fitch, Adams, and Joseph Dudley, examined works on politics, history, and feudal and civil law. The society, however, failed to attract wide support among practical-minded lawyers, and disinterest and busy schedules among the members soon led to the society's abandonment, just as Boston physicians had allowed a similar medical society to decay in the 1730s.[36]

The younger Otis argued for postcollegiate study at home as a means of maturing the outlook of law students before they embarked on formal legal training. He asserted that studying philosophy and the classics would help his brother Samuel avoid a common pitfall of young lawyers—lack of a broad education. "Early and short clerkships and a premature rushing into practice, without a competent knowledge in the theory of law, have blasted the hope of, (and ruined the expectations formed by the parents of) most of the students in the profession, who have fell within my observation for these ten or fifteen years past."[37] But lawyers needed more affirmative and ostentatious steps if they were to refute the opinions of such men as Justice Benjamin Dyer who remarked to Adams that lawyers were of no real value to society because they "live upon the sins of the People." "If all Men were just, and honest, and pious, and Religious etc.," he said, "there would be no need of lawyers."[38] Competence had to be demonstrable if lawyers' authority was to be accepted in the marketplace.

Lawyers rejected views like Justice Dyer's, and, basing their actions on the premise that both morality and law should govern society, they pushed for educational and ethical standards above the norm for colonial America. In 1770 young, ambitious lawyers in Suffolk County increased the formal activities of the county bar association, such as regular meetings and the appointment of committees to examine law students. They also agreed not to accept any student without the approval of the bar association and not to recommend any person not possessing a college education or an equivalent liberal education for admission to the inferior court of common pleas.[39] The new regulations also stated the need for a three-year term of study with a barrister even for candidates with a college or liberal education. But they ignored the need for some general supervision of the activities of apprentices. Taunton lawyer Robert Treat Paine, for example, probably had spent little more than one year engaged in legal studies, although he was formally a law student with Abijah Willard of Lancaster and Benjamin Prat of Boston from January 1754 to May 6, 1757, when he was admitted to the Suffolk bar. During this time Paine preached on Sundays, served as a chaplain at Crown Point, and worked as a surveyor in Massachusetts and Nova Scotia. Evidence indicates that his case was not an isolated one. Since most lawyers knew each other, they were not inclined to meddle in the intimate details of a compatriot's apprenticeship contract. When interpersonal contracts weakened later, lawyers replaced trust with written regulations and examinations.[40]

A necessary part of their personal profession was fraternal socialization, which had to be assimilated by neophytes through social and occupational interaction with experienced members of the profession. Attorneys began to view bar associations not only as formal vehicles for professional improvement but also as social centers that would strengthen their cohesiveness. James Hovey, a Plymouth barrister, regarded intercounty bar association meetings as important because they would cultivate "a good understanding between all, who are or shall be members of our Society." He suggested that an attorney of the inferior court be refused a recommendation for admittance to the superior court bar unless he cultivated and maintained a "good understanding with the Brethren of the Barr."[41] Although no formal action was taken on Hovey's suggestion, it underlined the importance of personal relations to a lawyer's career and the corporate nature of the profession.

Suffolk County lawyers continued their efforts to enlist province-wide support for a unified professional code. As early as 1764, Boston lawyers were soliciting suggestions from barristers in other areas for methods to improve the quality of legal practice.[42] But these attempts failed. Few regions outside of Boston held enough lawyers to sustain an active organization, and where lawyers became interested, they wanted their own association. These drives for intercounty cooperation often fizzled because the courts of general sessions and common pleas were organized by county, and the superior court held terms in each county. Lawyers, who were admitted by the separate county courts, logically organized on that geographical and political framework. In 1768 Essex County lawyers established their own bar association and introduced a minimum fee scale to the province's legal profession.[43] This attempt to raise professional incomes and reduce internal competition set a precedent that ultimately reaped a harvest of ill will.[44]

The Essex County lawyers' 1768 adherence to the Suffolk Bar Association's format and rules for professional advancement strengthened the belief of Suffolk lawyers that the bar association held the key to controlling their occupation and making it into a "learned profession." The Suffolk lawyers reacted optimistically to this growing interest in an improved and organized profession. Resuming attempts to organize the province's lawyers, they appointed Josiah Quincy, Jr., in March 1770 to prepare a circular letter to gain "the concurrence and assistance of the barristers and attorneys through the province" to the Suffolk County Bar Association rules. The turmoil following the Boston Massacre of March 5 caused a postponement of the action at the next recorded meeting, but the next spring the Boston lawyers were ready to try again. After sending copies of Quincy's letter to lawyers in the eastern counties of Plymouth, Bristol, and Barnstable, they invited all of the colony's superior court barristers and attorneys to meet during Harvard College's commencement in order to confer on the general affairs of the profession in the province. A notable lack of interest in other counties apparently killed the conference.[45] This apathetic response can be traced to the different concerns of lawyers in the commercially oriented eastern counties and the practitioners in the rural counties.

While the Suffolk and Essex lawyers had moved toward an autonomous profession with expanding influence in the province, trained lawyers outside the capital region struggled merely to be accepted as occupational experts. Untrained legal practitioners, or pettifoggers, as leading lawyers preferred to call them, thrived in rural Massachusetts, often providing the only legal services available. These irregular practitioners handled nearly 50 percent of the court cases (when an attorney was listed) at the York County Inferior Court in 1767. Such a serious drain on the limited potential income of the resident, trained lawyers, such as James Sullivan, William Cushing, and David Wyer, and the circuit-riding Boston lawyers, could not be ignored. In 1770 the trained lawyers mustered a concerted attack. Failing to gain the support of the judiciary, which was composed of nonlawyers, the attorneys agreed not to enter, argue, or in any way assist in the prosecution of causes when the writs were drawn by any person not regularly admitted and sworn, except in cases of necessity. This measure became so effective that by 1774, part-time or irregular practitioners entered fewer than 10 percent of the actions in the inferior court. Despite this initial success, lawyers apparently did not organize a formal county bar with admission or education standards in the Maine counties before the Revolution.[46]

Efforts to exclude untrained practitioners usually occurred as part of a broader effort to upgrade the occupation. When Essex County lawyers organized their county bar, they labeled irregular practitioners "a detriment to the public" and agreed not to enter, argue, or assist the prosecution of actions brought by irregular practitioners, and to challenge all writs and abatements of pettifoggers under English court rules.[47]

Not all legal practitioners moved with such visions. Central Massachusetts lawyers, frustrated by their unsuccessful attempts to exclude untrained practitioners, sought to turn their presence into a profit. In 1757 the Worcester County Inferior Court had ruled that anyone with a client's signed and sealed power of attorney could enter an action. Worcester County lawyers, planning to increase their fees, in 1773 stimulated the court into ruling that regularly sworn attorneys also needed signed and sealed powers of attorney for each client and allowed them to charge one shilling and six pence for this needless action. Efforts to enhance legal training or to exclude untrained lawyers did not materialize in this rural county before the Revolution.[48]

Lawyers' occupational aggressiveness sparked a clash in Hampshire County with superior court judges, who were determined to retain their dominant role in the courts. Antagonism between the judiciary and the legal profession stemmed in part from the adversary setting, but mostly from the absence of legal training among the judges, in contrast to the growing professional expertise of some lawyers. As a result, the bench feared that lawyers might infringe upon its judicial prerogatives through technical knowledge and legal legerdemain. With tempers still on edge from the Stamp Act confrontation, Joseph Hawley, a Northampton barrister, who was also a popular party political leader and recognized leader of lawyers in western Massachusetts, publicly criticized legal aspects of several court decisions. The superior court, dominated by eastern, crown (establishment) party men, disbarred him in 1767 because of "devisive injurious and scandalous Reflections on several of the Justices of this court, for what they did in court and as justices thereof." Chief Justice Hutchinson, a leader of the crown party, sympathized with Hawley despite their political differences, but asked, "How shall we save the honour of the court?" Benjamin Lynde, a justice of the court and another establishment politician, demanded an act of submission before Hawley could plead again. Other lawyers and mutual friends reconciled the antagonists, securing Hawley's readmission to trial practice in 1769. But the furor increased the belief within the profession that a legally trained and professionally oriented judiciary had become essential to the well-being of the legal profession.[49]

Hampshire County lawyers also had to overcome judicial reluctance to raise standards of legal education. The county court maintained that candidates for admission to the inferior court must have studied law for only one year. In 1773, however, lawyers disregarded the ruling and insisted on the three-year apprenticeship advocated by lawyers in Essex and Suffolk counties.[50] The adoption of this rule marks the first success of the eastern lawyers in extending the concept of standardized professionalization beyond the coastal counties.

More difficult than achieving rules by consensus is their enforcement, a truism that early bar association leaders quickly discovered. The basic reason for their inability to secure adherence to standard regulations was their voluntary nature, which did not bind anyone outside the county bar association's membership. Even when members failed to follow the regulations, bar associations did not possess the power to discipline them effectively. Association leaders, in short, could not control legal practitioners without the full support of the courts, and this they did not have.

Colonial judges were extremely reluctant to accept lawyers' arguments that only people acceptable to the legal guild could adequately advocate a client's interests in court. Being laymen they knew by experience that a lawyer's apprenticeship did not guarantee justice or that its absence ensured the prevention of justice. David Wyer, for example, while a law student and teacher in Falmouth, Cumberland County, Massachusetts, was allowed to argue a case in the York County Inferior Court in 1762. Irregular practitioners, moreover, such as Thomas Bragdon and John Frost, continued to enter causes in the inferior court after York lawyers had agreed to exclude them in 1770. In Middlesex County, Joseph Buckminister,

Joseph Haven, Josiah Stone, and Jonathan Maynard undertook business as formally untrained but apparently satisfactory practitioners. Hampshire County residents utilized self-instructed pleaders, such as Jabez Ward, Joseph Gilbert, William King, and Cornelius Jones.[51] Every court had its self-trained practitioners who had often proven essential to the cause of justice.

These men enjoyed the patronage of local residents for three major reasons: cost, the attraction of familiarity, and the scarcity of formally trained legal practitioners. Educated gentlemen, clerics, and "tavern lawyers" who were not dependent on the law for their everyday income could—and generally did—charge lower rates. Full-time lawyers often had to pacify disturbed clients when submitting their fees with words of consolation. Jonathan Sewall of Charlestown excused himself to Thomas Robie, who reacted hostilely to a charge of £2.14.8 in a losing cause for a debt of £11, by explaining: "The Clerk, Sheriff [and] lawyers have got it all and as much more out of my pocket. This, I hope, will afford you some *Christian* consolation."[52]

A paucity of well-trained lawyers made them unavailable to most people beyond the capital region except when they rode the court circuit. Just 4 lawyers resided in the Maine counties in 1760, and these had increased to only 8 by 1775. Edward Pope became merely the fourth trained lawyer in Bristol County in 1768. When Oakes Angier began practice in neighboring Plymouth County in 1769, he was the second regularly trained and sworn attorney. Essex County had 8 trained attorneys in 1760 and 12 in 1770; just 2 lawyers resided in Worcester and Hampshire counties in 1767. Throughout Massachusetts fewer than 80 trained attorneys and barristers practiced in 1775. By way of comparison, Virginia, with a more geographically dispersed population, reportedly had 183 lawyers practicing in the years 1760-1776.[53] This physical inability by trained and sworn lawyers to monopolize legal practice continually contributed to the profession's frustration.

Even within their limited associations, lawyers experienced severe disunity and, occasionally, outright revolt against their policies. Maintenance of the monopoly of arguing cases in the superior court assigned to barristers in 1762, for example, often proved impossible. A member of the Suffolk Bar and a member of a leading provincial family, Josiah Quincy, Jr., proudly recorded that in the 1769 August term of the superior court of Suffolk County, he had argued a case, although he was not a barrister. When barristers challenged the legality and propriety of his action, Quincy answered that he had no such scruple and would continue to manage all of his own business "though unsanctified, and uninspired by the pomp and magic of—The Long Robe." Another instance is provided by Timothy Langdon of Cumberland County who was admitted as an attorney of the superior court in 1772 after just one year's practice in the inferior court, despite efforts of leading lawyers to enforce a two-year minimum term of practice in the lower courts before being eligible for admittance to the high court.[54] Clearly not all lawyers accepted the formation of a restricted profession.

Efforts to improve educational standards for law students also proved divisive. In trying to create a learned profession, Boston lawyers wanted to accept only students having a liberal or college education. But not everyone in provincial Massachusetts willingly accepted this requirement as a prerequisite for legal education. The case of William Lithgow, who later became a United States district attorney, is one example of the county bar's inability to enforce this regulation. Originally the Suffolk Bar Association vetoed Samuel Quincy's proposal to accept Lithgow of Georgetown as a law student because he did not have a liberal education. A Biddeford barrister, James Sullivan, remained more impressed by the considerable regional influence of Lithgow's father than by the Suffolk association's rule, and he accepted Lithgow as a law student.[55] Like Sullivan, who also did not have a liberal education, Lithgow became a leader in the legal profession. His experience emphasizes an important point: county bar associations could control only lawyers within their geographic bounds, and no regulatory agency extended its jurisdiction over the entire province.

As one means of transgressing geographic lines and unifying practitioners, association organizers depended on a concept of professional brotherhood. It already existed, for example, in the local ministerial associations, innumerable social and political clubs, and in the Society of Gentlemen Practisers in London. When lawyers reorganized the Suffolk County Bar Association in 1770, they pointedly referred to it as a society or law club. Care was taken to call lawyers "gentlemen of the Bar," "brethren of the Bar," or "Brother Lawyers." Like their English counterpart, Massachusetts bar associations held their meetings in taverns not only for convenience but to stimulate social intercourse. They also held joint dinner meetings with the judiciary to improve working relations. Like other fraternal organizations, such as the high status Masons, the Suffolk Bar Association voted in 1770 to keep the transactions of the society secret from all people except members.[56] While membership remained small, the fraternal ties worked remarkably well.

Despite their organizational problems, lawyers' aggressive actions led to moderate prosperity for most lawyers and real wealth for a few practitioners in the three decades before the Revolution. Illustrating the possibilities was the exceptional case of the elder Otis, who by 1745 reportedly was realizing nearly £1,200 a year from legal work. He handled nearly half of all litigation in the Barnstable courts and also rode the circuit into Bristol and Plymouth counties. Sampson S. Blowers, a Boston lawyer, annually collected £400 for legal services at the peak of his career in the 1770s. Trowbridge, another successful Boston lawyer, purchased at least £1,241 worth of property between 1752 and 1760—187 acres of farmland, two houses, and a church pew. Theodore Sedgwick and Daniel Jones surmounted adversity to achieve solid prosperity in western Massachusetts. In 1767, Sedgwick, a Great Barrington barrister and politician, began as an impoverished pleader without land, income, or family connections. Only four years later, he had managed to purchase a house and garden, six and a half acres of farmland, twenty-three acres of pasture and woods, horses, a black house servant, and a cook. Jones, a Springfield attorney, accumulated enough financial and political capital to purchase twelve townships in neighboring New Hampshire. In the central Massachusetts town of Worcester, James Putnam amassed 1,259 acres in Worcester and Holden before the Revolution forced him to emigrate at the peak of his earning power.[57]

But not many lawyers could rank their incomes with Otis, Trowbridge, Sedgwick, or Putnam. Some existed on the fringes of the profession without much success. At least one—Jonathan Loring—

went bankrupt. Loring, although not trained to the bar, handled conveyancing work in Marlborough after 1740. When he could neither support his family nor pay his creditors, he filed bankruptcy papers before the Massachusetts Council. Ephraim Keith, a Taunton lawyer from 1765, did so little business in Paine's shadow that he was allowed to double as deputy sheriff for several years until 1771, when his law career became successful. Then he was forced to abide by the statute prohibiting sheriffs from advising legal clients.[58] Men such as Keith and Loring appear regularly in the records, but their numbers were small.

Inheritance was also a key to wealth for prerevolutionary lawyers. The younger Otis, politically more famous than professionally successful, nevertheless had no worries because of the family wealth and connections built by his father. Another Boston lawyer, Samuel Sewall, earned only about £50 a year in the 1760s and 1770s, but he could remain unperturbed because his hereditary estates were later valued at £27,140 by himself and £9,462 by the commission on loyalist claims.[59] The profession's rising economic and political status on the eve of the Revolution made it more attractive to the children of wealthy families, and the presence of these elite citizens in turn increased the status and attraction of the legal profession.

Lawyers' self-regulation actions appear to have aided their economic growth. The number of lawyers grew steadily but not uncontrollably in the prewar years (table 1), and the increase of lawyers did not seem to outstrip the concurrent climb in court cases (tables 2 and 4). Despite bar association efforts to structure competition through seniority gradations and fee schedules, lawyers were already becoming divided into a large average group and a small dominant group—a tendency that stiffened into a pattern after the war.

On the eve of the Revolution, lawyers of Massachusetts Bay, led by eastern, cosmopolitan practitioners, had established a firm basis for future attempts at improving the status and quality of the legal profession. By 1774 the colony's lawyers had a meaningful concept of a profession that, coupled with the necessary ability and will, had enabled lawyers to develop their own institution designed to control the occupation and protect their prerogatives. They had

TABLE 2 DOCKETED CASES IN SELECTED MASSACHUSETTS COUNTY INFERIOR COURTS OF COMMON PLEAS, 1760–1800

DATE	WORCESTER	HAMPSHIRE	MIDDLESEX	BRISTOL	BERKSHIRE
1760	238	308[a]	459	165	114[a]
1765	364	492	553	319	342
1770	479	315	475	429	473
1773	717	718	616	337	864
1774	509	331	314	186	484
1775	closed	closed	closed	closed	closed
1776	150	closed	46	218	closed
1777	208	closed	151	244	closed
1778	119	15	124	173	closed
1779	232	46	103	129	closed
1780	246	101	162	126	closed
1785	2,904	1,435	2,321	640	1,662
1790	1,955	669	1,216	298	574
1795	1,796	1,264	1,569	438	480
1800	1,871		2,544	645	

Source: Minute Books of Courts of Common Pleas for Worcester County, 1760-1800, Hampshire County, 1761-1797, Middlesex County, 1760-1800, Bristol County, 1760-1800, and Berkshire County, 1761-1798, as reported in Charles McKirdy, "Lawyers in Crisis: The Massachusetts Legal Profession, 1760-1790" (Ph.D. diss., University of Wisconsin, 1969), 215-216, 220-221, 225-226, 230 231, 235-236.

a. Cases for 1761 rather than 1760.

established a graded profession based on their perception of an English model, as adapted to colonial conditions. They had sought an occupational monopoly and the right to control entrance into the profession. They had attempted to raise the prestige of its members by devising educational standards and a regular program of legal study under lawyers' control. They had, in short, progressed well along what has become the standard path for aspiring professionals in America.

Divisions within the legal fraternity over the direction and form that the profession should take complicated organizational efforts, however. Regional differences, based on conflicting economic and professional interests, joined with local pride to prevent the spread of any unified program throughout the colony. Efforts to establish a province-wide bar association had failed, and many counties still did not possess even rudimentary county bar associations.

Lawyers discovered that without the courts' cooperation, they could not enforce their regulations or enjoy an occupational monopoly. Although concerned with their public image, attorneys and barristers had not yet fully considered the role of the profession in society. Consequently they had not faced and countered the reason for their unpopularity: that they achieved monetary success, in part, by exploiting human suffering and hardship. Moreover most laymen failed to perceive personal or societal benefits accruing from man-made restrictions designed to improve the quality of the legal profession and enlarge its members' economic benefits at their expense. Residents of Pittsfield, for example, could still petition the Provincial Assembly in 1775 for an elective judiciary because its absence has "afforded encouragement to our mercenary lawyers to riot upon the spoils of the people."[60]

NOTES

1. For an articulate exposition of the growth of English influence on the legal system in Massachusetts, see John M. Murin, "The Legal Transformation: The Bench and Bar in Eighteenth-Century Massachusetts," in Stanley N. Katz, ed., *Colonial America: Essays in Politics and Social Development* (Boston, 1971), 415-449.

2. George L. Haskins, *Law and Authority in Early Massachusetts: A Study in Tradition and Design* (New York, 1960).

3. Edmund S. Morgan, *Puritan Dilemma: The Story of John Winthrop* (Boston, 1958), 154-173; Richard S. Dunn, *Puritans and Yankees: The Winthrop Dynasty of New England, 1630–1717* (Princeton, N.J., 1962), 24-25; Charles Warren, *A History of the American Bar*, 3d ed. (New York, 1966), 68-71.

4. Morgan, *Puritan Dilemma*, 37-38; Roscoe Pound, "The Lay Tradition as to the Lawyers," *Michigan Law Review* 12 (June 1914): 634-635; Alan M. Smith, "Virginia Lawyers, 1680–1776: The Birth of an American Profession" (Ph.D. diss., Johns Hopkins University, 1967), 278-282.

5. Warren, *American Bar*, 68; Daniel J. Boorstin, *The Americans: The Colonial Experience* (New York, 1958), 24-26.

6. Warren, *American Bar*, 68-71; Nathaniel B. Shurtleff, *Records of Governor and Company of Massachusetts Bay in New England* (Boston, 1853-1854), 3:168, 4:563.

7. Zachariah Chaffee, Jr., and Samuel E. Morison, eds., *Records of the Suffolk County Court, 1671–1680, Publications of the Colonial Society of Massachusetts* (Boston, 1933), xxvi-xxvii, 9, 143, 186, 301, 514, 734, 742, 825 and 857. Boorstin, *The Americans*, 27-31. One of the senior fellows at Harvard, Reverend Jonathan Mitchell, at one point requested funds for a chair of law at Harvard, but no action followed. Samuel E. Morison, *The Intellectual Life of Colonial New England*, 2d ed. (Ithaca, N.Y., 1963), 32.

8. Chaffee and Morison, *Records*, xxvi-xxvii; Boorstin, *The Americans*, 27-31.

9. Business expansion can be seen in Bernard Bailyn, *The New England Merchant in the Seventeenth Century* (New York, 1964), 112-197. The changes in the legal system are available in Warren, *American Bar*, 74-79.

10. *Acts and Resolves, Public and Private of the Province of Massachusetts Bay. . . . 1692–1780* (Boston, 1869-1874), 1:467.

11. Ibid., 2:622-623.

12. Thomas F. Waters, *Ipswich in the Massachusetts Colony* (Ipswich, 1917), 2:99.

13. Smith, "Virginia Lawyers," 283-291; Paul M. Hamlin, *Legal Education in Colonial New York* (New York, 1939), 35-41.

14. George M. Bliss, Jr., *An Address to the Members of the Bar of the Counties of Hampshire, Franklin and Hampden. . . . 1826* (Springfield, 1827), 17; *The Charter and General Laws of the Colony and Province of Massachusetts Bay* (Boston, 1914), chap. 3, July 6, 1736, 540; *Acts and Resolves of Massachusetts*, 2:794; James H. Stark, *The Loyalists of Massachusetts and the Other Side of the American Revolution*, 2d ed. (Clifton, N.J., 1972), 225.

15. William Holdsworth, *A History of English Law* (London, 1938), 12:51-62.

16. Edwin Freshfield, ed., *The Records of the Society of Gentlemen Practisers in the Courts of Law and Equity Called the Law Society* (London, 1897), 1, 9, 13, 17-21; Holdsworth, *History*, 12:14, 52-77.

17. Governors William Shirley and Francis Bernard were also English lawyers who undoubtedly conveyed their knowledge of the profession to colonial lawyers. Bernard Bailyn, *The Ordeal of Thomas Hutchinson* (Cambridge, Mass., 1974), 40, 45; Alfred Z. Reed, *Training for the Public Profession of the Law* (New York, 1921), 76. Reed is not completely ac-

curate when he says that no New England lawyer attended the Inns of Court after 1733. John Gardiner, who practiced in Massachusetts from 1784 to 1793, was a product of the Inner Temple and was admitted to the rank of barrister in 1761. E. A. Jones, *American Members of the Inns of Court* (London, 1924), xviii-xx, 88; William T. Davis, *History of the Judiciary of Massachusetts* (Boston, 1900), 80.

18. "Records of the Transactions of the Annual Convocation of Ministers in the Province of New Hampshire, begun July 28, 1747," New Hampshire Historical Society, *Collections* 9 (1889): 1-67; Hamlin, *Legal Education*, 35-41; Michael Kraus, *Intercolonial Aspects of American Culture on the Eve of the Revolution* (New York, 1964), 207-208; "William Douglas to Cadwallader Colden, Feb. 18, 1735/36," Massachusetts Historical Society, *Collections,* 4th ser. 2 (1854): 188-189.

19. John Adams, *Diary and Autobiography of John Adams*, ed. Lyman Butterfield (New York, 1964), 3: 274.

20. Robert T. Paine to Thomas Paine, December 19, 1754, Robert T. Paine Papers, MHi.

21. Adams, *Diary*, 1:54, 235-236.

22. A professional lawyer is defined for the purpose of this study as someone who had training in the law, was admitted to practice by the courts, and had a regular and extensive practice of law that provided his chief occupational income. He might, of course, have had a larger income from inherited wealth, conjugal wealth, or from invested funds.

23. Robert Zemsky, *Merchants, Farmers and River Gods: An Essay on Eighteenth Century American Politics* (Boston, 1971), 49; Joseph Willard, *An Address to the Members of the Bar of Worcester County, Massachusetts, October, 1829* (Lancaster, 1830), 45; Adams, *Diary*, 1:235-236.

24. John Adams, *Legal Papers of John Adams*, ed. L. Kinvin Wroth and Hiller B. Zoebel (Cambridge, Mass., 1965), 1:xl-xli.

25. Governor Bernard later apologized for not appointing a lawyer as chief justice. Bailyn, *Thomas Hutchinson*, 47-54; Adams, *Diary*, 1:167-168, 2:41-42; Thomas Hutchinson to Richard Saltonstall, August 22, 1759, in Robert E. Moody, ed., *The Saltonstall Papers, 1607–1815* (Boston, 1972-1974), 1:429-431; John J. Waters and John A. Schutz, "Patterns of Massachusetts Colonial Politics: The Writs of Assistance and the Rivalry Between the Otis and Hutchinson Families," *William and Mary Quarterly* 24 (October 1967): 559-561.

26. Thomas Hutchinson, *The History of the Province of Massachusetts Bay from 1749 to 1774* (London: 1828), 3:104n; Zemsky, *Merchants, Farmers, and River Gods*, 10-38; John J. Waters, *The Otis Family in*

Provincial and Revolutionary Massachusetts (Chapel Hill, 1968), 61-131; Charles McKirdy, "Lawyers in Crisis: The Massachusetts Legal Profession, 1760-1790" (Ph.D. diss., University of Wisconsin, 1969), 34.

27. Zemsky, *Merchants, Farmers, and River Gods*, 10-38; Waters, *Otis Family*, 61-131.

28. Gerald B. Warden, *Boston, 1689–1776* (Boston, 1970), 153-162; Alan Day and Katherine Day, "Another Look at the Boston 'Caucus,'" *Journal of American Studies* 5 (April 1971): 29, 32.

29. Minute Books of the Superior Court, reel 2, MHi; Josiah Quincy, Jr., *Reports of Cases Argued and Adjudged in the Superior Court . . . 1761–1772* (Boston, 1865), 35; Charles Warren, *History of Harvard Law School and of Early Legal Conditions in America* (New York, 1908), 55. Warren places the date for the creation of barristers in 1760, but the superior court records pinpoint August 1762; the entry for August 1762 describes the occasion in *The Diaries of Benjamin Lynde and Benjamin Lynde Jr.* (Boston, 1880), 188; Reed, *Training*, 67-68.

30. James Hovey to Robert T. Paine, October 22, 1764, Paine Papers, MHi; Adams, *Diary*, 1:316.

31. Superior Court Minute Books, reel 6; Adams, *Diary*, 1:235-236.

32. Adams, *Diary*, 1:316; Adams, *Legal Papers*, 1:lxxviii-lxxix.

33. Hamlin, *Legal Education*, 35-41; Smith, "Virginia Lawyers," 189-190.

34. See chapter 4; Gerard W. Gawalt, "Massachusetts Legal Education in Transition, 1766-1840," *American Journal of Legal History* 18 (January 1973): 27-50; William J. Reader, *Professional Men: The Rise of the Professional Classes in Nineteenth Century England* (London, 1966), 9-11, 45-47.

35. Adams, *Legal Papers*, 2:39-47; "Records of the Transactions of the Annual Convocation of Ministers in the Province of New Hampshire," 4-5; Zemsky, *Merchants, Farmers and River Gods*, 35-36.

36. Adams, *Diary*, 1:252-253; Edward J. Forster, "A Sketch of the Medical Profession of Suffolk County," *Professional and Industrial History of Suffolk County Massachusetts* (Boston, 1894), 3:185-186.

37. James Otis to James Otis, Sr., 1760, quoted in William Tudor, *The Life of James Otis of Massachusetts* (Boston, 1823), 10-12.

38. Adams, *Diary*, 1:184.

39. George Dexter, ed., "Record Book of the Suffolk Bar," Massachusetts Historical Society, *Proceedings* 19 (December 1881): 147-179; Adams, *Legal Papers*, 1:lxxix. Although Boston physicians had no professional society in the years before the Revolution, several doctors in 1767 and 1768 supported a bill in the general court to prevent anyone from practicing

physic or surgery until he had "undergone a proper examination"; they were unsuccessful in their attempts, however. John J. Cary, *Joseph Warren, Physician, Politician, Patriot* (Urbana, 1961), 33.

40. Clifford K. Shipton and J. L. Sibley, *Biographies of Those Who Attended Harvard College* (Boston, 1873-1975), 12:465-467; see chapter 4.

41. James Hovey to Robert T. Paine, October 22, 1764, Paine Papers.

42. Hovey to Paine, October 22, 1764, Paine Papers.

43. Dexter, "Record Book," 149.

44. Concern for professional fees was not restricted to lawyers. An Essex County physician, John Warren, complained a few years later that "the People here are accustomed to being dealt so very easily with by their Physician, Doctor Holyoke having reduced the Fees to a very low Rate. . . . A Physician who should charge any thing nearly sufficient barely to support the Dignity of the Profession," he claimed, "or should attempt to make any innovations upon the Ancient Usage of the Town would at once throw himself out of Practice." J. Warren to unknown, January 29, 1775, quoted in Shipton and Sibley, *Bibliographical Sketches*, 12:32.

45. Dexter, "Record Book," 148-151.

46. William Willis, *A History of the Law, the Courts and the Lawyers of Maine . . .* (Portland, 1863), 83, 652; Adams, *Diary*, 2:44. Charles P. Whittemore, *A General of the Revolution: John Sullivan of New Hampshire* (New York, 1961), 4-5.

47. Dexter, "Record Book," 149.

48. Willard, *Address*, 45; Worcester County Inferior Court of Common Pleas Docket Books, 1760-1765, Court House, Worcester, Mass.

49. Superior Court of Judicature, Minute Books, reel 6, MHi; Thomas Hutchinson to John Cushing, July 30, 1767, "Cushing Letters," Massachusetts Historical Society, *Proceedings* 44 (March 1911): 524-525; Adams, *Legal Papers*, 1:ci.

50. Bliss, *Address*, 27; Adams, *Diary*, 2:44.

51. James D. Hopkins, *An Address to the Members of the Cumberland Bar . . . June Term, 1833* (Portland, 1833), 48; Shipton and Sibley, *Biographical Sketches*, 14:371; Willis, *History of the Law*, 83; Henry W. R. Taft, "Judicial History of Berkshire County," Berkshire Historical Society, *Collections* 1 (1892): 97; Samuel A. Drake, *History of Middlesex County* (Boston, 1880), 1:450.

52. Jonathan Sewall to Thomas Robie, November 8, 1773, in Henry Lee, ed., "Some Letters of Jonathan Sewall," Massachusetts Historical Society, *Proceedings*, 2d ser. 30 (January 1896): 410-411.

53. Abraham Holmes, *Address Before the Bar of the County of Bristol . . . June Term, 1834* (New Bedford, 1834), 12; Hopkins, *Address*, 77;

Willis, *History of the Law*, 331; William D. Northend, *Address Before the Essex Bar Association, December 5, 1885* (Salem, 1885), 55; Shipton and Sibley, *Biographical Sketches*, 16:5, 203; Smith, "Virginia Lawyers," 359.

54. Quincy, *Reports*, 27; Adams, *Diary*, 2:44.

55. Reader, *Professional Men*, 45-47; Willis, *History of the Law*, 105-106; Dexter, "Record Book," 150-151.

56. Dexter, "Record Book," 147-152; *Lynde Diaries*, August 6, 1770, 198.

57. Waters, *Otis Family*, 71-72; Shipton and Sibley, *Biographical Sketches*, 14:445-447, 15:359; deeds and farm account of Edmund Trowbridge, Dana Papers, MHi; Richard E. Welch, *Theodore Sedgwick, Federalist: A Political Portrait* (Middletown, Conn., 1965), 11; listing of land absentees, 1799, Lincoln Papers, MWA.

58. Shipton and Sibley, *Biographical Sketches*, 10:298-299; Ephraim Keith to Robert T. Paine, July 5, 1771, Paine Papers.

59. Waters, *Otis Family*, 71-72; Shipton and Sibley, *Biographical Sketches*, 14:269-270.

60. Memorial of Pittsfield to the Provincial Assembly, December 26, 1775, in J. E. A. Smith, *The History of Pittsfield, Massachusetts, from . . . 1735 . . .* (Boston, 1869-1880), 1:344.

They "Swarm and Multiply"

The American Revolution brought both disruption and opportunity to the legal profession. Disarray arrived quickly with court closures, the revolution of government, and the flight of refugee lawyers. And it lingered for a long time after the war as nationalistic Americans sought to Americanize the legal profession, the court system, and the common law. Lawyers were also badly divided over the desirability of retaining their Anglicized legal system and continuing to model their profession along English lines.

Despite the unsettling effects of the war, the Revolution opened new vistas to ambitious and perceptive practitioners. Lawyers emerged as a strong political force, symbolized by their control of the judiciary. The economic traumas of inflation and depression combined with geographic and political expansion to create unprecedented economic benefits and expanded opportunities in government for men of the law. What had appeared to be utopian plans for a large, prosperous, well-trained legal profession before the war became a reality in the postwar period. Lawyers did not fight to preserve what they had won before the Revolution.[1] Rather they continued to seek goals that they had set but had been unable to achieve before the war.

The legal profession suffered severely in the escalating conflict between colonists and the British government; patriot leaders forcefully closed the courts following attempts by British royal agents to enforce the Massachusetts Government Act in the summer and fall of 1774. Lawyers thus remained without any place to practice in most of the state until 1776. In western counties constitutionalists kept the courts inoperable until 1780. County conventions repeatedly urged residents to bypass the court system by settling civil suits through local arbitration.[2] How thoroughly court business was disrupted is evident in table 2.

Radical or populist-minded reformers in western Massachusetts hoped to use the revolt against the royal government to free themselves from all central government with its independent judiciary and fee-centered legal profession. They proposed the regional election of judges, which they believed would make the judiciary subject to the people's control, and the extensive use of arbitration to settle legal conflicts. Lawyers under this plan would rarely be needed. "Lawyers were Almost universally represented as the Pests of Society," complained Theodore Sedgwick, a Stockbridge attorney. "All persons who would pay Court to these extravagant and unreasonable Prejudices became their Idols," he lamented.[3]

The loyalist leanings of many lawyers damaged the profession as much as the court closings. British officials had wooed Massachusetts lawyers before the war, and many had accepted royal posts. Among these were Jonathan Sewall, James Putnam, Samuel Sewall, Robert Auchmuty, Jr., Edmund Trowbridge, and Daniel Leonard. Despite the growing union of Whig merchants and lawyers, most lawyers in Massachusetts hesitated to commit themselves to radical action as early as the Stamp Act crisis. A frustrated Adams confided to his diary: "The Bar seem to me to behave like a Flock of Pidgeons. They seemed to be stopped, the Net seems to be thrown, and they have scarcely Courage left to flounce and to flutter." Chief Justice Hutchinson happily congratulated the Suffolk Bar on its support and expressed the hope that it would serve as a future precedent to everyone and a good example to the community.[4]

By 1768-1769, however, crown officials believed that most Boston lawyers harbored rebellious sentiments. Governor Francis Bernard, an English barrister, had argued that having the posts of attorney general, solicitor general, and advocate general available for patronage and with fixed salaries would turn the lawyers toward the crown. But by 1768, he had become convinced that most attorneys acknowledged the "Cause of the People" as the winning side and were scurrying to it. In 1769 he asked the British government to postpone appointing an attorney general "because most of the leading lawyers have sided with the Faction."[5] When war came, the lawyers were more divided than Bernard had calculated.

Approximately 40 percent of the trained lawyers, particularly established barristers and holders of public office, remained loyal to Britain. Twenty-nine of the seventy-one lawyers looked at in this study who were practicing in the years 1773-1775 did not rebel, and only twenty-one emigrated or withdrew from practice. Eight loyalist lawyers joined with twenty barristers and twenty-two attorneys to provide continuity in legal practice and professsional organization during the war.[6] In a similar recent study, Charles McKirdy found that 38.3 percent (thirty-one) were loyalists. After exhaustive analysis, McKirdy concluded that most lawyers rebeled, but that age and geographic distribution do not explain why some remained loyal and others did not. Most young attorneys with no civil places, he argues, became patriots; older lawyers who were placemen split evenly between loyalists and patriots.[7] No single generalization appears to provide a concrete answer as to why some lawyers switched allegiance and others did not. Many had firm ideological convictions. But those who had no extensive loyalist family connections and who held no important government offices appear to have been more susceptible to radical ideology or perceived that their greatest opportunities rested with a victory for home rule.

Patriot lawyers often became unavailable for professional services and thus contributed to the profession's instability during the war. Adams and Paine went to Philadelphia in 1774 as delegates to the Continental Congress. Adams seldom practiced law again. Paine returned in 1777; he became the state's attorney general and then a justice of the supreme judicial court. James Sullivan, a Maine barrister and politically active legislator, moved first to Groton where he found little time to practice law; he later became a justice of the supreme judicial court and then the state's attorney general. Nathaniel Peaslee Sargeant, a Haverhill barrister, accepted a superior court seat in 1776 and handled few legal clients thereafter. Sedgwick, a leading lawyer from western Massachusetts, spent most of the Revolution purchasing supplies for the American army.[8] The withdrawal from practice by such a large number of patriot and loyalist lawyers inevitably weakened the profession. But this proved only temporary, as younger practitioners, no less able though less experienced in English law and traditions, filled these vacancies; and the profession gained the prestige and power that went with top positions in the government.

Just as the Revolution provided opportunities for merchants and traders, the decade of political upheaval after 1774 furnished lawyers with an excellent chance to attain political power in alliance with the commercial elite. Lawyers' expectations centered on the judiciary, a branch of the government that, based on English tradition, should have been dominated by barristers, but had not been in colonial Massachusetts. Of the ten chief justices between 1692 and 1776, only three were trained lawyers; of twenty-three associate justices, only three had received legal training. Twenty-two had attended Harvard College, but their educational backgrounds serve more as an indication of social and economic status than professional achievement. Their best qualification for the bench was an important connection with government leaders in England or the province.[9]

Some men had begun to study law to become community leaders or "public men," to use Blackstone's phrase. They perceived the judiciary as a major professional goal, a symbol of their status and achievement. Few positions in the colony's political system conferred the power, responsibility, and social importance of the province's judges.[10] A number of patriot lawyers, including Adams, the Otises, Quincy, Hawley, Paine, Sullivan, Sedgwick, and Sargeant, had been excluded from high judicial office before the Revolution. As leaders of the new system, they could be expected to exploit this new opportunity.

The appointment of politically partisan judges held particular importance during the Revolution because of the need for the law to appear on the right side. During the hostile years preceding the outbreak of war, government judges utilized their charges to the jury to defend the courts' integrity and the authority of the crown-provincial government rather than merely to analyze the legal business before the court. When the Whigs reorganized the judiciary, judges used the charge to the jury to propagandize and defend the revolution, self-government, high taxes, and other issues of public concern. As the months passed, these charges became more and more political in tone and less juridical in content.[11]

The political influence of lawyers, such as Adams, Hawley, the Otises, Sullivan, Sargeant, Sedgwick, Paine, David Sewall, William Cushing, and John Lowell, allowed them to execute part of their plans during the 1775-1776 reorganization of the courts. A measure of their success is the fact that all but one of the seven superior court judges appointed between 1775 and 1780 had been professional lawyers before the war. In 1782, a state law formalized the proposition that all justices of the supreme court be trained lawyers with the requirement that each "shall be an Inhabitant of this Commonwealth, of Sobriety of Manners and learned in the law." Only the appointment of Nathan Cushing in 1790 violated the spirit of this law before 1840. His selection reportedly cost the supreme judicial court much of the "veneration of the people."[12]

After the Revolution, the bench and the bar became so intermingled and mutually supportive that they were at times almost indistinguishable. Lawyers' rise to political power enabled them to capture nearly all appointive judicial and law offices in the commonwealth (table 3). This mounting evidence of political and judicial influence

TABLE 3 OFFICES HELD BY LAWYERS, 1780–1840

POSITION	NUMBER OF LAWYERS	NUMBER OF VACANCIES FILLED	PERCENTAGE
State circuit court of common pleas, 1811-1821	14	21	66.6
State court of common pleas, 1821-1840	6	6	100.
County courts of general sessions, 1807-1828	46	176	26.
County courts of common pleas, 1782-1811	37	89	41.5
County courts of probate	36	59	61.
County registers of probate	22	50	44.
Clerks of court	29	61	47.5
Registers of deeds	9	48	18.7
Sheriffs	21	73	28.7
County attorneys (prosecutor)	54	55	98.1
State supreme judicial court	20	21	95.2

Source: Compiled by comparing the listings of public officials in *Fleet's Pocket Almanack* and the *Massachusetts Register* with a file of trained lawyers in the state for these years.

Note: Includes the counties of Barnstable, Berkshire, Bristol, Dukes, Essex, Franklin, Hampden, Hampshire, Middlesex, Nantucket, Norfolk, Plymouth, Suffolk, and Worcester.

met with disgust and anger in other elements of society. But political antipathy toward lawyers had always been a recurring theme throughout Anglo-American history, and the war absorbed the attention of most laymen and lawyers.

As the Revolution widened, bar associations declined. The Suffolk County Bar met only occasionally and kept no records from mid-1774 to 1778. But some regulations were at least occasionally enforced.[13] John Thaxter, for example, felt constrained to ask Adams for a recommendation to the county bar association for admittance as an attorney to the court of common pleas in 1777.[14] Not until the fighting shifted southward and political stability returned to Massachusetts with a new constitution did lawyers return to institutional activities.

At their October meeting in 1780, the Suffolk barristers and attorneys agreed to charge law students a minimum of £100 sterling for their three-year apprenticeship. The adoption of this rule, which the Essex and Middlesex bar associations copied in 1783, signaled a renewed effort to ensure a well-trained but numerically restricted profession. By setting high fees for education, lawyers hoped not only to increase their incomes but also to discourage lower-class men from seeking entrance to the profession, which was increasingly becoming a preserve for gentlemen's and professionals' sons.[15]

Not all lawyers charged the established education fee. Theophilus Parsons, an Essex County lawyer, told James Sullivan's brother John that he charged clerks only £70 for three years of instruction. "At that time [1781] there was an agreement in Boston not to take less than £100 sterling for instruction," remarked Parsons, "and fault was found that I and the Gentlemen in this County took less." By 1785 lawyers in Essex County, including Parsons, were in theory charging the full £100 fee for a clerkship, yet according to Parsons, Worcester County lawyers, such as Levi Lincoln, still asked only £70 for instruction.[16]

Lawyers' interest in legal excellence also reemerged near the war's end, as evidenced by David Sewall's proposal to Lowell in 1782 that the state provide every shiretown with a law library. This suggestion languished until two decades later. Unlike the new Medical Society, which established a library in 1782, the bar associations delayed until 1804, when Boston lawyers sponsored

TABLE 4 LAWYERS' CASELOADS IN THE SUPERIOR AND SUPREME COURTS OF MASSACHUSETTS, 1760–1795

YEAR	BRISTOL	CUMBERLAND	ESSEX	HAMPSHIRE	MIDDLESEX	SUFFOLK	WORCESTER	YORK
1760	19-6		16-5	46-6			23-6	
1761	21-7	8-3	15-5	23-5			20-7	45-8
1762	39-7	9-6	41-7	25-6	22-5	72-11	15-5	25-6
1763	37-6	20-6	78-7	148-12	17-6	141-11	57-7	22-6
1764	35-6	43-7	75-7	183-13	20-5	70-16	56-4	10-6
1765	77-7	45-10	26-9	134-14	39-5	235-16	38-5	23-6
1766	64-6	38-10	80-10	45-11	28-7	184-16	38-6	21-5
1767	72-10		105-9	81-14	21-5		65-6	
1768	78-9		108-10	66-12			36-6	
1769	69-12		80-8					
1770	87-10		93-6					
1771	67-13							
1772	31-8							
1773	83-11	66-5						75-6
1774	9-4	58-6	62-9	8-7				53-7
1775[a]			*	*	*	*	*	*
1776	31-8	*[b]	128-11	20-6	*	66-16	10-6	11-5
1777	36-8	*	161-9	22-7		213-16	46-5	36-9
1778	6-4	*	16-6[c]	57-7	23-10		33-4	*[d]
1779	9-4	*	*	2-2	16-8			*
1780	8-5	*			21-11			88-5
1781	17-5	11-6						2-2
1782	62-7	3-3		29-11				12-4
1783	109-10	47-11		91-14	128-15			58-7
1784	67-10	44-8		85-16	90-11			51-8
1785		34-5		75-16				40-6
1786		17-5		41-18			196-17	46-9

1787	22-6		50-9		70-15	14-6
1788	29-6	108-16	32-8		38-9	25-7
1789	36-5	109-16	16-5		53-12	46-11
1790		108-15	26-8		59-16	27-6
1791		132-1	94-14		219-18	64-12
1792		175-10	76-14		179-20	63-14
1793		189-16	54-11[f]		187-17	93-16
1794		275-12	156-21		252-26	101-12
1795		272-14	168-26		268-25	125-12

Source: Compiled from Minute Books of the Superior Court of Judicature, and supreme court, reels 2, 4-7, MHi.

Note: The first number in each column represents the number of clients listing lawyers; the second figure represents the number of different lawyers listed on cases.

a. Courts were closed for the last terms of 1774, all of 1775, and the first terms in 1776.

b. In Cumberland County most cases were continued for nonappearance from 1775 to 1778. In 1779 and 1780, no attorneys were listed, and in 1781 and 1782, very few lawyers were listed.

c. In 1778-1779, few or no attorneys were listed.

d. In 1778-1782, few or no attorneys were listed.

c. In 1788-1789, few or no attorneys were listed.

f. In 1793, most cases did not list an attorney.

* Most attorneys not listed.

the establishment of the Social Law Library. Lawyers then quickly capitalized on their political power to obtain state support for law libraries.[17]

Practicing lawyers profited economically during the war if they lived in areas where civil or maritime courts still sat. After 1780 legal business skyrocketed, luring many lawyers back to private practice. Francis Dana and Paine temporarily refused seats on the state supreme court because they feared that the salary would not compensate for their lost business. Sullivan said he resigned from the supreme court at the end of the war because his depleted financial situation necessitated a return to lucrative private practice.[18] Adams, who was paid £500 sterling per annum plus expenses as congressional commissioner to France in 1778 and 1779, complained that this was "not half, I suppose of what I could have honourably earned at Home, in my Profession: not half, to be sure of what Some Gentlemen of the Bar have actually earned here, Since my Departure." Not until the courts opened in 1780 did attorneys in central and western regions have an opportunity to return their business to a sound financial basis, but even then legal practice in eastern counties appears to have been more lucrative.[19]

Some members of the legal profession enjoyed great occupational mobility during the war because most leading lawyers had left professional practice for political reasons. Thus even though business had declined, the number of practicing lawyers had been more drastically reduced, necessitating a compensatory response from the profession. A temporary end to some of the admission and graduation restrictions was the result. William Cushing informed Adams that five attorneys had been admitted at the first term of the superior court without the normal one-term delay because of "the Scarcity of Lawyers arising from deaths, toryism & running their country."[20] The remaining lawyers held advantageous positions when the courts resumed a full schedule.

As the war drew to a close, attorneys' economic opportunities changed dramatically for the better. Oft-continued actions were called, and long-delayed suits were entered. To judge by the number of lawsuits, almost everyone had some stake in a court proceeding in the 1780s (tables 2 and 4). Depressed economic conditions from 1783 to 1785 drove many indebted people over the brink, and without statutory bankruptcy protection, thousands appeared as defendants in the county courts and the state supreme court.

The explosion of lawsuits, representing only the tip of the pyramid of legal activity, not only aroused animosity toward lawyers and courts, but it stimulated a tremendous growth in the number of attorneys. Thirty-four trained lawyers were practicing in 1780; within five years, this had nearly tripled to 92 lawyers. By 1795 there were at least 112 and 200 by 1800. This development soon rendered the concept of a closely knit corporate profession a practical impossibility.

Most lawyers showed no apparent concern for these long-term implications, as hard-working lawyers angled to net the maximum cases they could handle—and sometimes more. Edward Pulling of Essex County, who had no cases in the superior court before 1780 and four in 1787, had nineteen actions in the Essex terms of 1788, thirty-two in 1791, and seventy-one in 1795. In Lincoln County, Silas Lee, who argued no cases in 1786, handled forty actions at the 1793 Lincoln term, sixty in 1794, and ninety-two in 1797. Worcester lawyer Lincoln entered four actions at the superior court's Worcester term in 1777; in 1786 he had sixty cases, and in 1795 he defended fifty-eight clients. Most lawyers, however, judging from the surviving records, were fortunate to enter five to ten actions per year at the supreme judicial court.[21]

The resurgence of professional prosperity and political stability after 1780 gave the superior court judges, now all trained lawyers, an opportunity to add prestige to the legal profession by renewing the right of the court to call distinguished practitioners to the rank of barrister. The bench justified this 1781 ruling at a Suffolk County court term as a sure way of promoting learning and literary accomplishments. Requirements for the distinction eschewed set periods of practice in favor of a close application to the study of the science, "a mode of conduct which gives a conviction of the rectitude of their minds and a fairness that does honor to the profession of the law."[22]

A 1782 general court act reorganizing the superior court further strengthened a stratified legal profession by granting the new supreme judicial court legislative sanction to establish rules and regulations for the admission of attorneys and barristers.[23] Lawyers still lacked direct institutional control over entrance to their ranks, but they did in effect control admission because the court, composed of trained lawyers, supported the same professional aims as bar association leaders and left effective control in the hands of the county bar associations.

Leadership continued to come from Boston. Members of the Suffolk County Bar in August 1783 reinstated their rule setting a maximum of three law students in a barrister's office at one time, thus evenly distributing the available, qualified apprentices throughout the profession's hierarchy. Theoretically students would receive better training and supervision if a master's attention was less fragmented, and a few lawyers could not monopolize clerkship fees.[24]

Suffolk County Bar Association organizers also sought to enforce its regulation that law students have a college degree or an equivalent liberal education. After April 1784, all law candidates who had not graduated from college had to pass an examination by a special committee, and it was not unusual for the committee to fail such candidates. The cases of John Gardiner and William Hill are examples. An examination committee composed of three premier lawyers—Paine, Lowell, and William Tudor—advised temporary refusal in July 1784 even though Gardiner and Hill were well versed in the Latin and English classics; the committee reasoned that "a course of study in the mathematics, in ethics, logic, and metaphysic was necessary previous to their admission as students of law."[25]

Recognizing the need for wider support for their regulations, some Boston lawyers promoted a state or regional bar association, or even joint meetings of the county bar associations. A tricounty bar meeting with members of the Essex and Middlesex bar associations appeared during the summer of 1784, but a proposal formulating one binding set of rules failed to carry.[26] Reasons for this hesitancy ranged from lawyers' localism to the institutional structure of the court system.

The concurrent appearance of new county bar associations reflected the reluctance of lawyers to abandon local control, but it also reinforced the existence of regionally differing regulations. One of the first postwar bar associations emerged in Worcester County in 1784, with most of its rules closely imitating the codes of Suffolk and Essex lawyers. But professional and cultural conditions in this rural region of central Massachusetts dictated adjustments to particular rules that had been designed for the commercial and cosmopolitan eastern counties. Any man seeking to study law in Worcester County who possessed a college degree or its equivalent liberal education had to undertake a similar three-year term of study in the office of an attorney of the supreme judicial court and to sustain a good moral character for a bar association recommendation. But in contrast to the eastern counties' refusal to accept law students without a college or liberal education, Worcester lawyers specifically provided a five-year term of study for people who came well grounded only in Greek and Latin. These looser regulations were partially caused by the relative scarcity of lawyers and aspiring college graduates in central Massachusetts. At this time only ten trained lawyers practiced in Worcester County; there were twenty-two in Boston itself. And because only one barrister, Lincoln, lived in the county, attorneys could not be expected to allow only barristers to have law students.[27]

In the immediate aftermath of the Revolution, the lawyers' greatest challenge for control over the practice of law came from the state legislature. During the Revolution, legislative supremacy became a dominant political principle as patriot leaders, sure of their control of the assembly, subordinated all other branches of government to the "voice of the majority." The legal profession was directly affected by the legislature's zealous exercise of its judicial function. The general court acted as a high court of appeals: granting new trials, examining witnesses, arresting people and committing them to jail, continuing actions, and remanding or reversing decisions. But it also interfered in matters normally handled by the judiciary, such as fraudulent transactions, defective titles, and loss of property in criminal proceedings. Lawsuits were arbitrarily extended and court sittings were changed, often to avoid legislative sessions, or to suit individual judges, lawyers, or litigants. Even after the general court transferred some of its power to the courts when it authorized the supreme judicial court to make rules for the admission of attorneys, it retained an active interest in the control of legal practice.[28]

Instead of trying to counter this action, politically active lawyers sought advantages in it. In the spring of 1784, lawyers supported a bill that eliminated one source of competition while trying to provide better legal services. This measure, based on similar prewar measures, forbade sheriffs and deputy sheriffs from appearing as legal counsel in court or before a justice of the peace in behalf of any suit, prohibited them from giving any legal advice, and denied them the right of drawing up any declaration, writ, or plea.[29] Suffolk County Bar leaders strengthened this act by ordering members not to solicit business outside their offices or hire anyone such as a sheriff or his deputy to engage clients for them.[30]

Any rejoicing by lawyers soon dissipated as dissidents began to demand the legislative destruction of a privileged legal profession. Sporadic verbal assaults on the legal profession had a long tradition in Massachusetts. But the Revolution's repetitive psychological, political, and economic crises produced radical outbursts against English law, traditional courts, and professional lawyers that threatened major alterations of the entire legal system. Conservatives and moderate political factions retained power during the 1780s, and, fearing social upheaval, they were reluctant to do any more than alleviate the worst complaints about the laws, the courts, and the economy.[31]

People had not lost animosities aroused by the wartime loyalism or neutrality of many lawyers. The reaction of the residents of Amherst and surrounding towns to the neutrality of Simeon Strong and Moses Bliss, two Hampshire County lawyers, is but one example of the depth of Whig antagonism. Strong, decidedly loyal in thought but neutral in action, was arrested on August 12, 1777, as an enemy of the American states. Lack of evidence set back the patriots and forced his release within a month. Refusing to be stymied, the selectmen of Amherst and ten neighboring towns petitioned the superior court to disbar both Strong and Bliss, arguing that they feared for peace and safety if people "who have always been viewed as Inimical to the Liberties of America by the People at Large, (or at least not friendly)" were permitted to practice law. The judges further frustrated the political powers when they denied the petitions because no particular crimes or gross immoralities were alleged or suggested. Even though both men refrained from court appearances, the dislike of lawyers and the judiciary in Hampshire County gained momentum.[32]

Legal assistance given to loyalists by patriot lawyers was unpopular, whether lawyers were upholding professional ethics, eager for business, or politically motivated. Sedgwick aroused the ire of

Sheffield area residents by defending loyalists such as William Vassall, David and Henry Van Schaak, and Elijah Williams.[33] In opposing the Massachusetts House bill in 1783 to prevent loyalists from recovering property by court action, Sedgwick lent further support to the belief that lawyers in Hampshire County lacked patriotism.[34]

Professional aid for loyalists extended beyond the western counties. Perez Morton, a young and promising attorney in Boston, petitioned the general court to prevent the seizure of emigrant Mary Swain's property by the Hopkinton Committee of Correspondence, Inspection and Safety in 1776. Almost simultaneously Thomas Russell, a Boston attorney, filed a plea in behalf of Charles Russell to restrain the Lincoln Committee of Safety.[35] In late eighteenth-century Massachusetts, many patriots were not willing to extend the right to legal counsel to "enemies of the people."

This ambivalent professional activity caused many laymen to link the legal profession with British sympathizers. One Salem citizen urged voters not to cast their ballots "for any who left the place of their nativity in the late troubles, none who had been timid, no lawyers, however good their character, as the profession is dangerous and damnable, to say no worse of it." Another irate critic demanded a bankruptcy act "regardless of the influence of *British Agents* or the gentlemen of a certain profession."[36] Lawyers who were Tories should not be placed in public office by patriotic laymen, critics claimed.

Patriot lawyers were no less reluctant to tar their opponents with the stigma of British association. Judge Sargeant, writing of the court closures in 1786, said, "The flagitious Tories, taking advantage of the Pressure of honest debts, high taxes, & scarcity of money have stirred up a true catalinian conspiracy against the government." Another barrister, Caleb Strong, claimed that attacks on lawyers "originate more from a Disposition unfriendly to regular Government and the Law itself than from the Conduct of those who practice it."[37]

But the wartime activities of some lawyers and the animosity already present in Massachusetts society only partially explain the hostility that mushroomed in the postwar period. Creditors with the conspicuous aid of lawyers brought the full force of the law to bear on people whose debts had escalated while court cases had often been postponed during the war. Some reasons were as personal as a bad experience in court; others were as idealistic as the desire to replace British law with American law. Certainly antipathy toward legal practitioners had deeper roots than just the malpractice of unscrupulous lawyers as some historians have said.[38]

Complexities in the entire English legal system baffled many laymen. The resulting frustration can be seen in this 1785 plea by "A Spectator": "The flagrant abuses in the execution of our laws . . . The embarrassments which we daily experience in almost every department of a judicial process . . . [and] The tedious delay: Intricasies-Labryrinths-Perplexities etc. which continually involve the most simple actions in our courts" demanded a simplified legal system.[39] To many lawyers, however, the intricacies of special pleading and the complexities of the common law were just the aspects of the system to be preserved, because they believed that each had been developed to resolve a specific legal problem and that the system worked very well.

Highflown American nationalism also spurred the rising tide of antilawyer sentiment. Many laymen felt that the complexity of the laws stemmed from their British origins and that cultural ties as well as political bonds should be severed. Newton residents echoed Bellingham citizens when they pinpointed the problem of provincial laws and the legal system as "being blended with the British codes, whereby, it becomes impossible for the people in general to understand them or to form from them a rule of conduct."[40] What emerged from this line of thought was a demand to simplify the laws, purging them of English influence.

The first attempts to eliminate or at least curb the use of English common law had been made during the war. The Massachusetts Constitution of 1780 allowed the use of only those elements of the common law that had been utilized in America since 1775—superficially a sweeping denial of English law. Consequently the general court that year appointed a committee to revise the acts and laws of the state and "make them consistent with the constitution and intelligible to the common people." The committee—Cushing, Sargeant, Sullivan, Paine, John Pickering, David Sewall, and James Bowdoin—received instructions to select, abridge, alter, digest, and "methodize" the acts and laws of Massachusetts.[41] This first attempt to simplify the state's statutes and to eliminate English laws stuttered and finally stopped by 1790. Despite mounting public pressure, the commissioners, all lawyers except Bowdoin, displayed no anxiety to adhere to the legislative charge and little ability to cope with the plethora of laws. Cushing, who was also chief justice of the state supreme court, exemplified the attitude of the commissioners when he reported that they had examined all former statutes "but by some late acts of the legislature the whole system of judicial proceedings have been so far deranged that it wants revision much more than it did at first."[42] He concluded that nothing could be done.

Cushing, like other commissioners, apparently misunderstood what had been asked of them. Advocates of this simplification urged the legislature to return the law to its pristine purity. If this were done, they claimed, British law and lawyers would fade away. When radical "republicans" such as Frederick Robinson, Robert Rantoul, Jr., and John Leland called for drastic revision of the common-law usage and procedures in the Massachusetts courts in the early nineteenth century, they were continuing demands that had been made in the 1780s. These critics wanted strict limitation, if not abolition, of the legal profession, and they planned to simplify and Americanize the common law so that laymen could manage the state's legal system and feel secure in its operation. Like the codifiers who followed them in the 1830s, these reformers rested their demands partly on anti-British sentiment, but they firmly grounded their case on the belief that the present system of justice was undemocratic and unfair. Throughout this fifty-year period, reformers fought to "rebalance the courts to the favor of the client" by curtailing the legal profession, eliminating common law, streamlining court procedure, and generally simplifying the law.[43]

Such reformers also reflected a form of anti-intellectualism that associated learning with elitism. Early in the War for Independence, residents of Worcester County were warned against men with intellectual training, particularly lawyers and physicians. "Democritus" cautioned readers of the *Massachusetts Spy* that "men of liberal education are not to be trusted with the reins of government," because, he claimed, they learn in college that the laity are their property.[44] One of the legal profession's chief opponents after the war, Benjamin Austin, son of a leading Boston merchant and a political ally of Samuel Adams, twisted the nascent professional status of lawyers to the advantage of their critics. Austin, utilizing the pen name "Honestus," advocated a simplified law code so that the principles of the law "would not be so exposed to be perverted, by the whims and fancies of a numerous body of professionalists." Instead, Austin claimed, men of leisure and ability should apply themselves to the study of law.[45] Austin soon became the leading spokesman for the antielitists.

Most members of the legal profession in Worcester, Hampshire, and Berkshire counties—the geographic regions where the most discontent resided—were not natives of the towns in which they practiced. This "foreign" character in rural areas reinforced the widespread distrust of lawyers. Of the forty lawyers practicing in the 1780s in these counties, twenty-two (55 percent) were newcomers. If this alone did not arouse the suspicion of the long-time residents, only twelve lawyers had begun practice by 1775, and therefore most were young in both age and experience.[46] In fact, studies of geographic mobility among lawyers, doctors, and ministers show that a majority were strangers in the town they practiced in throughout the period under study (tables 5, 6, 24-27). Many of them were from out of state or, in the case of the eastern district, migrants from the older, more settled region of Massachusetts. This development occurred despite efforts of county bar associations to exclude lawyers from other states and partly because county bar association efforts to discourage nonresident lawyers from riding the court circuit encouraged a broader residency distribution.

Beyond these factors, lawyers and sheriffs were also the most obvious agents of doom during the postwar depression. With lawsuits as the only effective means of debt collection, lawyers seemed to become "more numerous than locusts were formerly in Egypt and nearly as destructive." Even debtors who did not go to court would probably face an attorney, because attorneys were the major bill collectors for commercial men and money lenders.[47] The high costs of court astounded most people, and lawyers defended fewer debtors than creditors because debtors could not afford fees and did not perceive great benefits or security flowing from legal counsel. Despite periodic efforts to limit costs by law, assessed costs often equaled the value of a suit.[48]

TABLE 5 MOBILITY IN MASSACHUSETTS: LAWYERS, 1760–1840

GEOGRAPHIC LOCATION	COLLEGE GRADUATES, 1760–1809		COLLEGE GRADUATES, 1810–1840		NONCOLLEGE GRADUATES, 1760–1809		NONCOLLEGE GRADUATES, 1810–1840	
Practiced in native town	31.1%	(155 of 498)	31.1%	(215 of 690)	25.7%	(25 of 97)	24.2%	(39 of 161)
Practiced in one town, not native	37.5%	(188 of 498)	41.5%	(287 of 690)	40.2%	(39 of 97)	42.8%	(69 of 161)
Practiced in two towns	23.8%	(119 of 498)	21%	(145 of 690)	25.7%	(25 of 97)	25.4%	(41 of 161)
Practiced in three or more towns	7%	(36 of 498)	6.2%	(43 of 690)	8.1%	(8 of 97)	7.4%	(12 of 161)
Moved out of state	17.3%	(86 of 498)	17.8%	(124 of 690)	16.5%	(16 of 97)	19.2%	(31 of 161)
Moved into state	8.2%	(41 of 498)	14.4%	(100 of 690)	6.1%	(6 of 97)	12.4%	(20 of 161)

TABLE 6 MOBILITY IN THE EASTERN DISTRICT, MAINE: LAWYERS, 1760–1840

GEOGRAPHIC LOCATION	COLLEGE GRADUATES, 1760–1809		COLLEGE GRADUATES, 1810–1840		NONCOLLEGE GRADUATES, 1760–1809		NONCOLLEGE GRADUATES, 1810–1840	
Practiced in native town	4.7%	(6 of 127)	17.7%	(53 of 300)	14.2%	(6 of 42)	9.8%	(7 of 71)
Practiced in one town, not native	66.9%	(85 of 127)	47.3%	(142 of 300)	57%	(24 of 42)	53.5%	(38 of 71)
Practiced in two towns	19.7%	(25 of 127)	24.3%	(73 of 300)	21.6%	(9 of 42)	30.9%	(22 of 71)
Practiced in three or more towns	8.6%	(11 of 127)	10.6%	(32 of 300)	7%	(3 of 42)	5.6%	(4 of 71)
Moved out of state	18.8%	(24 of 127)	20.3%	(61 of 300)	9.5%	(4 of 42)	25.3%	(18 of 71)
Moved into state	85%	(100 of 127)	26%	(76 of 300)	70%	(23 of 42)	29.5%	(21 of 71)

What made the situation critical was the great number of court suits (tables 2 and 4). In Worcester County, for example, nearly 4,000 cases appeared on the dockets of the court of common pleas between 1784 and 1785.[49] In Essex County, Theophilus Parsons alone entered eighty writs at the April term of the court of common pleas in 1784. Lincoln entered 201 actions in one term of the Worcester County Court of Common Pleas. The leading lawyer in the county, Lincoln, to no one's surprise, soon became one of the largest landowners in Worcester County.[50] Paradoxically, the court system charged the costs of court cases to the loser—usually a debtor-defendant—regardless of who brought the suit. The prosperity of the legal profession not unexpectedly antagonized the residents of Massachusetts.

Lawyers, however, felt that the value of their services not only justified their fees, but that there were so many lawyers it was difficult to make a living. Just as business is seldom good for a businessman, the practice of law was rarely profitable to a lawyer. William Pynchon, a Salem lawyer, reported throughout the 1784-1786 period that legal business was poor. John Q. Adams complained in 1787 that the profession "is increasing rapidly in numbers, and the little business to be done is divided into so many shares, that they are in danger of starving one another."[51] John Forbes, a young Northfield practitioner, complained of riding 260 miles in one week scouting out business; he subsequently sought professional opportunity in Rhode Island. This same attitude still prevailed thirty years later when Rufus Choate discouraged an acquaintance from starting practice in Massachusetts because "of the scarcity of clients and the still greater scarcity of fees and neglect of merit."[52] But most professionals expected to build a practice over a number of years despite the uncertainties and penury of the early years. Prosperity followed persistence in the American myth. And for many lawyers with proper credentials and connections, it became reality. Established lawyers could be more confident of sustaining incomes. Yet even they depended on attracting the attention of clients. After the Revolution, the growing number of lawyers (as shown in tables 1 and 7) eroded one guarantee of legal success—a local law monopoly —except in the outlying districts, where business was scarce. Every shiretown or commercial center attracted a surplus of legal talent.

TABLE 7 INCREASE IN NUMBER OF LAWYERS BY COUNTY, 1800–1840

COUNTY	1800	1805	1810	1815	1820	1825	1830	1835	1840
Barnstable	3	2	5	9	7	11	8	8	8
Berkshire	20	21	31	34	35	38	36	36	40
Bristol	10	12	18	24	25	25	34	34	38
Dukes		3	4	3	3	3	3	4	
Essex	14	20	33	42	41	47	55	47	57
Franklin[a]				16	23	26	26	27	23
Hampshire	32	40	48	21	31	29	34	30	30
Middlesex	20	25	42	29	47	56	65	71	82
Nantucket			5	2	2	2	4	5	6
Norfolk	9	14	18	24	26	32	31	31	26
Plymouth	6	10	17	19	20	24	26	28	25
Suffolk	33	58	83	115	135	136	146	196	215
Worcester	18	33	44	56	63	65	77	74	62
Cumberland[b]	9	26	41	37	45				
Hancock	4	13	23	30	17				
Kennebec	12	26	33	31	43				
Lincoln	5	12	20	26	28				
Oxford[c]			5	7	13				
Penobscot[c]					13				
Somerset[c]			4	5	11				
Washington	1	4	4	3	7				
York	4	17	14	25	24				

Source: Composed from listing of attorneys and counsellors in *Massachusetts Register* for these years. Although the listings in the *Register* are occasionally incomplete, they do provide evidence of the great increase in lawyers throughout the state.

a. Franklin and Hampden were part of Hampshire and Berkshire counties before 1810.

b. This and the following counties became the state of Maine in 1820.

c. Not a county until the first numerical entry.

In fact, 80 percent of the lawyers lived in the fifty-four most commercial and cosmopolitan towns in the state.[53]

This growing number of lawyers limited the caseloads of most lawyers despite the general skyrocketing of litigation. The increase in the number of attorneys entering actions on the supreme court docket makes this evident. Five lawyers entered cases at the 1773 Cumberland term, but eleven attorneys did so in 1783. At the Essex term in 1774, just nine lawyers entered actions, but there were sixteen in 1788. Seven lawyers handled cases at the 1774 Hampshire term; there were fourteen in 1783 and twenty-eight in 1797. Five lawyers entered actions on the Lincoln term docket in 1786; twenty-two submitted actions at the county's 1797 supreme court session. The Worcester County court term saw an increase in lawyers from ten in 1774 to seventeen in 1786 and to twenty-five in 1795. There were few exceptions to this general trend.

Numerical growth also reduced the ability of a few lawyers to dominate the advocacy aspect of legal practice. Before the Revolution, a minority of barristers handled most cases tried before the superior court. They received internal aid from the graded system of professional practice that excluded more than half the sworn lawyers from advocacy roles in the highest court. A scarcity of resident lawyers made the practice of leading lawyers riding the judicial circuit with the judges of the high court very profitable and necessary to the smooth functioning of the legal system.

A study of the five leading lawyers in each court session, as measured by the number of cases handled in the superior court for ten counties between 1760 and 1770, reveals that only twenty-eight lawyers (56 percent of fifty hypothetical attorneys and barristers) appeared on the list. While seventeen appeared in the top five of just one county, eleven dominated in two or more counties. Trowbridge was one of the five leading lawyers in five counties ranging from York and Cumberland in the eastern district of Maine to Worcester, Middlesex, and Essex in the Bay region. Five other lawyers had one of the top five practices in three different counties.[54] The efforts of these dominant lawyers to maintain their status might have contributed to efforts to erect a statewide bar association in order to prevent county associations from restricting nonresident lawyers.

The increase in resident lawyers throughout the state and the restrictions of county bar associations against nonresident attorneys from other counties or states led to a greater geographic distribution of lawyers' caseloads in the supreme judicial court, evidenced by an examination of court dockets between 1785 and 1795. In the six counties studied, twenty-two lawyers appeared on the tabulation of the five leading lawyers in each county or 73 percent of a mathematical possibility of thirty. Although five possessed one of the top five practices in two or more counties, none approached Trowbridge's record. Moreover the counties they dominated were geographically contiguous and the lawyers normally lived in the county where their practice was largest. Daniel Davis and George Thacher, for example, were leading lawyers in the three Maine counties of Cumberland, Lincoln, and York. Parsons and Theophilus Bradbury appeared among the top five practitioners in the neighboring counties of Cumberland, and York, and also in noncontiguous Essex County. Only Sullivan, who rode the circuit after 1790 as state attorney general, placed among the head lawyers in widely scattered counties of Cumberland in Maine and Hampshire in western Massachusetts. Sullivan also ranked sixth in the Maine counties of Lincoln and York. Despite this wider distribution of legal business, a tremendous gap existed between the busiest and the least successful attorneys. Even among lawyers in the top five of a particular county, a broad differentiation in caseloads appeared. In the ten-year period for Hampshire County, Simeon Strong, for example, docketed 142 cases, but Sullivan, fourth on the list, had only 49. Lee argued 204 cases between 1786 and 1795 in Lincoln County; Thacher, who rated fifth, had only 60. This same pattern of a few leading lawyers—albeit a larger number—set apart from the main body of modestly successful practitioners appears to have continued in the years before 1850.[55]

The greater availability of local lawyers turned circuit riding from a lucrative expedition to a money-losing proposition. As early as 1790, Harrison G. Otis complained of the fruitlessness of circuit riding: "If these avocations into the country were as profitable as they are troublesome you would perhaps be reconciled to my apparent negligence but this is far from true."[56]

A study of supreme court cases for the 1820-1829 period confirms the death of circuit riding as a professional way of life. Eight annual sessions of the supreme court covering thirteen counties in Massachusetts as reported in the published court reports were used. The number of cases handled by each lawyer was tabulated, and every lawyer was ranked vertically by the number of cases. Although these published reports have a problem of selectivity—for example, they usually do not include continued cases—they nevertheless can be used to delineate the leading lawyers and which lawyers practiced in what county sessions. Only two lawyers, Richard Fletcher of Boston and Henry Hubbard of Pittsfield, appeared in the top five practitioners of more than one county. Fletcher had the fifth highest number of cases in adjoining Suffolk and Middlesex counties, and Hubbard was in the first five in neighboring Hampshire and Berkshire counties. Several others—including Lemuel Shaw of Boston and Elijah H. Mills of Northampton—handled a few cases in counties other than the county in which they appeared in the top five. Some lawyers had cases in several counties but never appeared as a leading lawyer in any one county.

As in the previous periods, the top lawyers clearly dominated particular sessions of the court. For example, William Baylies of West Bridgewater had 79 of 369 cases in the Plymouth County session over a ten-year period compared to his nearest competitor's 36 (thirty-four other lawyers divided the remainder). In Middlesex County, Samuel Hoar of Concord appeared as counsel in nearly one-third (92 of 299) of the reported cases, with 58 other lawyers dividing the remaining court appearances. This statistical study is backed by the business and personal papers of lawyers, reinforcing the conclusion that after 1800, lawyers usually attended the courts in counties other than place of residence when they had a prior commitment to a client. Lawyers regularly formed temporary partnerships with resident lawyers or simply referred business to a local contact in other parts of the state.[57] The disappearance of the circuit bar signaled the end of the profession as a fraternity of "gentlemen practisers of the law" and the emergence of the modern, dispersed, individualistic profession.

Most lawyers during this period believed that the excess of lawyers would lead to a decline in both the quality and profitability of law practice. Although no evidence has been found to substantiate these fears, the preceding studies do indicate that the increasing number of lawyers and their geographic distribution altered the nature of professional practice and the profession itself. Moreover most lawyers were justified in their complaints that they had little legal business in the courts. The reason, however, was not because there was a plethora of lawyers or a paucity of legal business but because a small group of lawyers, although it had increased in number as circuit riding ended, dominated court practice, leaving only a few cases for the vast majority of lawyers. Thus ironically, both laymen and lawyers found common ground in their desire to lessen the number of lawyers.

Despite the alleged predatory or confiscatory nature of much of their work, lawyers made little effort to relieve their clients and opponents. The bar associations' mandatory minimum fees—an attempt to counterbalance the increase in lawyers—seemed akin to doctors being forbidden to treat charity patients without normal payment (which they were not). Many people could not avoid concluding that the occupation was acting in its own interests against the interest of the wider community in general and the workingman and farmer in particular.[58]

Under increasing pressure from constituents, legislators moved forcefully against attorneys' and barristers' claims of an occupational monopoly in 1785. As part of a broader act regulating the admission of attorneys, the legislature ordered that the parties in court suits be allowed to plead and manage their own causes, personally or with the assistance of such counsel as they saw fit to engage.[59] The legislators clearly intended that the practice of law be open to anyone involved directly in a lawsuit or any person that a litigant might authorize as his attorney.[60] However, the use of the words, "the assistance of such *counsel* as they shall see fit to engage," was seized upon and exploited by lawyers like a technical error in a plea. They successfully stymied the law's design by arguing that "counsel" could be interpreted only to mean a professional lawyer.[61]

This law also replaced the legal profession's self-proclaimed standards for the admission of attorneys with minimum requirements, which were so general that they could easily have been interpreted as allowing admittance to almost every applicant. Each candidate was required only to be of good moral character, well affected to the constitution and government of the state, proficient enough to render him useful in the practice of law, and to have had an opportunity to qualify himself for the office. The courts, however, with many professionally oriented and highly trained lawyers on the bench, chose to restrict admissions to candidates with formal legal training, whereas a court system led by laymen might have thrown the profession wide open.[62]

The failure of these regulations to alleviate the inconsistencies and burdens of litigation led to more virulent verbal and political attacks on the legal profession as desperate people searched for a simple solution to complicated problems. Opponents extended their demands beyond open admission policies to the regulation of fees for lawyers and ultimately to the abolition of the entire profession. One critic satirically argued that the legal class could not be abolished because without lawyers, "Justice would be too easily attained—deception, oppression, intricacy, and chicanery, would cease; and this every honest man must certainly regret."[63]

Legislators on November 7, 1785, secured the appointment of a house committee to examine the laws making attorneys accountable for neglect of their duty, but no laws punishing faulty or unethical practices resulted.[64] Courts held a power of disbarment, but the obligation of regulating lawyers' ethics by default fell increasingly to the lawyers and their county bar associations.

After passage of the Act Regulating the Admission of Attorneys, trained practitioners moved to counteract the adverse public opinion through the newspapers. Under the pseudonym of "Agrippa," one attorney argued that the current distress was not the lawyers' fault; it instead resulted from monetary inflation and economic depression that followed every war. "Indeed it is inconceivable," he rationalized, "that less than one hundred men, of any description, and many of them not getting a subsistence should occasion such general distress through the state."[65] Such sophisticated arguments by lawyers' defenders failed to assuage their opponents. On the contrary, the entry of the lawyers into the war of words served only to escalate the verbal conflict.[66]

By the summer of 1786, protests of rural residents had shifted from the newspapers to raucous town meetings and county conventions. Even relatively quiet, eastern towns, such as Braintree, demanded laws that would "crush or at least put a proper check or restraint on that order of Gentlemen denominated Lawyers" whose conduct appears "to tend toward the destruction rather than the preservation of this Commonwealth."[67] The emotional appeal of such antilawyer outcries cannot be denied, but they were not the only focus of the written protests, and their importance to the overall protest movement can be easily exaggerated.

In late 1786 and early 1787, several town meetings and county conventions, including eight such bodies in central and western Massachusetts, sent petitions to the general court calling for further controls on the legal profession. Almost three times as many other petitions of grievances to the general court, however, did not even mention lawyers.[68] In the period's perspective, other issues seemed much more important; lawyers were only part of the larger problem of an increasingly complex and impersonal legal system and government.

The opposition to lawyers in central and western counties was stiffened by the people's struggle to lessen both political and economic dominance by the eastern counties. This emerged as a major issue in the constitutional struggle on both a state and federal level and, violently, in Shays's Rebellion. That most lawyers and state supreme court justices were easterners, traveling only on circuit into the western counties, increased hostility toward them as visible agents of eastern political and economic power.[69]

Economic disaster and political frustration led to a broad area of demands. Among those most often mentioned in 1785-1786 were the abolition of the court of common pleas, the removal of the state capital from Boston to a point farther west, the use of referees and justices of the peace to settle debt disputes without court actions, the use of the impost duties to lower tax rates, and the issuance of paper money. By the end of 1786, residents of central and western Massachusetts had concluded that their most immediate need was relief from tax liens, mortgage foreclosures, and public auctions of property for debt.[70] Consequently they turned their efforts toward prohibiting these actions and engaging in illegal activities that would apply pressure on the state's power structure.

Even as critics attacked the legal profession, some lawyers attracted respect among some elements of western Massachusetts, symbolized by their continued election to public office. It is impossible to determine exactly who voted for these men, but the fact remains that citizens chose numerous lawyers as representatives and senators throughout the state. Surprisingly, for example, Sheffield residents chose Sedgwick as their representative to the Berkshire County convention in August 1786. At the same time Thomas Gold, a Pittsfield attorney, sat in the Hampshire County convention. Both meetings roundly denounced lawyers.[71]

The selection of most lawyers probably depended on their political alliance with merchants, tradesmen, and artisans. Lawyers not only associated with merchants and tradesmen as legal advisers, but they often were business partners, giving them common interests and a similar perspective on society. Lawyers were frequently available for political activity; their flexible schedules and the recognized value of public notice for legal business made them efficacious spokesmen and representatives for the commercial community. Sedgwick and Gold probably were candidates of these elements. Sedgwick, who was a staunch opponent of leniency for debtors, lived for years under threats to his life. When replaced by Dr. Samuel Holten as a delegate to the Confederation Congress in 1786, Sedgwick wondered whether it was "because I am an old offending lawyer." Gold lost his post when Pittsfield residents became more radical. Colleagues of Gold from Pittsfield at the August convention had been two wealthy members of the local aristocracy; their replacements were more radical, small farmers. When small farmers and laborers challenged the political leadership of the landed-commercial elite, lawyers, already focal points of animosity, naturally served as lightning rods for the hostility directed at the moneyed class of the state.[72]

The dissension and antilawyer sentiment in Massachusetts was only part of a wide movement sweeping postwar America. This broad scope reinforces the thesis that it was the system of law rather than individual lawyers that aroused animosity. Historians have overwhelmingly focused on Massachusetts' court problems because of Shays's Rebellion. But hostility to courts and lawyers was endemic throughout New England and the North Atlantic states. Mobs threatened courts in Vermont and New Hampshire, while petitions to outlaw lawyers circulated throughout the region. In New Jersey Abraham Clark, a bitter foe of the organized legal profession, framed a law that altered and simplified legal procedure, sought to eliminate costly delays, and fixed a rigid schedule of fees. Many of the outspoken critics of the legal profession of the 1780s acquired more national importance as local leaders of the Jeffersonian Republican party.[73]

In Massachusetts an alarmed legislature suddenly became more conciliatory. The Act for Rendering Processes in Law Less Expensive, passed in November 1786, directed parties in suits before the court of common pleas to retain only one lawyer rather than the two attorneys permitted under the 1785 statute. More importantly, it required that all court actions, except those concerning real estate titles, be initiated before a justice of the peace with an appeal permissible to the court of common pleas, but judges were urged to arrange settlements by referees. Such action, the farmers claimed, would reduce the heavy overload in the county courts and provide less expensive justice by curtailing much of the court activity of lawyers. An emergency measure, the bill expired in two years, without providing permanent reform.[74] It deflected mounting antagonism away from lawyers but postponed needed alterations in the legal system and practice of law.

The commercial interests, despite their political and economic ties to the legal profession, were also tinged with antilegalism. In this period it was most evident in their support for the Referee Act of 1786, which called for the use of arbitration in civil suits. Despite the design of the legislature, practicing lawyers and the legally trained justices of the supreme judicial court soon negated its intent by reversing arbitration judgments on appeal for technical reasons. And in 1811 the court ruled that all questions of real estate were beyond the scope of the act.[75] Here as in the virtual nullification of the acts allowing laymen to practice law and prohibiting persons from retaining more than two lawyers, the alliance of bench and bar worked to enable lawyers and judges to solidify their control over the use of law in Massachusetts.

Without political and economic reform, these efforts to placate the people at the expense of the legal profession could not head off the armed closing of courts in Worcester, Hampshire, and Berkshire counties. The practice of the law became obscured in the attempt to reestablish law and order. Neither the followers of Shays and Luke Day nor the more peaceful delegates to the Hampshire County convention in January 1787 focused on the legal profession.[76] The regulation of lawyers in the acts of 1785 and 1786 may have satisfied them. Undoubtedly the Shaysites had come to recognize that lawyers formed only a small part of a more general quagmire: a system of indirect and unresponsive government and justice that proved to be incapable of meeting the demands and desires of debtors and dissident farmers, laborers, and artisans.

After overt rebellion had been crushed, however, the legal profession once again attracted the attention of reformers. Because the cost of justice remained a constant complaint, politicians lowered the state system of fees for all court officials, including lawyers. This move directly challenged minimum fee schedules in Suffolk and Essex counties, yet lawyers dared not publicly oppose it. Fees were fixed far below rates formulated during the war in 1778, which had, for example, allowed twenty shillings for arguing a case in the superior court and ten shillings in the inferior court. The regulations of 1787 allowed a maximum of twelve shillings for a case in the supreme court and six shillings a case in the court of common pleas or in the court of general sessions. The 1787 allowable charges most clearly approximated those set in 1701, but they were much lower because of the declining value of money over nearly a century. When the legislature attempted a further regulation of fees taxed by courts and also those charged by lawyers directly to clients, the members of the legal profession were able to muster enough support to defeat the proposal.[77]

The legislature, however, failed to pass other resolutions that not only had the support of some lawyers but would have more thoroughly reformed the legal system. Parsons, who later became chief justice of the state supreme court, introduced a bill to abolish the courts of common pleas and add three more justices to the supreme court. Justice would have been quicker and cheaper, according to Parsons, because many cases that originated in the court of common pleas, but were almost automatically appealed to the supreme court, would now originate in that upper court. The additional judges would have allowed more sessions of the supreme court to handle the case load. Other lawyers, such as Christopher Gore and Rufus King, supported the measure, but it did not pass—a failure Gore blamed on the weakness of governmental institutions.[78]

Even while resentment toward the legal profession was greatest, lawyers showed little overt concern. The Suffolk Bar met throughout the furor, and its records reveal little reaction to demands for its suppression. Along with the Essex Bar, it continued to restrain growth in the profession by enforcing restrictions on the number of law students allowed in each office and upholding the minimum fees for a clerkship. Yet the criticism seems to have been acknowledged by a tendency to loosen educational requirements within the Suffolk Bar. George Warren, for example, was permitted to enter the office of Perez Morton even though he had no college degree and his certificate of a liberal education proved to be unsatisfactory. Lawyers apparently believed that the outbreak of animosity would not demean their status in society. On the contrary, Gore argued that "lawyers are growing into consequence you may be assur'd."[79] The truth of Gore's prophesy became evident in the years after 1789. Once Shays's Rebellion had been pushed aside, lawyers resumed a strong political role, regaining lost seats in the house and senate and strengthening an already close alliance with the commercial establishment.

Lawyers were one of the dominant forces favoring ratification of the proposed federal constitution at the convention of 1788. Their overwhelming support became a rallying point for antifederalists. This is illustrated by the charges of Amos Singletary of the central Massachusetts farm community of Sutton: "These lawyers, and men of learning, and moneyed men, that talk so freely and gloss over matters so smoothly to make us poor illiterate people swallow down the pill, expect to get into Congress themselves; they expect to be the managers of this Constitution, and get all the power and all the money into their own hands, and then they will swallow up all us little folks, like the great leviathen."[80] In reality lawyers represented both rural and urban constituencies at the convention. Nineteen, or more than half of the lawyer delegates, came from the three eastern counties of Essex (nine), Suffolk (five), and Plymouth (five). Yet every county except York and Dukes sent at least one lawyer, and it is unknown whether any lawyers from those counties sought the office.[81]

The verbal, and occasionally physical, attacks of opponents produced only a temporary reduction in the number of lawyers sitting in the general court in 1786 and 1787 (table 8). Increasing numbers of lawyers won election to the House of Representatives

TABLE 8 LAWYERS ELECTED TO THE GENERAL COURT, 1760–1850

YEAR	SENATORS		REPRESENTATIVES	
	Number	Percentage	Number	Percentage
1760			4	3.5
1770			10	8.8
1780	3	10.3	3	1.5
1784	6	19.3	13	5.9
1785	5	16.1	15	6.8
1786	3	9.6	8	4.1
1787	2	5.6	11	4.1
1788	3	8.9	16	6.9
1790	4	11.8	19	10.5
1800	6	18.7	20	10.2
1810	6	15.0	41	7.6
1820	11	35.4	29	14.9
1830	15	37.5	59	13.0
1835	15	37.5	43	10.2
1840	15	37.5	25	7.1
1850	8	20.0	26	8.8

Source: Compiled from lists of members elected to the general court published in the *Acts and Resolves* for the appropriate years and compared with a list of all lawyers practicing in the state. Data for 1850 come from Poole's *Statistical View of the Executive and Legislative Departments of the Government of Massachusetts, 1850* (Boston, 1850).

peaking in 1830 with fifty-nine seats (13 percent) in the house and fifteen seats (37.5 percent) in the senate. Then a new round of antilawyer criticism, arising from a growing critique of "privileged and elite elements" in society, thinned the ranks of lawyer representatives. But legal practitioners maintained a constant hold on nearly 40 percent of the senate membership until the 1840s. Undoubtedly lawyers held more political offices than their simple numerical strength in the total population would seem to justify. They were never numerous or suitably united enough to control legislation affecting the profession against a determined opponent, although they could often muster enough support to modify drastically or deflect legislation altering legal practices.

In the House of Representatives, lawyers held a small minority of seats, rarely exceeding 10 percent. Between 1800 and 1815, just 190 lawyers comprised 9.7 percent of a house membership of 2,283. In 1810, for example, attorneys constituted 41 (7.6 percent) of the elected members. Practitioners held 29 of the elected seats (14.9 percent) in 1820, 9 (13 percent) in 1830, 43 (10.2 percent) in 1835, 25 (7.1 percent) in 1840, and just 26 (8.8 percent) in 1850. Most won election in the eastern counties of Suffolk, Essex and Middlesex—areas where most lawyers resided and prospered in alliance with the commercial and industrial elements of society.[82]

Testimony to lawyers' vigorous political activities lies in the number of lawyers winning elective office despite underlying hostility toward the legal profession. A study of the political involvement of 764 professional lawyers between 1760 and 1810 and of 1,222 trained lawyers from 1810 to 1840 reveals an extremely high degree of participation. Of the 764 lawyers before 1810, 338 (44.2 percent) won election to a political office on the local, state, or national level. After 1810, 403 lawyers (32.9 percent) achieved an elective post. Many more practitioners tried their political fortunes but failed to win and therefore remain uncounted in this study.[83] At least half of all professional lawyers in the state probably sought political office at some point in their careers.

With the burgeoning of political power, lawyers were better able to flex their professional muscles, seeking a way of circumventing the section of the 1785 act that allowed any person to plead his own cause or to choose anyone to argue in his behalf. Attorneys and baristers confronted the problem directly in the courts, where they had the advantage. When an untrained practitioner appeared to plead, they would challenge his right to act as an officer of the court without being sworn by the court, question his power of attorney, or challenge every motion and argument that he presented to the judges and jury. Gone was the friendly camaraderie that often marked courtroom confrontations. Through their social and professional connections with the judiciary, lawyers successfully stifled laymen in the courts and convinced clients that security lay in having professional attorneys.[84]

The experience of William Lyman, an irregular practitioner in Hampshire County, demonstrates lawyers' methods for destroying the effectiveness of this law. When Lyman appeared to plead four cases in the court of common pleas at the August term in 1789, the professional bar, led by Simeon Strong, Caleb Strong, and Moses Bliss, stepped to the fore. First, they challenged his right to act as an attorney on the grounds that he was not regularly sworn or admitted. At the same time another lawyer, Samuel Hinckley, offered to serve Lyman's clients at no charge, saying he feared that their causes would be lost because of Lyman's status. Lawyers then questioned the constitutionality of the section of the 1785 act that permitted Lyman to appear in court and requested that the court establish a rule that only sworn attorneys could practice before it. Lyman was finally prevented from arguing the actions when the judges, Eleazar Porter, a trained lawyer, and John Bliss, a relative of Moses Bliss, ruled that he did not have a legal power of attorney from his clients.[85] Since the clients apparently were attending at court, this was indeed a spurious argument. But a point had been made and upheld: people in court had best hire a professional lawyer or be willing to suffer the consequences. With this aggressive approach and with the aid of lawyer judges, the efforts of the profession to nullify the legislative restrictions on their occupational monopoly, as on the use of arbitration, generally proved successful.

Lawyers further frustrated reformers by evading the legislative prohibition of one client retaining more than two lawyers. Splitting a court suit, retaining law partners, and hiring consultants emerged as ways for wealthy or aggressive litigants to subvert this law. With the onset of corporate clients and the formation of multimember law firms rather than one- or two-man offices, this eighteenth-century attempt at providing equal legal counsel for rich and poor simply was not viable. By 1820 violations of this statute had become accepted practice.[86]

Lawyers often manipulated the courts in other ways for their own personal or professional advantage. For example, Sullivan, a barrister and former justice of the superior court, once asked for a two-week adjournment of the court of common pleas slated to sit at Groton so that he could attend the superior court session at Barnstable and return in time to serve his clients. He justified his request by saying, "The Gentlemen of the Barr who are above mentioned (John Lowell, Benjamin Hichborn, Perez Morton, and

Christopher Gore) *and who* have gone to Philadelphia had influence enough to procure an adjournment of Boston Court until their return." Judges Abraham Fuller, James Prescott, and Samuel P. Savage ordered the court postponed from May 3 to the first Tuesday in June 1783.[87]

The evasion of these laws and the manipulation of the judiciary by members of the legal profession marked the ultimate failure of reformers' efforts in the 1780s to control lawyers. It also marked the triumph of informal forces over institutions and statutes. Accomplished with the connivance and, occasionally, the direct aid of lawyer judges, the avoidance of these legislative acts reveals the power of the alliance of bench and bar. It was this alliance and lawyers' political power that increasingly enabled practitioners to deflect legislative control and defuse public criticism. As the postwar unrest drew to a close and Massachusetts embarked on a new venture in national government, lawyers stood on the threshold of unprecedented political, judicial, and commercial power.

NOTES

1. Other historical studies of this period claim that lawyers were fighting to preserve what they had won. Anton-Hermann Chroust, "The Dilemma of the American Lawyer in the Post Revolutionary Era," *Notre Dame Lawyer* 35 (December 1959): 64. James W. Hurst, *The Growth of American Law* (Boston, 1950), 252-253, argues that the departure of leading lawyers as loyalists and the general disfavor of the bar after the Revolution broke up the influence of the local bar associations. Charles McKirdy, "Lawyers in Crisis: The Massachusetts Legal Profession, 1760-1790" (Ph.D. diss., University of Wisconsin, 1969), has a main thesis that the legal profession reached its qualitative and institutional peak before the war.

2. Robert J. Taylor, *Western Massachusetts in the Revolution* (Providence, 1954), 76-100; petition to Provincial Congress, February 23, 1775, in J. E. Smith, *The History of Pittsfield, Massachusetts* (Boston, 1869-1880), 1:345; *Boston Gazette*, July 25, September 12, 19, October 3, 31, November 16, 1774.

3. Theodore Sedgwick to Aaron Burr, August 7, 1776, quoted in Clifford K. Shipton and J. L. Sibley, *Biographical Sketches of Those Who Attended Harvard College* (Boston, 1873-1975), 16:216. Attorneys and barristers of Hampshire and Berkshire counties met at Springfield on May 18, 1781, in hopes of alleviating some pressure. They promised to curb unnecessary expenses arising from excess and vexatious law suits. As a group they

pledged not to undertake frivolous suits and "by council, advice and persuasion check and controul a litigious spirit." The nobility of their verbal effort became tarnished when they swore not to give legal advice without "an adequate and honourable recompense and reward first paid or secured to be paid." Bar Proceedings, May 18, 1781, Sedgwick Papers, MHi; Thomas E. Andrews, ed., "The Diary of Elizabeth Phelps," *New England Historic and Genealogical Register* 119 (July 1965): 221. Taylor, *Western Massachusetts,* 79-83.

4. John Adams, *Diary and Autobiography of John Adams*, ed. L. H. Butterfield et al. (New York, 1964), 1:264, 2:56, 3:287-289, 313; "Thomas Hutchinson's Address to the Suffolk Bar, August, 1765," in Josiah Quincy, Jr., *Reports of Cases Argued and Adjudged in the Superior Court of Judicature of the Province of Massachusetts Bay . . . 1761–1772*, edited by Samuel Quincy (Boston, 1865), 197; Cadwallader Colden to the Secretary of State and Board of Trade, December 6, 1765, in *The Colden Letterbooks, 1760–1765*, NYHS, *Collections* 2 (1877):70-71; Milton Klein, "Prelude to Revolution in New York: Jury Trials and Judicial Tenure," *William and Mary Quarterly* 17 (October 1960): 440-443; General Thomas Gage to Secretary Conway, December 21, 1765, in Edmund S. Morgan, *The Stamp Act Crisis: Prologue to Revolution* (Chapel Hill, 1953), 184-185; Elias Boudinot to Hugh Gaine, [1765], Elias Boudinot Papers, DLC.

5. Francis Bernard to Lord Hillsborough, December 12, 1768, Francis Bernard to Board of Admiralty, March 15, 1769, Francis Bernard Papers, DLC.

6. Roscoe Pound, "The Legal Profession in America," *Notre Dame Lawyer* 19 (June 1944): 339. Some of the lawyers that Anton Hermann Chroust cites as loyalists in *The Rise of the Legal Profession in America* (Norman, 1965), 2:5-6, were not trained or regularly admitted lawyers in Massachusetts. Furthermore the figures he cites for the number of barristers and attorneys at the outbreak of the Revolution (2:8) appear to be inaccurate. In 1775 there were thirty-five barristers, not forty-four as Chroust claims. For example, he lists Samuel White and Richard Dana; White died in 1769 and Dana in 1772. Simeon Strong, also listed, was not admitted as a barrister until the 1780s. The number of attorneys was not "at least fourteen" but thirty-six. See table 1. *Mein and Fleeming's Register for New England . . .* (Boston, 1773); John Adams, *Legal Papers of John Adams*, ed. L. Kinvin Wroth and Hiller B. Zoebel (Cambridge, Mass., 1965), 1:ci, cviii, cxi, cxiii, xcix; George Bliss, Jr., *An Address to the Members of the Bar of the Counties of Hampshire, Franklin and Hampden . . . 1826* (Springfield, 1827), 26; Joseph Willard, *An Address to the Members of the Bar of Worcester County . . . 1829* (Lancaster, 1830), 39, 100; Franklin B. Dexter, *Biographical Sketches of the Graduates of Yale College, 1701-1815* (New

York, 1885-1912), 1:178-179, 390-391, 417, 511-512, 698-699, 2:775-776, 3:96-97, 444-448; *Biographical Directory of the American Congress, 1774–1961* (Washington, D.C., 1961), 980, 1456; William T. Davis, *History of the Judiciary of Massachusetts* (Boston, 1900), 185; William T. Davis, *Bench and Bar of the Commonwealth of Massachusetts* (Boston: 1895), 1:268, 270, 282, 2:164, 181, 336, 484, 515, 542; Benjamin Labaree, *Patriots and Partisans: The Merchants of Newburyport* (Cambridge, Mass., 1962), 11, 212-213; Harvard University, *Quinquennial Catalogue of the Officers and Graduates: 1636–1925* (Cambridge, Mass., 1925), 165; E. Francis Brown, "The Law Career of Major Joseph Hawley," *New England Quarterly* 4 (July 1931): 492-502.

7. McKirdy, "Lawyers in Crisis," 87-107. McKirdy estimates that there may have been as many as a hundred lawyers, but his list of eighty-one attorneys contains several untrained or nonpracticing men.

8. *Biographical Directory*, 1456; Shipton and Sibley, *Biographical Sketches*, 12:574-84; Davis, *Judiciary*, 99-103.

9. Emory Washburn, *Sketches of the Judicial History of Massachusetts from 1630 to the Revolution in 1775* (Boston, 1840), 241-317; John Cushing, "A Revolutionary Conservative: The Public Life of William Cushing, 1732-1810" (Ph.D. diss., Clark University, 1960), 32; Charles Warren, *A History of Harvard Law School and of Early Legal Conditions in America* (New York, 1908), 1:47-48.

10. Robert Zemsky, *Merchants, Farmers and River Gods* (Boston, 1971), 34; P. M. G. Harris, "The Social Origins of American Leaders: The Demographic Foundation," *Perspectives in American History* 3 (1969):192.

Many lawyers perceived power, responsibility, social and economic advancement, and preferment in politics, and they hastened to grasp them. Lawyers' zealous political participation is highly complex, but part of the answer must be that legal training produces men with necessary tools. A lawyer's skills of interpersonal mediation, conciliation, and verbal persuasion are highly applicable to politics. Moreover attorneys in private practice can arrange their business affairs in order to provide a flexible work schedule. They can also absent themselves from regular practice without undue inconvenience and without major obsolescence overtaking their professional knowledge. A lawyer's career, one can argue, could gain from politics through the acquisition of personal and professional contacts, knowledge, power, and prestige. Law quickly became the road to politics in large measure because politics, whether of election or preferment, had become the arena of power and status. This bonding of politics and law in the young republic was crucial to the development of both politics and the legal profession in America.

Some men began to study law not to become advocates but as the first step in a planned political career. They were little concerned with technical intricacies learned in apprenticeship. Issues of professional autonomy and control over education and advancement within the profession gradually lost their significance to these men. Politics subsequently involved lawyers in statewide and even national problems. When men with such backgrounds became leaders of the profession, they could easily see the advantages in a statewide system of regulation for lawyers. These men were not wed to local control. They did not fear centralized power. They sought it.

11. John D. Cushing, "The Judiciary and Public Opinion in Revolutionary Massachusetts," in George A. Billias, ed., *Law and Authority in Colonial America* (Barre, 1965), 169, 173-176.

12. Ellen E. Brennan, *Plural Office-Holding in Massachusetts, 1760–1780* (Chapel Hill, 1945), 41-46; John Q. Adams to John Adams, February 4, 1792, Adams Papers, MHi; William Sullivan, *An Address to the Members of the Bar of Suffolk County, Massachusetts, March 1824* (Boston, 1825), 41-42; Davis, *Judiciary*, 101.

13. George Dexter, ed., "Record Book of the Suffolk Bar," MHS, *Proceedings* 19 (December 1881):152-155.

14. John Adams to Abigail Adams, June 4, 1777, Adams Papers, MHi.

15. Dexter, "Record Book," 152-155; Fitch E. Oliver, ed., *The Diary of William Pynchon of Salem . . .* (Boston, 1890), 215.

16. Theophilus Parsons to John Sullivan, March 17, 1785, Washburn Autographs, MHi.

17. David Sewall to John Lowell, September 1782, John Lowell Papers, MHi; Walter L. Burrage, *A History of the Massachusetts Medical Society, 1781–1922* (Norwood, 1923), 389 395.

18. Diary of John Fell, August 6, 1779, DLC; Francis Dana to Elbridge Gerry, [1784], Gerry Papers, DLC.

19. John Adams to Elbridge Gerry, September 20, 1779, Knox College.

20. William Cushing to John Adams, July 29, 1776, Adams Papers, MHi; Thomas Cushing to Robert T. Paine, September 9, 1775, Paine Papers, MHi; Hector St. Jean Crevecoeur, "Letters from an American Farmer," in Oscar Handlin, ed., *This Was America* (Cambridge, Mass., 1949), 56; "Old Lincoln Street—The Daniel Henchman Farm," *Proceedings of the Worcester Society of Antiquity* 16 (1902): 261.

21. This information comes from a detailed study of the supreme court (superior court before 1782) minute books and a similar tabulation of all cases involving lawyers in some county courts of common pleas. Supreme court cases represented only a small part of a lawyer's trial practice. A comparison of suits in the county courts and the supreme court indicates that only approximately two in ten cases reached the supreme court.

22. Davis, *Judiciary*, 295.

23. Theron Metcalf, ed., *The General Laws of Massachusetts . . . to 1822 . . .* (Boston, 1832), 1:chap. 9, sec. 4, passed July 3, 1782, 66. Dexter, "Record Book," 145-146. Some states, including New York and New Jersey, gave similar powers to the courts, while other legislatures, as in Virginia and South Carolina, passed laws more directly regulating the profession. Chroust, *Legal Profession*, 2:245-269.

24. Dexter, "Record Book," 157; James D. Hopkins, *An Address to the Members of the Cumberland Bar . . . 1833* (Portland, 1833), 30; for a further discussion of this issue see Gerard W. Gawalt, "Massachusetts Legal Education in Transition, 1766-1840," *American Journal of Legal History* 17 (January 1973):33-35.

25. Dexter, "Record Book," 159-161. For the high percentage of lawyers that were college graduates, see chapter 4. Gardiner and Hill became law students the next year, presumably after acquiring the necessary education.

26. Ibid., 156-160.

27. Hollis R. Bailey, *Attorneys and Their Admission to the Bar in Massachusetts* (Boston, 1907), 32-33; Chroust, *Rise of the Legal Profession*, 2:133; William Coleman to William Plumer, Jr., March 29, 1787, William Plumer Papers, DLC; D. Hamilton Hurd, ed., *History of Worcester County* (Philadelphia, 1889), 1:lxxviii; *Biographical Directory*, 980; Thomas Fleet and John Fleet, *A Pocket Almanac for . . . 1785* (Boston, 1784), 81; Davis, *Bench and Bar*, 1:283-284, 524, 2:515; Davis, *Suffolk County*, 1:137; Shipton and Sibley, *Biographical Sketches*, 14:233-234; Although the commerce conducted in Suffolk County was much greater than that of inland Worcester County, the population of Worcester County more than doubled that of Suffolk County. U.S. Census Reports for 1790 and 1800.

28. Edward W. Corwin, "The Progress of Constitutional Theory Between the Declaration of Independence and the Meeting of the Philadelphia Convention," *American Historical Review* 30 (April 1925): 515-517; Massachusetts Records, Force Papers, DLC; Brennan, *Plural Office-holding*, 168-171.

29. *Acts and Laws of the Commonwealth of Massachusetts, 1782–1783* (Boston, 1890), chap. 44, 613-615.

30. Dexter, "Record Book," 158; Sullivan, *Address to the Members of the Bar of Suffolk County*, 45-46.

31. For a general view stressing the economic and political frustrations of the 1780s in Massachusetts, see Van Beck Hall, *Politics Without Parties: Massachusetts, 1780–1791* (Pittsburgh, 1972).

32. Decisions of the Superior Court by William Cushing, September 22, 1778, petition to the Superior Court, September 21, 22, 1778, in William Cushing Papers, MHi; Shipton and Sibley, *Biographical Sketches*, 15:93-94; Dexter, *Yale*, 437-438.

33. Richard E. Welch, Jr., *Theodore Sedgwick, Federalist: A Political Portrait* (Middletown, 1965), 22-24, 29-30.

34. Oscar Handlin and Mary Handlin, *Commonwealth: A Study of the Role of Government in the American Economy: Massachusetts, 1774–1861* (New York, 1947), 12-13.

35. Petition of Mary Swain, June 1776, petition of Thomas Russell, June 3, 1776, Massachusetts Records, DLC.

36. Oliver, *Diary of Pynchon*, October 9, 1780, 75; *Massachusetts Centinel*, November 2, 1785.

37. Nathaniel P. Sargeant to Timothy Pickering, August 10, 1786, Pickering Papers, MHi; Caleb Strong to Nathan Dane, June 24, 1786 quoted in Shipton and Sibley, *Biographical Sketches*, 16:96.

38. Chroust, *Rise of the Legal Profession*, 2:11-18, argues that the lawyers' ability to make money during a depression by malpractice and their natural alignment with creditors were the major causes of antipathy toward lawyers. The evidence also does not support the conclusion of Welch, *Sedgwick*, 46-47, that it was not the accredited bar but the buying of debts by third-rate legal hacks that brought public odium on the profession. Albert Farnsworth, "Shays' Rebellion," *Massachusetts Law Quarterly* (February 1927): 29-43, is even further from the mark when he asserts that because there were no bar rules for admission of attorneys before 1787, the debtor farmers were victimized by unscrupulous lawyers. Frank W. Grinnell, "The Judicial System and the Bar (1820-1861)," in Albert B. Hart, ed., *Commonwealth History of Massachusetts* (New York, 1928), 4:38-39, agrees with Farnsworth.

39. *Massachusetts Centinel*, September 24, 1785.

40. Instructions to Abraham Fuller in Francis Jackson, *History of the Early Settlement of Newton* (Boston, 1854), 208; instructions to Noah Alden, Bellingham Town Records, DLC.

41. Massachusetts Constitution of 1780, chap. 6, art. 6; *Acts and Laws of the Commonwealth of Massachusetts* . . . (Boston, 1890), 187-188, 810, 922; Cushing, "Public Life of Cushing," 177-192; Massachusetts Commission for Committee to Revise the Laws, November 29, 1780, Cushing Papers, MHi. On the persistence of British statutes in American law, see Elizabeth G. Brown, *British Statutes in American Law, 1776–1836* (Ann Arbor, 1964).

42. William Cushing, memoranda to the General Court, March 1788, quoted in Cushing, "Public Life of Cushing," 191-192.

43. *American Herald* (Boston), April 17, May 15, 1786; Richard E. Ellis, *The Jeffersonian Crisis: Courts and Politics in the Young Republic* (New York, 1971), 185-229.

44. *Massachusetts Spy* (Worcester), July 5, 1775; in a similar vein, see

"Plielutheros" in ibid., August 2, 1775.

45. *Independent Chronicle* (Boston), March 23, 1786.

46. John T. Hassam, "Registers of Deeds for the County of Suffolk . . . ," MHS, *Proceedings* 14 (1900-1901): 50-51; Welch, *Sedgwick*, 22-24, 29-30; Shipton and Sibley, *Biographical Sketches*, 14:233-234, 15:93-94; E. W. Carpenter and C. F. Morehouse, *The History of the Town of Amherst . . .* (Amherst, 1896), 60; Fleet, *Almanack for . . . 1785*; Davis, *Bench and Bar*, 1:284, 529, 536, 574, 2:164, 169, 180, 379, 461, 468, 484, 521-522, 564; Wroth and Zoebel, eds., *Adams Legal Papers*, 1:cx; *Biographical Directory* 980, 1456, 1548; Dexter, *Yale*, 1:437-438, 742-747, 2:775-776, 3:96-97, 444-448, 684-689, 4:160, 222; Labaree, *Colonial Newburyport*, 11, 212-217; Harvard *Quinquennial Catalogue*, 165; Hurd, *Worcester County*, 1:lxxvii; Smith, *History of Pittsfield*, 2:70.

47. *Massachusetts Centinel* (Boston), October 8, 1785; Marvin Mayer, *The Lawyers* (New York, 1966), 16-20.

48. Legal records of Dukes County, 1722-1800, DLC; Massachusetts Town Resolutions, 1773-1787, DLC.

49. Docket books, Worcester County Court of Common Pleas, 1784-1785, Courthouse, Worcester, Mass.

50. Theophilus Parsons, Jr., *Memoir of Theophilus Parsons* (Boston, 1859), 26; Lincoln Papers, MWA including writs, account books, deeds, and correspondence.

51. Oliver, *Diary of Pynchon*, 194, 256; John Q. Adams to Abigail Adams, December 23, 1787, in Worthington Ford, ed., *Writings of John Q. Adams* (New York, 1913), 1:36-39.

52. "Diary of John Q. Adams," 419; Rufus Choate to Edmund Carleton, June 1, 1823, quoted in Warren, *Harvard Law*, 1:366; John Forbes to Dorothy Forbes, April 16, 1791, Forbes Papers, MHi. For the difficulties of beginning practice, see also Theodore Sedgwick, "The Sedgwicks of Berkshire," Berkshire Historical and Scientific Society, *Collections* 3 (1899): 93; Leverett Saltonstall to William Minot, October 10, 1806, in Robert E. Moody, ed. *The Saltonstall Papers, 1607–1815* (Boston, 1972-1974), 2:348-49.

53. See Massachusetts Register for years after 1780, which contains an annual list of lawyers by residence. Hall, *Politics Without Parties*, 45.

54. This study and the following one were done by tabulating the cases for each lawyer in each court session. Minute Books of the Superior Court for Barnstable, Bristol, Cumberland, Essex, Hampshire, Middlesex, Plymouth, Worcester, and York counties, microfilm, MHi.

55. Minute Books of Supreme Judicial Court for counties of Cumberland, Essex, Hampshire, Lincoln, Worcester, York, microfilm, MHi.

56. Harrison Gray Otis to ?, January 14, 1790, Otis Letterbook, MHi.

57. A similar development in Tennessee is skillfully discussed in Daniel H. Calhoun, *Professional Lives in America: Structure and Aspiration, 1750–1850* (Cambridge, Mass., 1965), 59-87; Ephraim Williams, *Reports of Cases Argued and Determined in the Supreme Judicial Court of Massachusetts . . . 1804–1805* (Northampton, 1805), Dudley A. Tyng, *Reports of Cases Argued . . . 1806–1822* (Newburyport, 1807-1823); Octavius Pickering, *Reports of Cases Argued . . . 1822–1839* (Boston, 1824-1864). My conclusions are based on an examination of the papers of many Massachusetts lawyers, in particular the Lincoln Papers, Howe Papers, Burnside Papers, Goodwin Papers, Davis Papers, Kinnicutt Papers, Newton Papers, and Haven Papers, MWA; account book of Christopher Gore and Ellias Gray Loring cash book, MHB; Shaw Papers, Harrison Gray Otis Papers, and Cranch Papers, MHi.

58. For a discussion of the modern legal profession with this thesis, see Murray Teigh Bloom, *The Trouble with Lawyers* (New York, 1968), and Elliot A. Krause, *The Sociology of Occupations* (Boston, 1971), 171.

59. *Acts and Resolves of the State of Massachusetts, 1784–1785* (Boston, 1894), chap. 23, 476-477.

60. This position mirrored that of the superior court judges in 1778 as recorded by William Cushing during the hearings to disbar Strong and Bliss. The judges announced that "each Subject has an undoubted right to appear in said Court by himself or such other Persons not legally disqualified as he shall appoint." Decisions of William Cushing, William Cushing Papers, MHi.

61. *Acts and Resolves, 1784-1785*, 476-477; Journal of the Massachusetts House, May 1785-March 1786, 232, 240, M-Ar; Journal of the Massachusetts Senate, May 1785-March 1786, 198, 203, 208, M-Ar; *Independent Chronicle* (Boston), April 20, 1786; *Hampshire Gazette* (Northampton), April 7, 1790.

62. *Acts and Resolves, 1784–1785*, 476-477.

63. *Massachusetts Centinel* (Boston), November 16, 1785.

64. Journal of the Massachusetts House, November 7, 1785, M-Ar.

65. *Boston Gazette*, June 19, 26, 1786.

66. Articles defending lawyers were printed in *American Herald* (Boston), April 24, May 8, 1786; *Massachusetts Centinel*, November 16, 1785, April 8, 19, 22, 26, May 3, 20, June 3, 7, 14, 21, 28, July 5, September 9, 16, 1786. Other articles attacking lawyers appeared in *Boston Gazette*, April 17, 1786; *Hampshire Gazette* (Northampton), October 4, 25, December 27, 1786, February 14, 1787; *Massachusetts Centinel*, April 5, 12, 15, 22, 26, 29, May 6, 10, 17, 27, June 17, 24, July 12, 1786.

67. Petition of the Braintree town meeting, September 1786, in Charles F. Adams, *Three Episodes in Massachusetts History* (Boston, 1903), 2:895-897.

68. Petitions of the towns of Dracut, Ware, Stoughton, Braintree, Fitchburg, Hopkinton, Leverett, Shirley, Plymton, Swanzey, Taunton, Norton, Upton, Bedford, Acton, Methuen, Rowley, Groton, Grafton, and Lee in Shays' Rebellion Collection, MWA; "Roxbury Instructions," *Massachusetts Centinel*, September 9, 1786; petition of Worcester County Convention, August 26, 1786, MWA. In thirty-eight town resolutions, 1786-1787, in Massachusetts Town Resolutions, 1773-1787, DLC, only eight contained resolves against lawyers.

69. Lee N. Newcomer, *The Embattled Farmers: A Massachusetts Countryside in the American Revolution*, 2d ed. (New York, 1971), 98-100.

70. See note 68.

71. Welch, *Sedgwick*, 40, 47; Smith, *History of Pittsfield*, 1:86-87, 115-117, 122, 179, 181, 189, 203, 295, 311, 317, 358, 400, 406, 414, 442, 459. For a thorough discussion of Berkshire and Hampshire counties see Taylor, *Western Massachusetts*, 103-167.

72. Van Beck Hall, The Commonwealth in the New Nation, Massachusetts, 1780-1790" (Ph.D. diss., University of Wisconsin, 1964), 22-24; Welch, *Sedgwick*, 40.

73. William Plumer to John Hale, September 30, 1786, and to Jonathan Plumer, June 8, 1784, June 6, 1786, Plumer Papers, DLC; Irwin H. Polishook, *Rhode Island and the Union* (Evanston, 1969), 120-121; "Vermont at the Period of Shays' Rebellion, 1784-1787," in E. P. Walton, ed., *Records of the Governor and Council of the State of Vermont* (Montpelier, 1875), 3:357-380; Richard P. McCormick, *Experiment in Independence: New Jersey in the Critical Period, 1781–1789* (New Brunswick, 1950), 181.

74. *Acts and Laws of the Commonwealth of Massachusetts, 1786–1787* (Boston, 1893), chap. 43, 1786, 105-111.

75. Lawyers' and judges' successful efforts to curb the use of arbitration in commercial cases is ably discussed in Morton J. Horwitz, *The Transformation of American Law, 1780–1860* (Cambridge, Mass., 1977), 148-155. The idea of voluntary arbitration was revived in Adams, Massachusetts, in 1821 to eliminate lawyers in debt settlements. *Pittsfield Sun*, December 26, 1821, January 2, 1822.

76. "Address to the People . . . in the County of Hampshire from the Body Now at Arms," *Massachusetts Centinel*, January 6, 1787; Petition of the Hampshire Convention, January 4, 1787, *Hampshire Gazette* (Northampton), January 17, 1787.

77. "Petition of Hampshire Convention," *Hampshire Gazette*, January 17, 1787; Journal of the Massachusetts House, 1787, 155, 173, M-Ar; "Diary of John Q. Adams," MHS, *Proceedings*, 2d ser. 16 (November 1902): 342; *Acts and Laws of Massachusetts, 1786-1787*, chap. 73, passed

February 28, 1787, 232-233; *Acts and Resolves, Public and Private, of the Province of Massachusetts Bay, 1769–1780* (Boston, 1886), 5:chap. 17, passed January 24, 1778, 766; *Acts and Resolves of the Province, 1692–1714*, 1:chap. 7, passed June 20, 1701, 467. Richard B. Morris, "Insurrection in Massachusetts," in Daniel Aaron, *America in Crisis* (New York, 1952), 21-49, remains one of the best brief studies of the causes of discontent in this period and the effects of the efforts of the rebels. For a more recent and longer study, see Hall, *Politics Without Parties.*

78. Christopher Gore to Rufus King, June 28, 1787, in Charles R. King, *Life and Correspondence of Rufus King* (New York, 1894), 1:226-227.

79. Dexter, "Record Book," 161-162; "Diary of John Q. Adams," September 28, 1787, 325; John Q. Adams to Abigail Adams, December 23, 1787, in Ford, ed., *Writings of Adams*, 1:36-39; Oliver, ed., *Pynchon Diary*, February 5, 6, 1784, 174; Christopher Gore to Rufus King, June 28, 1787, in King, *Rufus King*, 1:226-227.

80. *Debates and Proceedings of the Convention of the Commonwealth of Massachusetts . . . 1788* (Boston, 1856), 202-203. They were not above using their positions in the judiciary for partisan purposes. Rufus King, a lawyer by training but a politician by preference, noted that all the justices of the supreme court favored the federal constitution. "Cushing the Chief Justice gave a solemn charge last week in *Bristol* to the Grand Jury," said King, during which he "enlarged upon our distressed situation, the danger of anarchy, and the well founded fear that we might yet lose our Freedom for want of Government and concluded in favor of the adoption of the Report of the Convention—this charge will be repeated on Tuesday at Cambridge." Rufus King to Henry Knox, October 28, 1787, Knox Papers, MHi.

81. *Debates and Proceedings*, 31-43, 87-92, 204, 318.

82. James M. Banner, Jr., *To the Hartford Convention: The Federalists and the Origins of Party Politics in Massachusetts, 1789–1815* (New York, 1970), 335. Both their professional aims and political interests differentiated cosmopolitan eastern members from their legal brethren in rural and western Massachusetts. Seldom could lawyers unite behind legislation favorable to the profession. Often they found themselves fighting rearguard actions against efforts to curtail their practices, curb their professional autonomy, or control their fee schedules. Some lawyers—among them John Gardiner, Levi Lincoln, Jr., and Robert Rantoul, Jr.—even introduced bills to limit or eliminate powers of the profession.

83. All lawyers known to have practiced in Massachusetts and for whom relevant data could be found are included in this study. It may be assumed with some certainty that a lower percentage of those lawyers for whom no evidence relating to their political participation or lack thereof could be

found have participated in politics. Therefore if this information were available, the percentages might slightly decline.

84. Trained lawyers and judges mingled socially during every session of the court, creating a personal familiarity that increased their professional identity. For particular examples, see Oliver, ed., *Diary of Pynchon*, 25, 136, 167, 225, 255, 291.

85. *Hampshire Gazette*, March 31, April 7, May 5, 12, 1790.

86. Docket books of the Massachusetts Superior and Supreme Court, 1761-1797, microfilm, MHi; Worcester County Supreme Judicial Court docket books, 1800-1830, Court House, Worcester, Mass.; Kennebec County Supreme Court docket books, Court House, Augusta, Maine; Williams, *Reports of Cases, 1804–1805*; Tyng, *Reports of Cases, 1806–1822*; Pickering, *Reports of Cases Argued, 1822–1839.*

87. James Sullivan to John Tyng, May 6, 1783, James Sullivan Papers, MWA; *Boston Gazette and the Country Journal*, May 12, 1783.

3

Lawyers under Fire

As social, political, and economic stability returned in the 1790s, lawyers became more aware of their powerful position in society and confident of their ability to maintain it. They thus became more willing to accept constructive criticism and to entertain plans for organizational reform. But neither the legal profession nor its critics could agree on a unified plan. Growing internal disputes over the philosophy of law, politics, the nature of legal education, and the profession's control mechanisms became critical to the profession. Members continued to utilize bar associations to achieve material advantages for their members and to elevate professional ethics and cultural standards.

Simultaneously the Enlightenment idea that nature and nature's law provide a pattern to order society increasingly influenced some younger, more scholarly lawyers' approach to law and the legal profession. Enlightened lawyers viewed law as a dynamic, organic body rather than a diffuse aggregation of legal cases and statutes. Just as scientists of the eighteenth century searched for generalizations about nature, philosophers, lawyers, and theologians sought natural laws governing society, human nature, religion, politics, and economic life. This view of law as a science clashed with the traditional utilitarian approach to law and the profession, and it spawned major changes in the training of lawyers and the practice of law.

Laymen also divided into factions over legal reform. One group of radical reformers, led by Benjamin Austin, Jr., Thomas Allen, and John Leland, sought the destruction of the legal profession, the simplification and Americanization of the law, and the reconstruction of the court system. Moderate reformers hoped to alleviate some of the worst problems by reconstituting the court system, making procedural changes, enlarging rather than reducing the power of judges, Americanizing law, and making it more understandable and uniform by reducing it to written form either in statutes or court reports. Another faction, small in size like the radicals, wanted to strengthen the power of judges and leave procedural questions and the interpretation of the law in the hands of judges and lawyers of their own persuasion. As a result, lawyers who often favored moderate reform found themselves in the advantageous position of peacemakers and compromisers when court reform resurfaced as a powerful political concern.[1]

All these reforms swirled about the legal profession in 1789 as Massachusetts began life under the new national political system that spurred aspirations of rising social and economic status throughout society. Most lawyers looked to the future, confident that their frustrations would be eased by new opportunities for law practice and for lucrative and power-laden appointive posts. More than any other occupational group, they quickly leaped into the broadened political arena and seized a dominant position in the federal judiciary and the state's congressional delegation (tables 9 and 10).

The federal judiciary, staffed by trained lawyers, reinforced this lawyer-government tie by the traditional structure of a graded profession. When the United States District Court for Massachusetts met at its first session in Boston on December 1, 1789, Judge John Lowell, a Massachusetts barrister, ruled that all gentlemen ranking as barristers and attorneys of the state supreme court who took the oath to the United States would be admitted as counsellors and attorneys of the district court with equal rank. Subsequently the United States Supreme Court strengthened this artificial stratification the next year with the rule that candidates for admission as counsellors or attorneys to the Supreme Court must have held that rank in their state supreme court for three years. The erection of a graded profession on a national level may have been influenced by William Cushing, a trained Massachusetts lawyer, who sat on the United States Supreme Court. These rules preserved the graded profession in Massachusetts because judges and lawyers had apparently become disinterested as evidenced by the very few promotions of attorneys to the rank of barrister after 1784.[2]

While the seniority system of the profession was being bolstered by the federal courts, lawyers' privileges again came under attack from within the legal profession. John Gardiner, a barrister trained in England, spearheaded this ambitious effort. The major thrust of his 1790 reforms was to mold the profession and the entire legal system to the needs of a changing society. One subsidiary aim was to destroy the exclusive nature of the profession, particularly lawyers' control over training and admission standards.[3]

John Gardiner, the son of Dr. Sylvester Gardiner, a wealthy loyalist émigré, was born in Boston, but at an early age went to study in England. Admitted as a barrister of King's Bench in 1761 after preparing at the Inner Temple with Sir Charles Pratt, later lord chancellor of England, he practiced privately and served as an assistant to Lord Mansfield. These connections earned him the post of attorney general of the island of St. Christopher, where he sat out the war. The end of the Revolution reawakened hopes of restoring the family fortune in Massachusetts, and Gardiner returned to Boston, where he successfully reacquired large tracts of family land in Maine. As the only practicing lawyer in the state who had been trained at the Inns of Court, he aroused much jealousy and resentment for both professional and nationalistic reasons. After an unsuccessful attempt to practice law in Boston, he moved to family lands in rural Pownalboro, Maine. There, despite his English connections, residents not only accepted him but continuously elected him representative to the general court from 1789 until his death in 1793.[4]

His reforming zeal was also suspected on other grounds. Political ambition probably played a role in his reforming zeal. In November 1790 (ten months after his plan was presented), he offered himself as a candidate for the United States Congress. Another contributing cause of his action was undoubtedly the Suffolk Bar's 1784 rejection of his son, John Sylvester, as a student. His embittered attacks on the bar associations, which often overshadowed his other substantive reforms, probably grew out of this experience.[5] His less than objective motivations, when combined with the prevalent Anglophobia, presented opponents with more than enough ammunition to defeat most of Gardiner's proposals.

He introduced the "proposed law, or code" in January 1790 in

TABLE 9 OCCUPATIONS OF MASSACHUSETTS MEMBERS OF CONGRESS, 1789–1840

YEAR	LAWYERS	DOCTORS	MINISTERS	MERCHANTS	MANUFACTURERS	FARMERS	OTHERS[a]
1789	5	0	0	3	0	1	0
1791	5	0	0	3	0	0	1
1793	7	3	0	5	0	0	1
1795	11	1	1	4	0	1	0
1797	9	0	1	3	0	2	1
1799	12	0	1	3	0	3	2
1801	9	1	1	2	0	0	2
1803	9	2	1	4	0	0	2
1805	8	0	2	5	0	3	1
1807	11	0	2	4	0	2	2
1809	12	0	0	5	0	3	1
1811	8	0	1	6	0	4	2
1813	16	1	1	5	0	2	0
1815	18	1	1	3	0	1	0
1817	21	0	0	3	0	0	0
1819	18	3	1	3	0	0	1
1821[b]	10	2	0	3	0	0	0
1823	10	0	0	3	0	1	1
1825	11	0	1	3	0	0	2

1827	11	0	1	2	0	0	2
1829	10	0	1	2	0	0	2
1831	11	0	0	2	1	0	1
1833	12	0	0	2	1	0	1
1835	10	0	0	1	3	0	0
1837	12	0	0	1	2	0	0
1839	16	0	0	0	2	0	0
Total	292	14	16	80	9	23	25

Source: Biographical Directory of the American Congress, 1774–1961 (Washington, D.C., 1961).

Note: Of the twenty-two members of the Massachusetts delegation to the Continental Congress, there were ten lawyers, seven merchants, one physician, one brewer, one farmer, one teacher, and one retailer.

a. Includes teachers, retailers, shipbuilders, and distillers.

b. Maine became a separate state.

TABLE 10 OCCUPATIONS OF MAINE MEMBERS OF CONGRESS

YEAR	LAWYERS	PHYSICIANS	MINISTERS	MERCHANTS	MANUFACTURERS	FARMERS	OTHERS
1821	6	0	1	2	0	1	0
1823	6	0	1	0	1	1	0
1825	8	0	0	0	1	1	0
1827	7	0	0	0	1	2	1
1829	6	1	0	1	0	1	1
1831	6	2	0	0	0	0	1
1833	9	1	0	1	0	0	0
1835	8	1	0	1	0	0	1
1837	9	0	0	3	0	0	0
1839	9	0	1	0	0	0	0
Total	74	5	3	6	3	6	4

Source: Ibid.
Note: Until 1820 Maine was a district of Massachusetts.

the Massachusetts legislature, then sitting as a committee of the whole, which referred the plan to a committee composed of one member from each county.[6] Arranged in twenty-one sections, Gardiner's bill, which suggested over fifty changes in Massachusetts law and legal practice, initially met only scattered, verbal resistance from professionals such as Dr. Charles Jarvis and Dr. William Eustis, and a judge of the court of common pleas, William Spooner. Gardiner's main opponents, the lawyers, remained quietly in the background despite a vicious verbal attack and a group of professionally castrating proposals.[7]

There could be no question that the profession's autonomy was threatened by Gardiner's bill. Among his proposals were plans to declare all bar meetings unlawful; to provide for the admission of law students by the supreme court upon a certificate of good moral character from the selectmen of their town and from their minister; to require all law students to attend the sessions of the supreme court and take notes; to allow any man to draw his own writs; and to prevent the charging of fees for travel and court attendance that were not actually performed. The first two ideas may have stemmed from his son's rejection by the Suffolk Bar, but the final two restrictions, which were rooted in the excess charges of many lawyers, had been repeatedly demanded. In summary, Gardiner accused the lawyers of usurping the power of the general court and the judiciary by deciding court cases before trial and by controlling admission to the legal profession.[8]

Gardiner did not spare the judiciary either. He designed a radical program for preventing conflict of interest in the execution of justice, most of which was adopted in the next century. He argued that judges should be restrained from any practice as lawyers under penalty of permanent forfeiture of the right to hold state office—a reform still sought by some. Lawyers and clerks of court should be prohibited from exercising the functions of a justice of the peace in any civil action, Gardiner proposed. He would also have prevented sheriffs, deputy sheriffs, coroners and constables from filling any writ except in their own cause or practicing law or giving any legal advice.[9] Gardiner naively hoped to institutionalize the impartiality of justice.

One of the most novel and potentially the most popular proposal, at least among debtors, was Gardiner's plan to provide free legal service for the poor by allowing "all poor persons to sue or defend, in all civil actions, and to defend in all criminal prosecutions, for offenses not capital without paying any fees to any lawyer or officer." Those without means to pay would have to prove their disability by affidavit before the courts would appoint an attorney. Support from the legal profession for this measure might have succeeded in countering complaints of excessive fees. An almost universal belief in self-help and rugged individualism almost certainly ensured that the plan never left the committee stage, but lawyers' opposition helped defeat it.[10]

There were still more proposed limitations on the activities of lawyers. Special pleading was to be abolished and everyone would be allowed to draw their own writs. Deeds were to be unsealed and written plainly to state intent in a short form of conveyance. All claims against one person were to be brought in a single action rather than a multitude of suits. Gardiner also wanted to outlaw champerty (contingency fees) and maintenance, or the aiding of lawyers in one suit by a lawyer not directly employed in the same suit.[11]

Other measures were aimed at aiding special interest groups in the state. One, specifically designed for many of Gardiner's Maine constituents, was a quieting act to allow a person living on land for a certain, unspecified length of years to assume ownership for a specific sum. Such a bill finally was enacted in the next century, thus solving the longstanding problem of squatters in Maine. If enacted in 1790, it would have removed a major cause for the separatist movement in the eastern district. Another proposal would have eliminated incarceration for debt except between merchant and merchant. Indebtedness, however, remained a crime in Massachusetts for another forty years.[12] These special interest bills met the same storm of opposition that greeted most of Gardiner's sweeping plans.

The depth and breadth of Gardiner's reform program proved to be detrimental because it antagonized a great spectrum of powerfully connected men. In the legislature, professional men surfaced as leaders of the anti-Gardiner movement. Doctors Jarvis and

Eustis consistently opposed him. Judge Spooner spoke against Gardiner's call for a meeting of the house as a committee of the whole to consider his plans without regard for parliamentary rules. Lawyers Samuel Sewall, John Bacon, and Thomas Ives attacked Gardiner's bills that proposed to allow any person to appoint anyone as his attorney and to limit court taxation for travel and attendance fees. Lawyers Parsons and Jonathan Mason, Jr., publicly and privately led a propaganda barrage against the entire program.[13]

An anonymous writer denounced Gardiner's proposals for the elimination of special pleading and the curtailment of bar associations as a plot "to convince a New England yeomanry, that English fees and English practice are the only proper fees and practice for the Order in Massachusetts." Even the editor of the *Cumberland Gazette* in Portland, Maine, reversed his previous support for Gardiner, observing that "while Mr. Gardiner shews himself acquainted with the laws and practice in England, he exhibits a great degree of ignorance and misapprehension in the constitution, laws and practice of the Courts of law in this Country."[14] The persistent prejudice against English law that had often hurt the legal profession became an ally in the defeat of Gardiner's reforms.

Some critics accused him of being a stalking horse for the legal profession, while most lawyers were alienated by his ideas and his intemperate speeches. Even potential allies, such as James Sullivan who sympathized with much of Gardiner's program, became estranged. Sullivan remarked that Gardiner had little support because he was "reforming the Law and abusing every Body."

Most of Gardiner's plan failed to generate any enthusiasm in the legislature. Gardiner and two other lawyers, Bacon and Abraham Holmes, comprised a subcommittee to draft bills from Gardiner's recommendations. The assignment of two professional lawyers indicates the legislative attitude toward Gardiner's bill, particularly given Bacon's outspoken opposition. Consequently the subcommittee reported out only three measures: A Bill for the Annihilation of Special Pleading; A Bill to Prevent Actions at Law Being Brought Without the Knowledge of the Plaintiff and for Allowing Everyone to Constitute any Fellow Citizen his Attorney; and a Bill to Prevent Fees from Being taxed in Any Bill of Costs hereafter for Travel Not Performed. Proposals to prevent judges from acting as lawyers and lawyers and clerks of court from acting as justices of the peace in any civil actions, albeit part of Gardiner's code, were independently introduced.

Of these measures, only one became law at that time.[16] Lawyers and their supporters could not prevent the passage of the bill to keep open the practice of law to laymen and to allow the people to prosecute or defend their own causes. The preamble explicitly stated that its aim was to clarify doubts that had arisen in some of the judicial courts since the 1785 act respecting the rights of persons to act as attorneys other than those who had been admitted in the form proscribed by law.[17] Thomas Dawes, Jr., a young Boston attorney, appealed to the state's attorney general, Paine, to urge the governor to veto the bill. "The consequences I need not mention —to say the least, the Courts would be worse than Town Meetings," pointed out the elitist lawyer. Nevertheless Governor John Hancock signed the measure into law on March 6, 1790.[18] The tradition that a man has the right to represent himself in court still remained to frustrate lawyers' monopolistic aims.

Another of Gardiner's proposals that ultimately was enacted was the abolition of what was considered the most English of legal arts: special pleading. The object of special pleading was to default the writ or plea of an opponent without testing the facts of the case. Robert Auchmuty, for example, won a case from James Otis when the judge abated a writ because the defendant was listed in the writ as a yeoman. Auchmuty claimed that his client's militia commission as a captain had raised the defendant above the rank of yeoman to the status of gentleman. On this basis the judge dismissed the case. Many lawyers considered this technical pleading indispensable to the practice of law and the proper functioning of the courts, and their countermoves reduced Gardiner's initiative to mere legislative maneuvering.[19] At their urging, the general court authorized a study to revive parts of the British statute law that had been adopted by the courts of law but not included in the laws enacted by the legislature since 1775. The house and senate appointed four lawyers for the task, but their efforts never extended beyond their committee. Meanwhile Gardiner's bill for the annihilation of special pleading, which had been reported out of committee, languished and faded into the background, but the idea would not die.[20]

Because of their own aspirations, professional lawyers made sure they found the time to aid judges, many of whom had trained and worked as lawyers and had many lawyers for friends. Practitioners contributed to sidetracking Gardiner's plan to prohibit judges from practicing law anywhere within the state. Then they threw their political muscle behind efforts to secure a salary increment for justices of the supreme judicial court. Parsons and even Gardiner spoke in favor of increasing the judges' salaries. The measure passed, allowing the chief justice £370 per annum and the other justices £350 per annum.[21] The interdependence and mutual assistance of the judiciary and the legal profession was a well-established political and economic fact.

With Gardiner's plan safely defeated, some lawyers turned their attention to nurturing the potential power and institutions of an autonomous profession.[22] Lawyers at opposite ends of the state organized bar associations in regions where lawyers had only recently been under withering attack. Lawyers founded the Berkshire County Bar Association in 1792 and issued rules that closely resembled those of the Worcester County Bar. In order to staunch the influx of attorneys from Connecticut and to halt the outflow of law students to the Litchfield Law School, they refused to credit legal studies performed outside Massachusetts toward admission to practice. Noncollege graduates could enter the profession, but they had to study between four and seven years in the office of an attorney of the supreme court. College graduates, who presumably were better prepared in Latin, Greek, philosophy, and similar areas, had to study law for the standard three-year term.[23]

Minimum prices for legal services were set at more than double the rates judges could assess under state law. Minimum rather than maximum fees were always used by lawyers in their quest to end competition within the occupation and to raise professional incomes, much as European guilds had determined wage prices in the past and labor unions would bargain for wages in the future. Berkshire lawyers agreed to charge 2.5 percent for debt collection and a minimum of twelve shillings as a retaining fee in all cases. They also set a minimum fee of twelve shillings to appear in the court of common pleas for a continuance or an appeal and an additional fee of twelve shillings for every term that each case was in court. One attorney would argue a case in the court of common pleas for five dollars, but if a client hired two or more lawyers, he could pay each only four dollars. In the supreme court the advocacy fee for one lawyer was eight dollars, but for more than one lawyer, their fee was six dollars each.[24] Such actions by the Berkshire lawyers reflected both in insensitivity for clients' purses and a sense of the profession's security.

Lincoln County lawyers also organized early in the 1790s and promptly adopted a provincial stand that extended the Berkshire rule of disallowing legal studies completed outside the state to include men trained in different counties within Massachusetts. In 1794, for example, Lincoln County attorneys refused to recommend Thomas Rice for admission to the court of common pleas because he had studied law in Worcester County. In Boston similar strictures were voted, but they then were amended to demand evidence of the bar association's consent in the county in which the student had studied—a fair request given the lawyer's reliance on personal knowledge to judge aspirants to the profession. It was a move that produced occasional inconvenience but only rarely outright rejection.[25]

In the decade after 1784, a sharp rise in the number of lawyers in Worcester County and a desire to improve training produced stronger preparation requirements for law students. In 1784 only ten lawyers resided in Worcester County, but eight gained admittance to the county court of common pleas, and the supreme court admitted twelve new attorneys for the county between 1785 and 1795. In 1795 members of the county bar assoociation stiffened its rules to require seven years of study instead of five for aspirants without a college education. Moreover in a move to weed out prospects with weak academic backgrounds, committees were formed to examine prospective law students. But the effort failed to halt professional expansion; eighteen lawyers began practice in the court of common pleas between 1795 and 1805.[26] Yet the extension of stronger regulations to Worcester County and the initiation of examinations probably contributed to raising the quality of lawyers in rural, central Massachusetts.

Lawyers were also buoyed by the organizational efforts of two other learned professions: doctors and ministers. Both the Boston

Medical Society, founded in 1780, and the Massachusetts Medical Society, established in 1781, imitated bar associations' form and function. Precedents for the doctors, in addition to the lawyers' organization, could be found in the Medical Society of New Jersey (1766) and the Medical Society of Litchfield, Connecticut (1767). A fee table, not surprisingly, had also been one of the first concerns of the Boston Medical Society. Congregational ministers moved in the same institutional direction in 1790 when they strongly recommended that all clergymen join ministerial associations that could issue credentials based on educational requirements to prospective candidates. These self-regulatory agencies soon were exercising as much power as bar associations.[27]

The idea that voluntary associations could furnish the necessary means to establish order in the professions gained momentum after the Revolution (and it still exists today with an intricate system of county, state, and national organizations, such as the American Bar Association and the American Medical Association). Professional associations were joined by agricultural societies, temperance societies, antislavery societies, women's rights groups, religious reform organizations, and intellectually oriented societies as people tried to use moral voluntarism to control and reform American society. Civic aspirations and cosmopolitanism led to a proliferation of formal voluntary associations. At least 1,900 voluntary societies were created in the period 1760 to 1820. Before the Revolution these groups had been largely restricted to Boston and to society's elite, but in the postwar period they proliferated throughout the state and encompassed all social groups. Each in its own way sought centralized power over an aspect of life through a voluntary cohesiveness.[28]

As the legal profession expanded, legislators sought to capitalize on the boom by levying a progressive excise tax on a lawyer's admission to each court level—twenty dollars for the court of common pleas, thirty dollars for attorney of the supreme court, and forty dollars for barrister. The tax had precedent in New England; lawyers had been taxed in Connecticut since 1756.[29] Motivation for the Massachusetts taxes, however, remains a mystery because they seem too small to have raised a substantial revenue or discouraged entrance into the practice of law.

The increased number of attorneys turned Boston lawyers' attention to ensuring high incomes. Fee rates adopted in 1796 by the Suffolk County Bar Association were designed not to fix standard fees but to prevent competition from lawyers who might lower charges to clients and thus cheapen the value of legal services. This new fee table was more than double the cost of legal service in other parts of the state. The Berkshire Bar in 1792, for example, had set a minimum charge of three dollars to argue a case in the court of common pleas and five dollars to argue a cause in the supreme court. In comparison, the Suffolk rate for the former was five dollars and for the latter, ten dollars. Small wonder that a foreigner visiting Boston in the 1790s reported: "The profession of the law is unhappily one of the most lucrative employments in the state. The expensive forms of the English practice, which good sense and the love of order ought to suppress, are still preserved here and render advocates necessary. These have likewise borrowed from their fathers, the English, the habit of demanding exorbitant fees."[30]

Increasing costs for legal services and the rise of political parties in Massachusetts brought the predictable result: a resumption of outbursts against attorneys in the press and demands for reform. Jeffersonian Republicans in particular fueled antilawyer feelings by partisan attacks on the legal profession—even though many lawyers, including leaders on both the state and national level, were party members. Political parties gave critics an organizational strength that they had previously lacked, and politicians saw antilawyer sentiment as an issue on which to capitalize. Usually they urged voters to exclude legal practitioners, especially their opponents, from political office as a means of destroying the profession's power. William Manning, a Billerica "farmer" who expressed his dislike for all professions in a politically astute pamphlet, *The Key of Liberty*, made a telling statement on this point. He complained that, despite all the criticism of lawyers, nothing had been done because the voters sent these "fee officers" as representatives to make the laws. "Unless the people can be brought to calculate more upon the opporation of these little selfish principles, on mankind, & purge the Legislatures from fee officers," he argued, "they cannot be governed by laws very long." Lawyers, more secure in their power, reacted less harshly than in the past and accepted the criticism as part of normal politics.[31] Although some lawyer politicians quite probably were hurt at the polls, the legal profession continued to enlarge its influence within political parties.

For lawyers in politics, there was no consensus beyond participation. An examination of the party affiliation of 304 lawyers between 1790 and 1860 demonstrates their division. No attempt has been made to determine why a lawyer entered a particular party or whether a lawyer adhered to his political label once he had been elected to office. What is important is that trained lawyers were associated with every major political party or faction; in commercial counties they tended to be Federalists, and in the western or rural counties they became Jeffersonian Republicans in these early years of the Republic. Evidence does not permit even the conclusion that lawyers belonged chiefly to the conservative parties, though a majority of the lawyers studied adhered to either the Federalists or, later, to the Whig party. Historians are still ambivalent about identifying these parties as either liberal or conservative. In Massachusetts many of the legal reforms, such as limited codification, statutory revision, abolition of special pleading, and court reorganization, came under Whig auspices. Few lawyers, with such notable exceptions as Gardiner, Robert Rantoul, Jr., and Henry Sedgwick, would be found on the radical side of legal or governmental reforms. Lawyers, like other politicians, reflected their constituencies.

Table 11 provides a statistical breakdown of party affiliation as determined by the party label that lawyer politicians claimed or were assigned by contemporaries during elections. The small number of Republican party members undoubtedly can be attributed to the fact that this analysis included only lawyers practicing before 1840 and that no newspapers were consulted for the post-1840 period.

James Banner's recent study of politics in Massachusetts shows that only 19 percent of the 178 lawyer members of the Massachusetts House from 1800 to 1815 whose party affiliation could be determined adhered to Jeffersonian Republicanism. He asserts that Jeffersonian Republican lawyers were certainly proportionately overrepresented in the general court and that lawyers became disposed toward Federalism by social origins and training, as well as by the structure and ethic of the legal profession. This conclusion

TABLE 11 LAWYERS' PARTY AFFILIATION

PARTY	NUMBER	PERCENTAGE OF WHOLE
Jeffersonian Republicans	40	13.1
National Republicans	29	9.3
Whigs	74	24.4
Democrats	49	16.1
Free Soil	7	2.3
Republican	11	3.6
Federalist	94	30.9

Note: Based chiefly on personal papers and contemporary newspapers.

echoes Jackson T. Main's study of political parties in Massachusetts, which argues that in the 1780s, lawyers always voted with merchants and lesser traders to form the commercial-cosmopolitan party in the state legislature—the same type of men who formed the Federalist party. But Banner's claim that the 19 percent figure for Jeffersonian Republican party affiliation among lawyers was an overrepresentation is unsupported by additional evidence. Banner makes no effort to establish the party affiliation of lawyers who were not representatives to the general court. Nor does he take into account that nearly half of the lawyer representatives came from the heavily Federalist regions of Essex and Suffolk counties and the Connecticut River Valley, where Jeffersonian Republicans could hardly expect election.[32] Both these omissions only limit Banner's argument, however. Certainly a majority of successful lawyer-politicians upheld the Federalist party—70 percent of the 134 Federalist or Jeffersonian lawyers included in table 11. But the fact remains that lawyers maintained both a high degree of participation and variable partisanship despite their strong and numerous ties to the commercial class. The *Salem Gazette* chided the Jeffersonians on this score: "Democrats hate lawyers: they have . . . therefore chosen a lawyer for governor, a lawyer for lieut. governor . . . in this town they have chosen the only democratic lawyer that could be found in it for representative."[33]

During these early years of the Republic, many people feared that lawyers would gain control of both the judicial and legislative branches of government. "The making of lawyers legislators, seems to defeat the grand principle of keeping the Legislative Department distinct and separate from the Judiciary," stated Jeffersonian Dr. Nathaniel Ames, brother of Dedham's Federalist lawyer, Fisher, in February 1799. If these two departments were in the same hands, Ames claimed, then "tho' the forms under the real sovereignty of the people are still observed to amuse them, the substance is gone."[34]

Lawyers' domination of the state's congressional delegation was particularly galling to the agrarian interest. As tables 9 and 10 show, over 290 lawyers served in Congress compared to 80 merchants who comprised the next highest occupational group. "A Plain Voter" from Cambridge queried: "Do we intend to put the whole government under the direction and control of this order of men? I should not be satisfied for my own part, with even nine Clergymen out of fourteen delegates, good and pious as they are," he said. "But to have nine lawyers and not a single Farmer, is really too much," he lamented. In rural, western Massachusetts, antilawyer sloganeering became a standard campaign tactic. Yet lawyers still won elective office. Ephraim Williams constantly faced the argument that his opponent Thompson Skinner should be elected because "we have now one Lawyer in Congress from this County, and that is more than their proportion, considering this district consists of farmers and mechanics."[35]

In the state legislature, which did not present the same geographic and occupational obstacles to service as the national Congress, lawyers did not approach the same dominant position in membership. But they did hold the most seats of any profession and were far ahead of their numerical proportion. During the 1800-1815 period, for example, 190 lawyers (9.7 percent) sat as members of the general court. At the same time, there were 116 doctors (5.9 percent) and 59 clerics (3 percent). But legal practitioners held a high number of seats for their small numbers in comparison to say farmers (941, or 47.9 percent), merchants (346, or 17.6 percent), or artisans (213, or 10.8 percent), most of whom came from the eastern and commercial areas of the state (table 8). Only occasionally did a rural town, such as Groton where 6 of 23 delegates between 1780 and 1840 were lawyers, send a high number of law brokers to the general court.[36]

Candidates seldom expected to attract votes simply because they practiced law. One halfhearted exception came in 1796 when "Farmers for Bradbury" answered the rhetorical question, "Is an extensive knowledge of the law any disqualification for a Representative to Congress?" with a resounding, "Certainly Not."[37] The growing political clout of lawyers ensured application of the precept that judges should have been legal practitioners.[38]

Lawyers did dominate the highest judicial offices, such as the supreme court, courts of common pleas, probate courts, and county attorney (table 3). They certainly held more than their proportionate share (based on population of course rather than expertise) of minor posts. For one profession to claim a preemptive right to an entire branch of government and then nearly to succeed in enforcing that claim was certain to arouse animosity in large segments of the electorate.

As they grew more confident of their power, legal practitioners even argued that minor posts, such as court clerk, should be filled by men trained in the law; however, they were not successful despite heavy-handed pressure (table 3). Nathaniel Ames said that he was forced to resign his office as clerk of the Norfolk County Inferior Court of Sessions and Common Pleas because lawyers would not honor any writs signed by him as a nonattorney and in general harassed him both in and out of court. An attorney replaced him. In 1833 the Berkshire Bar Association made an overt effort to influence the appointment of a court functionary. They notified Solomon Strong, a judge of the court of common pleas, that thirty-six members of the bar association recommended the appointment of Joel Davis of Lenox as court crier because his "character, circumstances, and acquaintance with the members of the Bar, render him a suitable person."[39] It was virtually impossible for a judge who had to depend on lawyers for the smooth working of his court to disregard such a plea. By 1840 legal training had joined party affiliation as a prime determinant of political preferment.

Critics of the legal profession opposed the control of the courts by trained lawyers, expressing fears of potential conflicts of interest, as well as the dominance of the group or class of men over the executive, legislative, and judicial branches of the government which might be used to extend their special interests. In 1784 a Massachusetts act expressly forbade a judge to counsel either party in a suit before his bench. But only one judge was removed from the bench before 1840 for indiscretion in accepting fees and acting as an adviser in cases pending before his own court; he was James Prescott, Middlesex county judge of probate, impeached and ousted by the Massachusetts House in 1821.[40] This action curbed neither the abuses nor the accusations, however. Even in 1839 the Committee on Agriculture in the Massachusetts House wholeheartedly supported a reduction of the salaries of judges and court officials: "All those officers are allowed to practice in the courts, and many of them, it is presumed, find their practice more profitable in consequence of holding an official station."[41] Court officials continued to practice law throughout the six decades after the Revolution.

Efforts to remove all or most lawyers from the judiciary became part of general judicial reform from 1790 to 1840. Some Jeffersonian Republicans hoped that the appointment of all judicial posts by the governor would weaken the power of the legal fraternity, assuming that a Jeffersonian were governor. In 1811 Elbridge Gerry, the Jeffersonian Republican governor, brought the appointment of county attorneys and court clerks under the executive wing, but this function was restored to the courts in 1814 by the general court. When this approach did not work, critics pushed for short terms of appointment and finally returned to the Berkshire Constitutionalists' demand for the election of judges and other court officers. In Massachusetts judges never became elected officials, but district attorneys had to seek popular election after 1856.[42] Given the lawyers' demonstrated ability to win elective office, there is little doubt that they would have maintained their dominance of the courts as well as the states' governing bodies and congressional delegation.

Conversely legal practitioners realized that their public image could adversely affect their professional practice. John Adams, for example, warned his son that "the purest Spirit of Popularity that we have in this Country is adulterated if not poisoned with ancient mawkish prejudices against the Profession and Professors of Law, which it is difficult to overcome." He added, "It deserves your consideration whether the highest Rewards are given to the cultivation of the law or not." Occasionally citizens took drastic action that ended a man's practice. In Lynn a deputation of angry citizens, affronted by the idea of a resident lawyer in their town, visited

Benjamin Merrill shortly after he hung out his shingle as the town's first lawyer. Merrill quickly grasped their message and sought refuge and a practice in Salem.[43]

Public criticism was just one reason why lawyers' political activities were not always self-serving. Another one, on a personal and professional level, was that their political involvement often raised serious obstacles to professional preferment, particularly if their political views clashed with the administration in power or the majority of the populace in the region where they practiced. Before the Revolution, John Adams complained that even a talented lawyer would be a failure in Boston if he was "not obstinately determined never to have any connection with Politics or does not engage on the Side of the Government, the Administration and the Court." Joseph Story, a Salem lawyer who became a Jeffersonian because of his idealism, his father's allegiance, and the opportunity for advancement in a growing party, warned of the same dangers of adhering to a political minority. Story claimed that many avenues of professional advancement had been closed to him "in a county where all the judges and lawyers are pertinaciously federal."[44] Sullivan, another highly successful lawyer and Jeffersonian politician, recalled in 1804 that he had suffered "every abuse" that Federalist lawyers such as Nathan Dane, George Thacher, and Parsons could administer to him with the full support of the "greatest part of the Bar." These attacks, Sullivan claimed, stemmed from his political loyalties.[45] Story, Adams, and Sullivan reaped handsome rewards when their own party gained power, however.

The time-consuming nature of a political career often loomed as a more crucial block to legal business. Harrison Gray Otis, who became one of the wealthiest lawyers in Boston through inheritance and real estate speculation, refused legal business in 1799 because "my avocations [politics] at this moment prevents me." Two years later Otis happily wrote to a London merchant that he had retired from politics and stood ready to resume his professional career.[46] Another lawyer, Robert P. Dunlap of Maine, even sought economic aid from bar association members. Arguing that he was "busily legislating for lawyers," Dunlap, a state representative in the assembly, wanted the "brotherhood" to maintain his practice during his politically caused absence.[47]

One of the best expositions of the labyrinth of dangers to a professional career posed by politics is a letter of Connecticut Valley counsellor and United States Senator Elijah Mills. "You must have misapprehended . . . , some part of my letter in relation to Mr. Lathrop," he began. "I most certainly wish him success and think him deserving of it. Still, I know full well the motives which induced his nomination, and the objects of those who promote it with us," he said. "First, Mr. Lathrop at present fills a place which our good brother Bates is very desirous of filling, and which he is certainly well qualified to fill with advantage to the country and credit to himself," Mills continued. "Secondly, Mr. Bates had a great deal of professional business, which, if he was sent to Congress, the young aspirants at the Bar—Forbes, Ashmun, Clark, etc., think they should share among them; and thus Lathrop, Bates, and myself being disposed of they could cut and carve business for themselves," he concluded. "But I have no idea of being disposed of in this way," he warned. "Hence I say that if their plans in the election of Lathrop for governor, and Bates as his successor in Congress should be successful, I should return home with a prospect of taking at least my share of professional labor and profit."[48]

The lawyer politicians tended to be highly successful in their profession, both before and after they won a major elective post (congressman, senator, governor, lieutenant governor). Few lawyers, however, simultaneously held a major political office and maintained a lucrative legal business. Of the twenty-two leading lawyers in six counties—Essex, Cumberland, York, Hampshire, Lincoln, and Worcester—for the 1785-1795 period only four—Theophilus Bradbury, George Thacher, Samuel Sewall, and Caleb Strong—were major politicians during the same period. However, all but three of the twenty-two men later held an elective office as governor, congressman, or senator.[49]

When multimember law firms emerged in the nineteenth century, leading lawyer politicians could expect to maintain their professional income. One early beneficiary of the ability to turn political office into professional profit was Daniel Webster. His national political reputation and power enabled him to maintain a highly lucrative legal career in Boston and Washington before both state and federal courts and agencies. Improved means of communication and transportation when combined with changes in the structure of professional practice, gradually eliminated much of the danger of both short- and long-term economic loss from participation in politics.[50]

Many lawyers saw career dangers in judicial appointment, the backbone of political patronage. Some, chiefly the most financially successful, claimed that judges were underpaid and that to appeal to top lawyers, the positions would have to be made more lucrative. Trowbridge in 1771 testified to this sentiment when he suggested that "some one Lawyer might be found in each County who would take a Seat upon the Inferiour Bench, if he could be made a Judge of Probate at the same Time." Financial problems grew graver during the inflation that occurred during the Revolution, and in 1780, the general court authorized bonus payments to justices of the superior court after three judges threatened to resign. By then their £7,000 salaries were worth only £100 lawful money as valued in 1775. In contrast the chief justice of the superior court before the Revolution had received £300 per annum and the four associate justices had each received £250 with independently collected fees, usually sufficient to cover expenses. In 1786 salaries were raised. The chief justice received £375 and the four justices £350, but the fees were then deducted from the salary. In comparison the Hollisian Professor at Harvard received £100 and the Harvard president had a salary of only £200. The high court justices had salaries well above the £100 per annum income level used as a base to determine entrance into the upper-middle class in revolutionary America.[51]

Leading lawyers, nevertheless, continued to perceive judicial salaries as lower than their potential professional incomes and refused to make this sacrifice. As a result Sullivan resigned, and Paine refused to accept appointment to the supreme court. Paine said he preferred the office of attorney general because "I hoped my Office would have yielded me more income which my family wanted than a judgeship." Theodore Sedgwick, a wealthy, politically powerful lawyer who became a justice of the Massachusetts supreme court, echoed the now standard cry that it was necessary to provide adequate, permanent provision for "the support of the Judges, other wise you will have Judges who are no lawyers."[52] Critics seized on lower judicial salaries as one way to curb the dominance of the legal profession within the judiciary.

The legal profession, keenly aware of these dangers, tried to maintain order in its own house. Lawyers of Hampshire and Berkshire counties petitioned the state attorney general, Sullivan, to prosecute vigorously any member of the legal profession who was guilty of buying securities or loaning money with the object of creating suits in violation of state law. And the Suffolk County Bar in 1800 appointed a standing committee of three lawyers to enforce its bar rules.[53]

Efforts to police the profession included tighter regulations for out-of-state lawyers. Candidates who had studied law in other states would not be recommended for admission until they had studied for one year in Suffolk County, according to that county association's 1800 rules. This requirement would be waived if they had practiced in the highest court of their state for four years, but candidates would still be examined on their knowledge and personal character. The Norfolk County Bar after 1804 reserved the right to examine every candidate from another state, and Hampshire County lawyers the next year required all non-Massachusetts candidates to study a minimum of eighteen months with an attorney of the supreme court in their county.[54]

Lower training requirements in some neighboring states and desires to curb competition partly motivated efforts to restrain nonresident lawyers. In Connecticut and Rhode Island, for example, the period required for apprenticeship was two years for college graduates and three years for nondegree holders—a variation of one to four years from Massachusetts rules. Yet the standards for New York, Vermont, and New Hampshire equaled those of the Bay State.[55] Lawyers, nevertheless, increasingly came from out of state: 8.2 percent of the lawyers entering practice in the state before 1810 were nonresidents but this grew to 14.4 percent for the years 1810 to 1840 (table 5).

Lawyers in Bristol, Plymouth, and Barnstable counties hoped an intercounty organization would be able to enforce higher uniform standards. But this latest multicounty institution of Massachusetts lawyers did not survive the supreme court's refusal to accept certificates of recommendation from the Old Colony Bar because they were not given by the county bar in which the candidate had studied.[56] Suffolk and Essex counties' legal leaders accentuated this divisiveness when they adopted a rule of extreme localism forbidding any lawyer, even if previously admitted to practice in the state courts, to open a law office in either county without its prior approval.[57]

Problems of internal control and conflicting regulations cried for statewide standards. Lawyers of Cumberland and Hampshire counties, for example, lacked written rules until 1805. Essex and Worcester county lawyers had let their bar association decline and were forced to reorganize in 1806 and 1809, respectively. York County did not have a formal bar association until 1811, relying on the so-called Old Bar for the district of Maine. Rules fluctuated widely where they did exist. Suffolk County required noncollege graduates to study five years and non-Harvard graduates to study for four years. Norfolk and Hampshire counties, in contrast, made individual decisions on each noncollege graduate. Students in Suffolk County had to pay an annual apprentice fee of $150; in Maine the rate stood at $150 for the three-year period, and Hampshire County lawyers charged $250 for a three-year clerkship.[58]

Lawyers' frustrating attempts at intercounty control are highlighted by an episode in the history of the Norfolk County Bar. In September 1805 the bar association members voted unanimously not to allow any "gentleman of the profession" to maintain more than one office at any time in the same or different towns. They then directed that Perez Morton, a leading lawyer who had offices in Dedham and Boston, be notified of the vote and requested to "immediately relinquish and discontinue, both directly or indirectly, either or the other of said offices." Then, realizing the futility of this action, they voted to ask assistance from the Suffolk Bar if Morton did not comply. The intransigent Morton carried on this "unethical behaviour" even when he became state's attorney general in 1810.[59]

Seeking to gain support for uniform standards, lawyers in Middlesex and Suffolk counties simultaneously called for a statewide meeting of attorneys and barristers during the summer of 1805 at Niles Tavern in Boston. But plans to create a code for legal education and admission standards failed. Only the lawyers of Essex County responded by adopting the 1805 rules of the Suffolk Bar.[60] The lawyers' failure to enforce standardization through voluntarism led to the imposition of statewide regulations by the Massachusetts Supreme Court.

This action by the high court justices with the support of other leading lawyers desiring centralized and uniform quality control came in the midst of a long and bitter battle to reform the state's legal system. Radical Republicans, conservative Federalists, and moderates from both parties were fighting a triangular battle in the gubernatorial elections and in the state legislature. Lawyers appeared on all sides of the issues, but moderate lawyers including Jeffersonians—Sullivan, Morton, and Story—and Federalists—Sewall, Sedgwick, and Otis—engineered the reform program that eventually emerged.

Two major programs confronted each other: one supported largely by radical populists and Jeffersonians and the other backed by Federalists and moderate Republicans. The more radical Republicans wanted an elective judiciary, which they believed would increase the reliance on jury members to interpret the law and to cross-examine witnesses and lawyers. They desired to eliminate dependence on lawyers whose interests, they charged, were "not congenial with the general welfare of the community," and they wanted to erect a system of reference that would act as a substitute for the lower courts, where, they thought, lawyers controlled the proceedings as judges and advocates. They also wanted to simplify the common law or replace it because of its uncertainty and its reliance on lawyers who "sport with their client with a parade of wonderful learning and investigation."[61]

The platform expounded by lawyers—Sewall, Sedgwick, and Otis—and supported by moderates of both political persuasions became a successful alternative. The publication of court records as a means of making court decisions available to lawyers and judges was a key part of this general scheme and a vital step in keeping the common law a viable system in the Bay State (adopted 1805). Moreover the publication of reports on state and national levels was a necessary step if American precedents were to replace British cases in common-law arguments. The design also included extending the power of the courts of common pleas (passed 1803); reducing the number of supreme court justices to five and introducing *nisi prius* (passed 1804); increasing the salary of judges (passed 1807); and circumscribing the powers of juries to interpret the law (accomplished by the judiciary).[62]

The supreme court's decision to set statewide standards for the legal profession can be seen as a product of this general desire to upgrade court decisions and expedite the judicial process. The rules, adopted at the supreme court's Suffolk term in March 1806, brought the legal profession in Massachusetts under a uniform code for the first time. One of the more significant innovations was to require an examination of every candidate for counsellor or attorney by a court-appointed Committee of Examiners for each county to determine the quality of legal attainments and the moral character of each candidate. Rejected aspirants could appeal to the supreme court. Qualifications for examination included at least seven years beyond a grammar school education, dedicated to literary acquisitions, of which three years must have been spent in the office of a Massachusetts barrister or counsellor. To qualify for an examination for counsellor, a lawyer must have been an attorney at the supreme court for a minimum of two years. Counsellors could practice as attorneys, but attorneys could not advocate causes on issues of fact in the supreme court.[63]

These rules reflected the ambitions of the cosmopolitan lawyers of Suffolk and Essex counties to impose their high standards on the profession. Extended education, lengthy and regulated training, and a graded advancement system remained vital elements in the profession. The introduction of court-appointed examiners was a creative effort to have the elite of the profession impose high entrance requirements after the traditional system based on personal relations and individual judgment had collapsed.

But even the supreme court justices could not avoid dealing with the regional differences that divided the profession. When the supreme court circuit reached the western counties in 1806, it came under heavy pressure from the bar associations to lower educational standards. Requirements of training for the bar had traditionally been more lenient in western areas, reflecting the rural and semi-isolated nature of the region and the lack of a local college. Opportunities for study were fewer, and requirements for practice seemed less demanding in those counties than on the cosmopolitan commercial coast. The judges quickly backed down and permitted candidates to pursue an education equal in advantages to a "liberal education" rather than seven years of "literary achievement."[64]

Organization men within the profession for the first time wholeheartedly accepted the primary institutional role of the judiciary in formulating regulations for legal education and admission standards. In exchange the profession finally acquired a statewide code of standards and a formal means of enforcing these regulations. Although the Massachusetts Medical Association had been granted the power to license doctors by the legislature in 1781, the regulatory power of the bar associations had never been approved by the state government. The principle that lawyers could best determine the qualifications of individual candidates for admission was given legal standing by the appointment of the examiners, even though ultimate authority plainly rested with the court—a body assumed by lawyers to be permanently composed of trained lawyers.

One historian in a recent study of Berkshire County has charged that politics inspired the formation of rules for admission of attorneys by the supreme court because the Federalist bench wanted to exclude Jeffersonian Republican lawyers from the profession.[65] Rather than an issue of Federalists versus Jeffersonian Republicans, however, evidence indicates that this action centered around the belief of most legally trained judges and lawyers that only an expert, highly organized legal profession could make the legal system work. An analysis of the examiners—positions that most likely would be filled entirely by Federalists if politics were the dominant influence—seems to downgrade partisanship as the motivating force.

Even though the supreme court justices overwhelmingly affirmed Federalist tenets, the examiners of attorneys and counsellors reflected the legal profession's political divisions. In a study of 120 politically active lawyers throughout the state, 87 (72.5 percent) were Federalists and 33 (27.5 percent) were Jeffersonian Republicans. A survey of the 46 lawyer examiners shows a similar breakdown. Of 30 examiners whose political affiliation could be determined, 23 (77 percent) adhered to Federalist views and 7 (23 percent) to the Republican party. Ironically one of the examiners for Berkshire County, Barnabas Bidwell, was a leading Jeffersonian Republican in the county; shortly after his appointment as examiner, Sullivan, the Republican governor, named him state's attorney general.[66] Motivation for court-established regulations sprang more from the inability of leading lawyers to persuade county bar association members to conform to uniform, strict standards at a time when many lawyers were concerned with general rules of law and standard interpretations of law.

These regulations failed to restrict the quantity of attorneys practicing at the supreme court, but they may have increased the ratio of professional lawyers having a college or liberal education. Of the forty-three lawyers admitted to the rank of supreme court counsellor or attorney in Suffolk County between 1807 and 1810, thirty-seven possessed a college degree. In Kennebec County eight of the nine lawyers admitted to the rank of attorney in the same years had a college degree, but only two of the six practitioners admitted to that rank in the five years before 1807 had possessed a college degree. Nevertheless in both counties the number of admissions to supreme court practice increased over the previous five years.[67]

If the formulators of these rules had hoped they would assuage the public's antipathy toward the legal profession, they were mistaken. Notwithstanding their organizational, educational, and political progress, lawyers remained under a cloud. William Bentley, a sometimes broadminded minister in Salem, summarized the profession's public image in his comments on the death of Governor Sullivan. "Nothing was objected to him seriously, but what belonged to his habits as a lawyer & of this character the people are the most jealous as it is the only one to which the people of this county [Essex] generally attribute dishonesty."[68]

Lawyers' refusals to observe the state law of allowing a person to conduct his own court case or appoint anyone he chose as his attorney, regardless of legal training, reinforced this distrust. The Suffolk bar repeatedly threatened its members with disbarment if they did not disassociate themselves from all actions entered in the courts by irregular practitioners. And then even attorneys of the court of common pleas whom the bar association had refused to recommend as attorneys to the supreme court were included in this prohibition. Lawyers of Essex County, where Bentley said most people distrusted lawyers, adopted the same rule in 1806, and Worcester County lawyers followed suit in 1809.[69]

Despite their conspiracy to continue an illegal monopoly through the coercive force of professional institutions, lawyers did try to regulate professional ethics. Bar association rules forbade lawyers of Essex and Suffolk counties to maintain an office with a justice of the peace, justice of the court of common pleas, or deputy sheriff (unless a lawyer held one of the first two offices himself, a not uncommon occurrence). Worcester County lawyers were also warned not to purchase notes of securities for the purpose of bringing suit for payment.[70] But efforts were more verbal than real.

The absence of a workable code of ethics can be traced in part to the emphasis placed on income rather than public service by bar association rules, which presumably reflected many lawyers' private beliefs. Originally designed as vehicles for the advancement of professional standards and status, bar associations had become, in large measure, a means of curbing internal competition by regulated fees and a controlled seniority system. To many laymen the establishment of minimum fee schedules symbolized a haughty disdain toward lawyers' clients.

Minimum costs for court suits, meanwhile, skyrocketed, spurred by the bar associations' adoption of differential rates for the various county, state, and federal court systems. A recognition of the progressive importance of court cases and the additional skill needed in higher courts furnished some justification for the fee scales. But the need to make the scale conform to the professional hierarchy and the real desire to collect larger fees were two more reasons. In 1796 Suffolk County lawyers, for example, were required to charge a minimum of five dollars to argue a case in the court of common pleas and ten dollars in the state supreme court. By 1805 these rates had risen to ten dollars and twenty dollars, respectively. While new rates in 1810 retained the same prices for court suits, lawyers substantially advanced charges on noncourt actions such as debt collection, divorce, advice on property, and the issuance of writs. Lawyers in Essex and Worcester counties followed the same general policies, although the rates tended to be lower outside of Suffolk County. In each instance, the rules urged lawyers not to construe them as excluding higher fees.[71]

Partly because of bar association efforts to curb internal competition and maintain high fees, most lawyers earned a moderate income. The few wealthy ones almost invariably acquired their riches outside of the courtroom. Sometimes their wealth came either from their parents or wife. Pliny Merrick, a country lawyer in Brookfield,

Worcester County, parlayed an inheritance of $1,564.44 and a successful law practice into a fortune in real estate worth $125,941.04 at the time of his death in 1814. Naturally enough, his son, also a lawyer, was quite wealthy.[72] As the power and wealth of some lawyers climbed, the status of the profession also improved as more wealthy and aggressive men perceived it as an opportunity for greater power, fame, and riches.

Other legal practitioners acquired wealth by the time-honored American means of land speculation. Access to the court records, an expertise in the instruments of land purchase and ownership, and familiarity with both debtors and moneyed men gave lawyers several unique advantages over most laymen in efforts to purchase or retain land. The collection of case fees, moreover, gave attorneys the usually scarce but essential liquid capital for land speculation in postrevolutionary America. The profession of law, in short, presented an opportunity to cash in on an expanding agricultural society where land steadily climbed in value as the population burgeoned.[73]

An examination of tax records indicates that some lawyers were virtually propertyless, however, and only a few older lawyers with long years of practice were wealthy landowners. Worcester County tax records provide a good example. The county contained a predominantly agricultural economy with strong local industry and a diverse transportation network, making it more typical of the state as a whole than the urban, eastern counties of Essex or Suffolk. (See table 12.) Nineteen of the fifty-eight lawyers in Worcester County (32.6 percent) possessed no taxable land or dwellings. These nineteen, however, had practiced an average of just 6.6 years and averaged 32.5 years of age in 1815, far below the average of 12.3 years of practice and 39.3 years of age for all the lawyers in Worcester County at this point. Twenty lawyers owned less than $2,000 in taxable real estate. These men had averaged 9.1 years of practice and 35.4 years of age. Nineteen lawyers owned a minimum of $2,000 in taxable real estate. These men were an average of 48.5 years old and had practiced an average of 21 years. There were exceptions, such as Levi Lincoln, Jr., and Bezaleel Taft, Jr., both of whom had inherited their wealth. The five lawyers of these nineteen men who held more than $5,000 in taxable real estate had practiced an average of 25.2 years and averaged 49.5 years in age.

Two lawyers, Lincoln of Worcester and Foster of Brookfield, were the largest landowners in their respective town.

Based on these tax valuations, only slightly more than 50 percent of the lawyers could be considered moderately prosperous or upper-middle class, and just two would rank as wealthy by contemporary local standards.[74] But clearly the older lawyers with more years of practice dominated the economic side of the profession, thus supporting the view of a stratified legal profession.

This interpretation is reinforced by comparing an 1834 valuation of lawyer's property in the town of Worcester (table 13) with that of 1815. Samuel Burnside, for example, paid no tax in 1815, but in 1834 he faced taxes on $15,350 in real and personal property. Newton's property valuation rose from 0 in 1815 to $31,800.[75] In 1834 only three lawyers in Worcester held less than $2,000 in taxable personal and real property, and they had practiced slightly less than an average of 6 years. The eleven lawyers owning more than $2,000 had been practicing an average of 16.4 years.

Professional incomes in postrevolutionary Massachusetts also showed a diamond pattern—a few rich and poor lawyers at either end of the bulk of moderately prosperous lawyers. An eminently successful Boston counsellor, Lemuel Shaw, grossed just $200 during his first year of practice in 1804-1805. By 1806 he was protesting that the weight of business prevented visiting his seriously ill father. And by 1830 he was reportedly receiving annual legal fees in excess of $15,000. From his lucrative practice in Essex County, Story reaped $7,000 in 1811, and in 1816 could coolly reject an offer of $10,000 per annum to practice in Baltimore, Maryland. Webster, another dominant lawyer, reported an annual income hovering around $15,000 between 1819 and 1844.[76] Income of this magnitude, rare though it was, most likely occurred in eastern Massachusetts.

More typical of a law practice's value in Massachusetts was a net income of well under $1,000 per year—not inconsiderable but not riches by any means in a society that considered $2,000-3,000 per annum a gentlemanly income. But it was still far above the average monthly wage rates of agricultural workers of $11.90 in 1818 or $11.60 in 1830 or the monthly wages of laborers of $13.50 in 1818 and $12.00 in 1830. Then as now, skilled tradesmen and artisans could earn as much or more money than many professionals, but

TABLE 12 VALUE OF LAND, LOTS, AND DWELLINGS OWNED BY WORCESTER COUNTY LAWYERS, 1815

AGE	YEARS OF PRACTICE	NAME	TOWN	VALUE	HIGHEST VALUE IN TOWN
32	10	Samuel Eastman	Hardwick	$ 557	$7,300
35	6	Ephraim Hinds	Barre		4,443
61	32	Eleazar James	Barre	3,370	4,443
c.31	5	Nathaniel Houghton	Barre		4,443
30	8	Lewis Bigelow	Petersham	1,602	4,698
49	20	Joseph Proctor	Athol	1,243	10,362
37	13	Samuel Swan	Hubbardston	691	4,616
39	11	Alexander Dustin	Westminister	2,512	5,773
35	15	Solomon Strong	Westminister	1,539	5,773
31	5	Samuel Cutting	Templeton	1,036	3,627
48	18	Lovell Walker	Templeton	1,295	3,627
30	5	Isaac Goodwin	Sterling	736	5,997
c.31	4	John Davis, Jr.	Lancaster		6,188
50	28	William Stedman	Lancaster	5,417	6,188
50	28	William Stedman	Worcester	2,591	18,628
38	13	Moses Smith	Lancaster	1,103	6,188
44	6	Joel Harris	Harvard		
40	17	Abijah Bigelow	Leominister	1,413	7,756
c.55	24	Asa Johnson	Leominister	2,057	7,756
c.29	3	John Shepley	Fitchburg	196	6,296
31	6	Calvin Willard	Fitchburg		6,296
44	19	Zabdiel Adams	Lunenburg	2,889	3,807
35	6	Daniel Henshaw	Winchendon	991	5,809
53	29	Seth Hastings	Mendon	4,694	10,597
38	9	Warren Rawson	Mendon	2,473	10,597
51	23	Benjamin Adams	Uxbridge	2,649	12,364
35	7	Bezaleel Taft, Jr.	Uxbridge	3,179	12,364
34	4	Sumner Bastow	Sutton	518	9,190
34	11	Samuel M. Crocker	Douglas		9,190
41	21	Francis Blake	Worcester		18,628
33	10	Levi Lincoln, Jr.	Worcester	8,478	18,628
66	39	Levi Lincoln	Worcester	18,628	18,628
60	34	Nathaniel Paine	Worcester	4,710	18,628
39	14	William E. Greene	Worcester	7,348	18,628
61	28	Benjamin Heywood	Worcester	3,925	18,628
35	10	Estes Howe	Worcester		18,628
38	15	William C. White	Worcester		18,628
33	5	Rejoice Newton	Worcester		18,628

TABLE 12 continued

AGE	YEARS OF PRACTICE	NAME	TOWN	VALUE	HIGHEST VALUE IN TOWN
59	35	Edward Bangs	Worcester	2,198	18,628
32	5	Samuel Burnside	Worcester		18,628
31	4	Levi Heywood	Worcester	1,177	18,628
27	4	Enoch Lincoln	Worcester		18,628
26	2	Gardner Burbank	Worcester		18,628
44	14	Nathaniel P. Denny	Worcester	3,666	18,628
39	14	Liberty Bates	Charlton	1,189	9,420
30	5	Frederic Bottom	Charlton		9,420
c.27	2	George Davis	Sturbridge	471	7,222
42	10	Daniel Gilbert	North Brookfield	2,747	5,652
29	4	Jesse Bliss	Brookfield	353	7,458
58	35	Dwight Foster	Brookfield	7,458	7,458
24	1	Pliny Merrick	Brookfield		7,458
34	9	Elisha Hammond	Brookfield	3,729	7,458
54	11	Amos Crosby	Brookfield	549	7,458
29	5	Jacob Mansfield	Western	254	9,067
32	7	Rufus Putnam	Rutland	981	5,883
33	5	Jonathan Morgan	Shrewsbury		6,319
31	4	Andrew A. Ward	Shrewsbury		6,319
32	5	William J. Whipple	Dudley		5,966
37	4	Nahum Harrington	Westboro		5,180

Source: United States Tax Valuation 1815, Worcester County Collection, I-II, MWA.

an indeterminable part of a lawyer's compensation came in the form of prestige and power.[77]

Many law brokers found more than moderate prosperity elusive. Christopher Baldwin, a young Worcester attorney who became librarian of the American Antiquarian Society, reported in 1830 that although he made $500 per year, it cost him that much to live. Another young attorney, Benjamin R. Curtis, who conducted John Nevers's legal practice in Northfield when he became sheriff, estimated its value in 1832 at only $800 per year. Two years later Curtis moved to Boston where he became a partner with his cousin, Charles

TABLE 13 WORCESTER VALUATION AND ASSESSMENT, 1834

AGE	YEARS OF PRACTICE	NAME	REAL ESTATE VALUE	PERSONAL PROPERTY VALUE	
37	16	Charles Allen	$8,200	$1,650	
34	9	Christopher C. Baldwin	0	600	(income)
51	24	Samuel Burnside	5,700	9,650	
47	19	John Davis	3,300	12,200	(stock, money at interest)
32	1	George Folsom	0	300	
34	9	Thomas Kinnicutt[a]	6,700	13,100	
30	7	Henry Paine	0	200	
56	31	Charles G. Prentiss	2,100	400	
21	1	Benjamin F. Thomas	1,650	1,600	(stock)
33	6	William M. Towns	4,000	100	
52	29	Levi Lincoln	27,800	11,000	(personal property and money at interest)
33	9	William Lincoln	26,700	4,950	
40	17	Pliny Merrick	14,600	1,300	
52	24	Rejoice Newton	27,850	3,950	

Source: William Lincoln Papers, Worcester County Collection, MWA.

a. Kinnicutt's personal account book values his investments at $55,660.74 for 1834 and $45,032.16 in debts. Thomas Kinnicutt Papers, MWA.

P. Curtis, and received a $500 a year guarantee or half the profits accrued from cases in the court of common pleas, debt collection, and conveyancing. Samuel Burnside, a Worcester lawyer, confided to a friend that between 1818 and 1823 , he had an income of only $2,084.84, exclusive of apprentices' fees, an average of $416.97 a year. Ellis Gray Loring, a Boston lawyer who set his net worth in 1830 at nearly $20,000 in real estate, notes, bills receivable, and cash, reported his legal practice income at $2,176.84 in 1830, and $3,707.17 in 1832; it slipped to $792.86 in 1831. Much of his total income came from rentals.[78]

Lawyers often prospered by diversification, functioning as accountants, real estate agents, commission merchants, bill collectors, and estate managers. Only rarely did an attorney decline nonadvocacy business. Most lawyers, such as Levi Lincoln, John Hancock's Worcester agent, gladly ran errands for a suitable fee.[79]

Lawyers in commercial regions were the business omnibudsmen. Boston lawyer Christopher Gore acquired great wealth by charging a 1.25 to 5 percent commission on business negotiations, estate management, and debt collection. Some fees were as low as £1.15.3 on October 3, 1786, and as high as £10.9 on July 11, 1786. But most important, they were numerous. For legal cases requiring political as well as legal savvy, Gore charged high fees. In 1805, he received $900 for speaking on behalf of "the sponsors of a bridge from Lechmere's Point before the Genl. Court." Loring performed similar tasks in Boston but collected much smaller fees: $4 for a writ, $1.02 for a debt collection of $53.12, and $20.41 for "services."[80]

In agricultural areas of the state, such as Berkshire County, which had only one bank and limited industry in 1818, a lawyer's practice was restricted. According to Increase Sumner, a Berkshire lawyer and judge, it consisted mainly of collecting debts, conveyancing, and giving legal advice.[81] Opportunities for wealth existed —Sedgwick and Jones are examples—but the ambitious lawyer had to engage in several occupations to claim them. His chances were greater if he practiced in the commercial eastern counties of Suffolk and Essex, which not surprisingly attracted a greater number of lawyers than did the rural, western, and central regions.

Curbs on internal competition and the hierarchical nature of the fee system received renewed justification when the Massachusetts Supreme Court revitalized the seniority system in 1806. In 1805 only nine barristers were practicing in the state, but by 1810, more than fifty counsellors resided in Suffolk County. The Suffolk Bar followed the example of the courts by drawing the bounds between counsellors and attorneys. Attorneys were prohibited from arguing all issues in fact and all questions of law arising on writs of error, certiorari and mandamus, on special verdicts, on motions for new trials, and in arrest of judgment. Attorneys, in short, could not advocate any cause in the supreme court without a counsellor as a colleague.[82]

While bar organizations concentrated on training, rank, and money, the personal-fraternal aspects of the brotherhood, so apparent in the eighteenth century, had begun to disappear. Changing word usage to address lawyers was symbolic. Although lawyers persisted in referring to each other as "gentlemen of the bar," they discontinued the practice of addressing other lawyers as "brother."[83] Moreover the system of circuit riding that had helped turn lawyers into a subsociety had declined late in the eighteenth century as an increasing number of lawyers began to reside in more geographic areas. Nevertheless sessions of the county and supreme court did attract many lawyers, who, according to Leverett Saltonstall, tended to congregate at one inn if they did not reside in the shiretown. As Saltonstall remarked on one such occasion while in Castine, Maine: "In the evening I remov'd my quarters to Mr. Masons where several of the Attorneys put up as would be pleasant to cultivate an acquaintance with them."[84] The collapse of the circuit-riding system marked a profound shift within the legal profession from the ideal of a corporate brotherhood of gentlemen linked by close personal knowledge to a highly individualistic, competitive, and impersonal profession.

The bar associations at the same time became less social and more business oriented. Meetings were less frequent, and committees assumed many functions previously performed by the entire membership. Essex County lawyers after 1806 were fined if they did not attend just two meetings a year, while the Worcester County Bar and the Suffolk County Bar met only annually. An indication of the attendance at the meetings is given by the Suffolk rule that only twelve members compose a quorum—this in a county where more than seventy counsellors and attorneys of the supreme court were eligible to attend.[85]

New action by the supreme judicial court muted these psychological shifts and temporarily strengthened the bar associations. The justices acted in March 1810 when they realized that the system of examiners had proven "inadequate to the purpose therein contemplated."[86] The bar association of the county, in which the candidate had studied and practiced, now replaced the Board of Examiners. That institution's recommendation became a legal prerequisite for admission to the court of common pleas and all subsequent grades, including counsellor in the supreme court.[87] For the first time in Massachusetts history, lawyers had the formal legal power, as well as the practical right, to control entrance into the profession and to regulate advancement within professional ranks, albeit under the courts' aegis.

There were some restrictions on the bar associations by the court's rules and a right of appeal to the court if a candidate felt that he had been unjustly denied a recommendation by the county bar association. The standards, constant for the next twenty-five years, remained high—in essence copying those of the state's stronger bar associations in Suffolk, Essex, and Worcester counties. College graduates had to study in the office of a counsellor for three years; nondegree holders faced five years of study in a counsellor's office. In a significant reversal of the 1806 rules, a college degree became the only acceptable evidence of a liberal education. The maintenance of the traditional seven-year program of advancement for college graduates to the highest professional rank emphasized the elevated position of the counsellor.[88]

Geographic provincialism was bolstered by the supreme court's requirements. Not only did candidates from within the state need the recommendation of the bar association of the county in which they had studied or currently practiced, but the court adopted the rules of the Suffolk, Essex, and Hampshire bar associations that aimed to exclude practitioners from other states. College graduates who had practiced law in the highest court of their state for one year still had to study in the office of a Massachusetts counsellor for a year before being admitted as an attorney of the supreme court. Nonresident lawyers without a liberal education had to have practiced for two years in the highest court of their state. Even then they faced three years of study in the office of a Massachusetts counsellor before admission to practice in the supreme court. The court specifically ordered the bar associations not to except anyone from these standards.[89] With these rules, the bar associations achieved their peak of institutional autonomy, and the profession had its most complex formal standards before the twentieth century.

Lawyers had reached this point by persistent efforts and in spite of public opposition. Their political power ascended rapidly during the revolutionary era when men knowledgeable in the law were needed to recast the government. Through political influence and by gaining recognition of the need to appoint legally trained men to the bench, they secured control of the judiciary. The tremendous numerical growth of trained lawyers from about 71 in 1775 to at least 493 in 1810, with their political and judicial influence and economic power combined with their commercial connections, made lawyers the strongest professional group in the state's society. In the nineteenth century, lawyers replaced ministers as the spokesmen and leaders as law replaced religion as the dominant force in the state.

NOTES

1. For a solid study of judicial reform and politics, see Richard Ellis, *The Jeffersonian Crisis: Courts and Politics in the Young Republic* (New York, 1971).

2. Charles Warren, *The Supreme Court in United States History*, 2d ed. (Boston, 1926), 1: 23, 49: George Dexter, ed., "Record Book of the Suffolk Bar," MHS, *Proceedings* 19 (December 1881): 164; William T. Davis, *History of the Judiciary of Massachusetts* (Boston, 1900), 98-99; John Adams, *Legal Papers of John Adams*, ed. L. Kinvin Wroth and Hiller B. Zoebel (Cambridge, Mass., 1965), 1: ciii; *Salem Gazette*, February 16, 1790; *Boston Gazette*, February 13, 1790.

3. Gardiner's suggestions have received only brief mention from leading legal scholars who failed to recognize the broad range of his proposals to adapt the practice of law to the demands of society for inexpensive and responsible legal service. Charles Warren, *A History of the American Bar*, 3d ed. (New York, 1966), 218-219; Anton-Hermann Chroust, *The Rise of the Legal Profession* (Norman, 1965), 2:20. Richard Ellis fails to mention Gardiner's proposals as a predecessor of Republican reform of the legal system in his book *Jeffersonian Crisis.*

4. William Willis, *A History of the Law, the Courts, and the Lawyers of Maine, from Its First Colonization to the Early Part of the Present Century* (Portland, 1863), 117-123; Theophilus Parsons, *Memoir of Theophilus Parsons* (Boston, 1859), 162-163; *Herald of Freedom*, February 2, 1790; *Massachusetts Centinel*, January 10, 1790.

5. Dudley Hubbard to George Thacher, November 29, 1790, MeHi; Parsons, *Memoir*, 162-163; *Herald of Freedom*, February 2, 1790; *Massachusetts Centinel*, January 10, 1790.

6. *Massachusetts Centinel*, January 20, 27, 1790.

7. Ibid., January 20, 23, 27, 30, 1790; *The Salem Gazette*, January 26, February 2, 1790; Massachusetts House, *Journal*, 1789-1790, 180-181, M-Ar.

8. *Massachusetts Centinel*, January 27, 1790.

9. Ibid., *Salem Gazette*, February 2, 1790.

10. *Massachusetts Centinel*, January 27, 1790; *Boston Gazette*, January 25, 1790; *Western Star* (Stockbridge), February 23, March 2, 30, 1790.

11. *Massachusetts Centinel*, January 27, 1790.

12. Ibid. On the separation of Maine, see Ronald F. Banks, *Maine Becomes a State: The Movement to Separate Maine from Massachusetts, 1785–1820* (Middleton, 1970).

13. *Massachusetts Centinel*, January 20, February 6, 17, March 10, 1790; *Berkshire Chronicle* (Pittsfield), March 11, 18, 1790; Parsons, *Memoir*, 163-173.

14. *Massachusetts Centinel*, January 16, 1790; *Cumberland Gazette* (Portland), February 15, 1790. The support of Gardiner is given in an editorial on February 1, 1790, in the *Cumberland Gazette*. An article by "Junius" in the Boston *Independent Chronicle*, February 11, 1790, accused Gardiner of the same charges and added that he had failed in Boston as a lawyer because of his lack of knowledge of American laws and courts. This was also the thrust of an article in the *Boston Gazette*, February 8, 1790, by Theophilus Parsons. Other articles opposing Gardiner appeared in the *Herald of Freedom*, February 2, 1790; *Massachusetts Centinel*, February 10, 1790; *Western Star*, February 23, March 1, 2, 9, 16, 30, 1790; *Berkshire Chronicle*, March 18, 1790.

15. *Massachusetts Centinel*, January 16, 1790; James Sullivan to Elbridge Gerry, February 3, 1790, Gerry Papers, MHi.

16. Articles supporting Gardiner appeared in *Herald of Freedom*, February 12, 1790; *Boston Gazette*, January 25, 1790; *Western Star* (editorial), February 23, March 2, 1790; *Independent Chronicle*, February 18, 25, 1790. For action on the program, see *Western Star*, February 12, 23, March 30, 1790; *Massachusetts Centinel*, January 27, February 6, 17, 20, March 10, 1790; *Boston Gazette*, March 1, 1790; Journal of the Massachusetts House, 1789-1790, M-Ar.

17. Journal of the Massachusetts House, 1789-1790, 232, 238-243, 254, 258, M-Ar; *Acts and Laws of the Commonwealth of Massachusetts, 1788–89* (Boston, 1890), chap. 58, passed March 6, 1790, 511.

18. Thomas Dawes to Robert T. Paine [1790], Paine Papers, MHi; *Acts and Laws of the Commonwealth of Massachusetts, 1788-89* (Boston, 1890), chap. 58, 511.

19. Josiah Quincy, Jr., *Reports of Cases Argued and Adjudged in the Superior Court of Judicature of the Province of Massachusetts Bay . . . 1761–1772*, ed. Samuel Quincy (Boston, 1865), 237; John Adams, *Diary and Autobiography of John Adams*, ed. L. H. Butterfield et al. (New York, 1964), 1:190-198; William D. Northend, *Address Before the Essex Bar Association, December 8, 1885* (Salem, 1885), 40-41; Parsons, *Memoir*,

221. One legal historian has noted that one of the important symptoms of the emerging instrumentalism of law in the nineteenth century was the decline in the significance of technicalities or form in case decisions. Morton Horwitz, "The Emergence of an Instrumental Conception of American Law, 1780-1820," in *Law in American History*, ed. Donald Fleming and Bernard Bailyn (Boston, 1971), 324-325.

20. *Berkshire Chronicle*, March 18, 1790. The unwillingness of some members of the legal profession to abandon English law and practices created a crucial division of the legal community in the first decades of the nineteenth century. Proponents of English law practices appeared adamant. Parsons was one. He sustained the ancient and intricate art of special pleading as chief justice of the Massachusetts supreme court after 1806, refusing to consider cases if the complex writs or pleas were not technically accurate. Isaac Parker, Daniel Webster, and Theron Metcalf are only three of the many lawyers who supported English law and procedures through writings in law journals and literary reviews. Other lawyers—Joseph Story was one —sought the best from both American and English law and procedures. A lifelong defender of special pleading, Story made a plea for American law in his *A Selection of Pleadings in Civil Actions* (Salem, 1805). Story recognized that laws and customs in Massachusetts differed too much from those of England to rely solely on British law books. Explaining his attempt to adapt special pleading to local court interpretations, Story wrote that although a variety of English books pertained to this general subject, the difference of American customs, statutes, and common law was such "that they will be found, in many instances, inadequate to supply the necessities of our own judicial practices." English law and legal procedures had to be molded to the American environment.

By the 1830s the destruction or reduction of special pleading had become psychologically essential to popular, radical legal reformers because of its symbolic and real power in maintaining the influence of English common law and a privileged legal profession. Maine, moreover, in 1831 had required both plaintiff and defendant in all civil suits to plead the general issue. This goal became assured when the philosophically moderate lawyers who composed the Commission to Revise the General Statutes recommended its abolition in their 1834 report to the legislature. Special pleading lingered through 1835, nevertheless. Then a committee on codification in the Massachusetts House placed the issue squarely on the line when it stated that the worst abuse of the common-law system was special pleading because "every person, who undertakes to manage his own cause in a court of justice has to encounter these tremendous pleas and is sometimes thrown into confusion, to the infinite amusement of the bench and bar." Shortly after, the lawmakers approved legislation, which the governor signed on April 16, 1836, bringing an end to special pleading in civil suits by allowing only pleas in the general issue. The supreme judicial court reinforced this enactment with new court rules that set down regulations for pleas in the general issue.

Even though many lawyers had favored special pleading, little organized opposition to the measure appeared because of the divided opinion among concerned lawyers and a general disinterest within the profession. Most lawyers no longer utilized the finer techniques of special pleading and found the everyday details that it required a needless bother. Lawyers now spent most of their time preparing legal papers that would keep their clients out of court rather than working on adversary actions in court.

Story's remarks to James J. Wilkinson help to understand the moderate's position of mild opposition. "While in England your Courts have by the new rules given a new vigour to Special Pleading, we in Massachusetts have by a recent statute positively abolished it, & substituted the general issue in all cases," Story explained. "I confess myself opposed to this change & deem your present system far preferable to ours, as to certainty & convenience & saving of expense," he said. "I think our recent enactment grew out of a restless love of innovation, combined with a desire of some members of the profession to find an apology for their indolence or want of skill," Story lamented. "How it will work remains to be shewn." The editor of the *Hampshire Gazette* also unveiled this posture with a parable: "The older members of the profession have groaned at the thought of this fell stroke at the Science, as they would at losing a tooth, but they seem to rejoice that the defective thing has been removed, now that the operation is over." And in fact most lawyers, especially those engaged in commercial law, seemed relieved at the passing of special pleading despite some verbal protestations.

Richard E. Welch, Jr., "The Parsons-Sedgwick Feud and the Reform of the Massachusetts Judiciary," *Essex Institute Historical Collections* 92 (April 1956): 184; Charles B. Brown, ed., "Review of Literature," *American Register* 1 (1807): 176; Isaac Parker, "Inaugural Address . . . ," *North American Review* 3 (May 1816): 21-24; Daniel Webster, "Review of Henry Wheaton's *Reports of Cases . . . ,*" *North American Review* 7 (December 1818): 63; Theron Metcalf, "Review of Dudley A. Tyng's *Reports of Cases . . . ,*" *North American Review* 7 (July 1818): 184-85; see Horwitz, "Emergence of an Instrumental Conception," 324-325; Joseph Story, *A Selection of Pleadings in Civil Actions* (Salem, 1805); "Legislation of Maine," *American Jurist and Law Magazine* 6 (October 1831): 441-446; *Report of the Commissioners . . . to Revise the General Statutes of the Commonwealth*, pt. III (Boston, 1834), 154; "Report of Codification

Committee to the House," *Boston Advertiser*, February 1, 1836; *Pamphlett Laws of Massachusetts* (Boston, 1835), 13: chap. 273, signed April 16, 1836, 1000; *Essex Register* (Salem), January 25, 1836; *Columbian Centinel*, January 14, 25, 1836; Supreme Judicial Court, *Rules of the Supreme Judicial Court of Massachusetts* (1836), 31-40; Journals of the Massachusetts House and Senate, M-Ar; Emory Washburn, "Address to the Members of the Worcester County Bar," in Joseph Willard et al., *Addresses Before the Members of the Bar of Worcester County* (Worcester, 1879), 130; Joseph Story to James John Wilkinson, December 26, 1836, quoted in Massachusetts Historical Society, *Proceedings*, 2d ser. 15 (October 1901), 221; *Hampshire Gazette*, April 27, 1836.

21. *Massachusetts Centinel*, February 24, 27, 1790.

22. *Salem Gazette*, June 8, 1790; *Massachusetts Centinel*, June 12, 16, 1790; *Cumberland Gazette*, June 21, 1790; *Western Star*, June 29, July 20, 1790, March 3, April 1, 1791.

23. Berkshire County Bar Rules, April 1, 1792, Sedgwick Papers, MHi.

24. Ibid., 1792, MHi; see also Richard D. Birdsall, *Berkshire County: A Cultural History* (New Haven, 1959), 230-233.

25. Dexter, "Record Book," 167; William Willis, "Thomas Rice," *Maine Historical and Genealogical Recorder* 9 (May 1898): 130.

26. Docket books of Worcester County Court of Common Pleas, 1785-1805, Court House, Worcester, Mass.; Docket books, Massachusetts Supreme Judicial Court, 1785-1795, microfilm, MHi.

27. *Independent Chronicle*, February 19, 1789; Caleb Strong to Moses Bliss, January 27, 1790, Greenough Papers, MHi; William Cranch to His Mother, April 8, 1792, Cranch Papers, DLC; Dexter, "Record Book," 166; David H. Calhoun, *Professional Lives in America: Structure and Aspirations, 1750-1850* (Cambridge, Mass., 1965), 104; Walter L. Burrage, *A History of the Massachusetts Medical Society, 1781–1922* (Norwood, 1923), 19, 239, 280-281.

28. Ralph S. Bates, *Scientific Societies in the United States*, 2d ed. (New York, 1958), 16-18; Rowland Berthoff, *An Unsettled People: Social Order and Disorder in American History* (New York, 1971), 254-274; Richard D. Brown, "The Emergence of Urban Society in Rural Massachusetts, 1760-1820," *Journal of American History* 56 (June 1974): 38-42.

29. *Acts and Laws of the Commonwealth of Massachusetts, 1796* (Boston, 1896), chap. 80, sec. 4, passed February 27, 1796, 450-452; George C. Groce, Jr., *William Samuel Johnson: A Maker of the Constitution* (New York, 1937), 25.

30. Dexter, "Record Book," 167-169; Birdsall, *Berkshire County*, 230-233; Jean Pierre Brissot quoted in Oscar Handlin, *This Was America* (Cambridge, Mass., 1949), 75.

31. William Manning, *The Key of Liberty . . . (1798)*, ed. Samuel E. Morison (Billerica, 1922), 33-34. Other antilawyer articles appeared in the *Independent Chronicle*, March 2, 30, 1797, and *Western Star*, October 17, 24, 31, 1796.

32. James M. Banner, Jr., *To the Hartford Convention: The Federalists and the Origin of Party Politics in Massachusetts, 1789–1815* (New York, 1970), 184-187, 289-293, 365; Jackson T. Main, *Political Parties Before the Constitution* (Chapel Hill, 1973), 83-119.

33. *Salem Gazette*, January 27, 1807.

34. Diary of Nathaniel Ames, quoted in Charles Warren, *Jacobin and Junto: or Early American Politics as Viewed in the Diary of Dr. Nathaniel Ames, 1758–1822* (Cambridge, Mass., 1931), 179; *Debates and Proceedings in the Convention of the Commonwealth of Massachusetts, 1788* (Boston, 1856), 204, 318; *Independent Chronicle*, January 8, 1795, March 19, 1794, March 2, 1797; *Western Star*, October 31, 1796, October 27, 1800; *Journal of the Debates and Proceedings in the Convention of Delegates Chosen to Revise the Constitution of Massachusetts, 1821* (Boston, 1853), 47.

35. *Independent Chronicle*, January 8, 1795; *Western Star*, October 17, 1796.

36. Banner, *To the Hartford Convention*, table 7, 365; "Members of the General Court," in Samuel A. Green, ed., *Groton Historical Series* 2 (1890): 116-120; *Independent Chronicle*, March 2, 1797.

37. *Impartial Register* (Salem), November 4, 1796, October 27, 1800.

38. *Western Star*, April 14, 28, May 5, 1795; James Sullivan to Elbridge Gerry, March 22, July 30, 1789, Gerry Papers, MHi; Theodore Sedgwick to Harrison G. Otis, February 7, 1803, January 5, 1804, Otis Papers, MHi; Joseph Story to Charles Sumner, January 22, 1844, William Story, ed., *Life and Letters of Joseph Story* (Boston, 1851), 1:390; Joseph Story to Daniel Webster, January 10, 1824; editorial, *Law Reporter*, 2 (February 1840): 318-319.

39. Nathaniel Ames's diary, September 30, 1796, August 21, 1797, in Warren, *Jacobin and Junto*, 177-178; Berkshire Bar to Solomon Strong, February 7, 1833, Taft Papers, MHi.

40. *Massachusetts Centinel*, August 26, September 2, 1786; *Independent Chronicle*, March 2, 1797; Davis, *Massachusetts Judiciary*, 276-277.

41. "Report of the Committee of Agriculture in the Massachusetts House," *Law Reporter* 1 (March 1839): 341-342.

42. Frank W. Grinnell, "The Judicial System and the Bar (1820-1861)," in Albert B. Hart, ed., *Commonwealth History of Massachusetts* (New York, 1928), 4:59; Willis, *History of the Law*, 515; "Massachusetts Legislation," *American Jurist and Law Magazine* 6 (October 1831): 427-431; William Lincoln, *History of Worcester, Massachusetts, from Its Earliest*

Settlement to September, 1836 (Worcester, 1862), 342; *Law Reporter* 2 (February 1840): 317-319.

43. John Adams to John Q. Adams, February 14, 1795, quoted in William Kent, *Memoirs and Letters of James Kent* . . . (Boston, 1898), 67-69; Alonzo Lewis and James R. Newhall, *History of Lynn, Essex County, Massachusetts* . . . (Boston, 1865), 370.

44. John Adams to Abigail Adams, June 29, 1774, Adams Papers, MHi; R. Kent Newmeyer, "A Note on the Whig Politics of Justice Joseph Story," *Mississippi Valley Historical Review* 58 (December 1961): 481-491; Joseph Story to Gabriel Duvall, March 30, 1803, in Story, *Life and Letters*, 1:102-103.

45. Story, *Life and Letters*, 1:96-97; James Sullivan to ?, in Warren, *Jacobin and Junto*, 179.

46. Samuel E. Morison, *The Life and Letters of Harrison Gray Otis: Federalist, 1765–1848* (Boston, 1913), 1:31-44; Harrison G. Otis to Jarvis Duff, November 7, and to Harrison Gray, April 27, 1801, Otis Papers, MHi.

47. Robert P. Dunlap to J. Sewall, January 11, 1822, Sewall Family Papers, MWA.

48. Elijah H. Mills to Henrietta Mills, February 28, 1824, in Henry C. Lodge, ed., "Extracts from the Familer Correspondence of Hon. E. H. Mills," Massachusetts Historical Society, *Proceedings* 19 (September 1881): 42.

49. This statement is based on a comparison of the table of leading lawyers compiled from the supreme judicial court records and utilized in the study of economic status with a listing of officeholders.

50. Bernard Barber, "Some Problems in the Sociology of the Professions," in Kenneth Lynn, ed., *The Professions in America* (Boston, 1965), 29-31; Maurice G. Baxter, *Daniel Webster and the Supreme Court* (Amherst, 1966), 14; John D. Darling, *Political Changes in Massachusetts, 1824–1848: A Study of Liberal Movements in Politics* (New Haven, 1925), 18.

51. Adams, *Diary*, 2:41-42; *Acts and Resolves, 1779-1780*, chap. 856; *Boston Magazine* (November-December 1786): 429; Donald R. Adams, Jr., "Some Evidence of English and American Wage Rates, 1790-1830," *Journal of Economic History* 30 (September 1970): 506, 516.

52. Robert T. Paine to John Adams, April 13, 1789, in Ralph Davol, *Two Men of Taunton* (Taunton, 1912), 325-328; Theodore Sedgwick to Harrison G. Otis, February 9, 1803, Otis Papers, MHi.

53. Address of Hampshire and Berkshire Lawyers, 1798, Taft Papers, MHi; Dexter, "Record Book," 174.

54. Dexter, "Record Book," 174; Hollis R. Bailey, *Attorneys and Their Admission to the Bar in Massachusetts* (Boston, 1907), 35-37.

55. Frank S. Smith, "Admission to the Bar in New York," *Yale Law Journal* 16 (May 1907): 515-516; Alfred A. Reed, *Training for the Public Profession of the Law* (New York, 1921), 83-84; W. Raymond Blackard, "Requirements for Admission to the Bar in Revolutionary America," *Tennessee Law Review* 15 (February 1938): 120-121.

56. Reed, *Training*, 74-77; Abraham Holmes, *Address Before the Bar of the County of Bristol . . . 1834* (New Bedford, 1834), 13-14; Blackard, "Requirements," 120-121; Norfolk County Bar records in Bailey, *Attorneys*, 34. In 1788 New Hampshire county bar associations had formed a federation, and by 1795 Connecticut lawyers had organized a statewide bar association.

57. Suffolk County Bar Association, *Rules and Regulations of the Suffolk County Bar . . . 1805* (Boston, 1805), 4-5; Essex County Bar Association, *Rules and Regulations of the Bar in the County of Essex . . . 1806* (Salem, 1806), 5-6.

58. James D. Hopkins, *An Address to the Members of the Cumberland Bar . . . 1833* (Portland, 1833), 30; Old Bar Record Book, MHB; Tristram Gilman to Estes Howe, Jr., July 28, 1802, Howe Papers, MWA; Northend, *Address Before the Essex Bar*, 50-51; Suffolk County Bar Association, *Rules . . . 1805*, 8; Worcester County Bar Rules, 1809, in Lincoln Papers, MWA; Hampshire County Bar Rules, 1805, in Bailey, *Attorneys*, 34-35; Essex County Bar Association, *Rules . . . 1806*, 5-6.

59. Frank Smith, *A History of Dedham, Massachusetts* (Boston, 1936), 371; Davis, *Judiciary*, 285, 287.

60. Solomon Stoddard, Jr., to Wiliam Sullivan, May 30, 1805, quoted in Bailey, *Attorneys*, 35-36; Essex County Bar Association, *Rules . . . 1806*, 1-27.

61. Ellis, *Jeffersonian Crisis*, 199-203; for evidence of a much less politically oriented approach to judicial reform than that proffered by Ellis, see Samuel Sewall to Joseph Story, January 2, 20, 1807, Theodore Sedgwick to Joseph Story, December 9, 1807, Story Papers, DLC.

62. Ellis, *Jeffersonian Crisis*, 187-191; Samuel Sewall to Joseph Story, January 2, 20, 1807, Theodore Sedgwick to Joseph Story, December 9, 1807, Story Papers, DLC; Ellis, *Jeffersonian Crisis*, 157-191; William E. Nelson, *Americanization of the Common Law* (Cambridge, Mass., 1975), 167-168; Warren, *American Bar*, 331; James Sullivan, *History of Land Titles in Massachusetts* (Boston, 1801), iv-v; John Anthon, *American Precedents . . .* ,3d ed. (Brookfield, 1821), iii; Story, *Selection of Pleadings*, iii-iv.

63. Dudley Tyng, *Reports of Cases Argued and Determined in the Supreme Judicial Court of Massachusetts, 1806-1822* (Boston, 1808-1823), 2:72-75, 105.

64. Ibid., 105.

65. Birdsall, *Berkshire County*, 234-235.

66. See table 11. For a listing of examiners, see Tyng, *Reports*, 2:75-76, 4:410, 454, 5:488; Franklin Dexter, *Biographical Sketches of the Graduates of Yale College, 1701–1815* (New York, 1885-1911), 4: 387-388.

67. Docket books, 1800-1810, Kennebec County Supreme Judicial Court, at Augusta, Maine; Bailey, *Attorneys*, 45.

68. William Bentley, *Diary of William Bentley . . . 1803 . . . 1810* (Salem, 1911), 3:401. See also *Independent Chronicle*, April 7, 1806; *Eastern Argus* (Portland), March 21, 1806.

69. Suffolk County Bar, *Rules . . . 1805*, 7; Essex County Bar, *Rules . . . 1806*, 8; Worcester County Bar Rules, 1809, MWA.

70. Suffolk County Bar, *Rules . . . 1805*, 6-7; Essex County Bar, *Rules . . . 1806*, 8-9; Worcester County Bar Rules, 1809, MWA.

71. Dexter, "Record Book," 167-168; Suffolk County Bar, *Rules . . . 1805*, 7-8; Suffolk County Bar, *Rules . . . 1810*, 11-13; Essex County Bar, *Rules . . . 1806*, 9; Worcester County Bar Rules, 1809, MWA.

72. Warrant of Partition and the Commissioner's Return of Richard Dana's Estate in Charlemont, Buckland, and Heath, Dana Papers, MHi; will of Edmund Trowbridge, Dana Papers, MHi; court appraisal of Rev. Merrick's Estate, deeds to Pliny Merrick, 1788, 1789, 1794, 1800, 1803, 1805, 1807, Merrick Papers, MWA; Richard B. David, "The Early American Lawyer and the Profession of Letters," *Huntington Library Quarterly* 13 (February 1949): 194-195.

73. Docket books, Worcester County Court of Common Pleas and Supreme Judicial Court for Worcester County, 1780-1800, Worcester County Court; Lincoln, *History of Worcester*, 193-197; listing of land absentees, 1799, Levi Lincoln's account book, 1776-1782, deeds to Levi Lincoln, deeds to Levi Lincoln, Jr., Lincoln Papers, MWA; will of Edward D. Bangs, Bangs Papers, MWA; deeds of Samuel Haven, Haven Papers, MWA.

74. These tax lists are occasionally misleading. For example, the father of Bezaleel Taft, Jr., of Uxbridge was the largest landowner in the town. Also, the father of Pliny Merrick of Brookfield had died the previous year with an estate valued at more than $100,000

75. Jackson T. Main argues in *Social Structure*, 276, that most lawyers were well-to-do. Chroust takes the same position in *Legal Profession*, 1:52, but in 2:87, he estimates that lawyers' incomes were modest on the whole. An earlier tax list for Worcester in 1798 lists the three Worcester lawyers in this way: Edward Bangs, $1,650; Levi Lincoln, $19,222; Nathaniel Paine, $1,155. Assessors' lists, 1798, Worcester Papers, MWA.

76. Leonard Levy, *The Law of the Commonwealth and Chief Justice*

Shaw (Cambridge, Mass., 1957), 10, 17; Lemuel Shaw to Mrs. Oakes Shaw, January 21, May 6, 1805, August 29, 1806, Shaw Papers, MHi; Chroust, *Legal Profession*, 2:89; Joseph Story to Stephen Whate, February 26, 1816, Story Papers, MHi; Baxter, *Webster and the Supreme Court*, 14.

77. Donald R. Adams, "Some Evidence of English and American Wage Rates, 1790-1830," *Journal of Economic History* 30 (September 1970): 506, 516. A spot comparison with ministers and college instructors, also members of the intellectual elite, indicates that most lawyers had no greater direct compensation in fees or salary. College teachers, for example, received comparable salaries—$2,000 in the 1830s and $4,000 in the 1860s at Harvard; $600 at Dartmouth in 1805; $700 at Bowdoin in 1825; and $700 at Williams in 1835. Ministerial salaries were higher compared to other professionals in the eighteenth century, but they lost their dominant status during the first half of the nineteenth century. Seventy to 100 pounds sterling plus housing with lifetime tenure was termed an adequate compensation before the Revolution. During the nineteenth century, lifetime permanency for ministers evaporated, and their incomes collapsed; $500 to $700 became the average annual income (plus any fees they received). Unlike the legal profession, moreover, teachers and ministers had fewer prospects of greatly increasing their incomes through larger and more numerous fees, political connections, business ventures, or land speculations. Frederick Rudolph, *The American College and University* (New York, 1962), 193. These figures were arrived at through a composite view of ministers' salaries listed in studies that were utilized in compiling the statistical studies cited in this and the next chapter.

78. Diary of Christopher Baldwin, May 1, 1830, MWA; Benjamin R. Curtis to George W. Phillips, February 11, 1832, Curtis to George Tichnor, September 1833, April 24, 1834, Benjamin R. Curtis, Jr., ed., *A Memoir of Benjamin Robbins Curtis* (Boston, 1879), 1:54, 63-66, 68-69; Samuel Burnside to Isaac Goodwin, Goodwin Papers, MWA; cash book of Willis Gray Loring, MHB. The income pattern set by the profession in the late colonial and early national periods apparently is still holding firm. In 1963, of 132,891 lawyers who were solo practitioners and filed income tax returns, only 4 grossed more than $1 million. In the same year, 43,078 attorneys grossed less than $5,000, and nearly 12,000 soloists actually lost money. More than 150,000 other lawyers practiced in multimember firms, in corporations, or in the government. A more inclusive study in 1966 indicated that the median income for all lawyers was approximately $13,000. Marvin Mayer, *The Lawyers* (New York, 1966), 13-14, 16.

79. John Hancock to Levi Lincoln, August 8, 1782, Hancock Papers, MHB.

80. Account book of Christopher Gore, MHB; cash book of Ellias Gray Loring, MHB; see also Saltonstall, Otis, and Strong Papers, MHi; Caleb Cushing Papers, DLC.

81. "Address of Increase Sumner," in William C. Richards, *Great in Goodness: A Memoir of George N. Briggs, Governor of the Commonwealth of Massachusetts, 1844–1851* (Boston, 1866), 73. See also Burnside, Lincoln, Newton, Bangs, and Sewall Papers, MWA; Thacher Papers, MeHi; Sedgwick Papers, MHi.

82. *The Massachusetts Register* . . . (Boston, 1805-1810); Suffolk County Bar, *Rules . . . 1810*, 28.

83. Among the many examples are William Jewett to James C. Jewett, January 22, 1804, Howe Papers, MWA, and William Eustis to Barnabas Bidwell, September 15, 1808, Taft Papers, MHi.

84. Subsociety is defined here as a group with common interests and attitudes that are strengthened by strong bonds of friendship. *The Saltonstall Papers,* ed. Robert E. Moody (Boston, 1972-1974), 2:283, 328, 372, 396, 432.

85. Essex County Bar, *Rules . . . 1806*, 3; Suffolk County Bar, *Rules . . . 1810*, 3; Worcester County Bar Rules, 1809, MWA. See Charles Page Smith, *James Wilson: Founding Father, 1742-1798* (Chapel Hill, 1956), for a discussion of this practice in Pennsylvania.

86. Rules of the Supreme Court, Tyng, *Reports*, 5:382.

87. Ibid., 382-385.

88. Ibid.

89. Ibid. Many states, including New York and New Jersey, restricted out-of-state lawyers, but Massachusetts was the most exclusionary. Chroust, *American Legal Profession*, 2:251-256.

Education and Regulation in the Entrepreneurial Age

Early in the nineteenth century Massachusetts passed over the watershed from a rural, small-town society to an industrial, urban-cosmopolitan society. This turning point in the state's (and indeed the nation's) economic and political development was evidenced by the emergence of the factory system, modern internal transportation, intense economic growth and competition, occupational specialization, and political democratization. Within the legal profession, this critical transformation was most clearly evident in efforts to reform and modernize the training of law students after 1810. Aggressive, entrepreneurial-minded professionals in the Bay State sought to mold the profession to the demands of this commercially oriented society. Many of them were also advocates of more structured and standardized training—proponents of professional schools. It is no coincidence that the triumph of professional schools began during this egalitarian and entrepreneurial age.

Like members of other colonial professions—religion and medicine—lawyers were convinced that society would respect and reward highly trained specialists. They therefore turned to education to raise their occupation's status from an artisan to a professional level. They assumed that a regular system of training would ensure their competence, establish their professional authority, and gain entry into a higher socioeconomic stratum. A college education, they believed, prepared a person socially and culturally for the role of a gentleman, and they relied on apprenticeship to provide technical knowledge, special skills, and the subculture that would separate the professional from the layman.

Reliance on education exposed the legal profession to anti-intellectual critics who reacted with hostility to the technical expertise and elitist attitudes that mushroomed among the learned guild of professional lawyers. Confusing efforts to lower admission standards for legal practice while demanding greater skills from lawyers reflected laymen's resentment of the emergence of a professional elite in a society that increasingly required legal specialists for its smooth functioning.

While some people decried the exclusivity of legal education, a growing number of lawyers hoped to strengthen and broaden legal training. Convinced that law was a science and not just a technical skill, these men rejected the apprenticeship system. With visions of a unitary bar, they protested that clerkship was inadequate for uniformly instructing students in the general principles of the law or in the new fields of commercial law. They wanted to shift learning from the work situation to special training institutions where an abstract and systematic body of theory, sufficiently complex to demonstrate their professional claim to unique competence over legal activities to a doubting public, could be developed. Because law schools were seen as a better setting for the lecture-discussion method and more suitable for large-scale, uniform instruction than an office, they came to be considered the progressive means of training. The growing influence of these beliefs, when contrasted to the absence of a law school in Massachusetts until well into the nineteenth century, creates an apparent paradox that requires historical examination.

This reluctance to supplement or replace a purely clinical system with lecture courses in a state that contained an ambitious, educated, and cohesive legal profession has been explained in several ways by legal historians. Arthur Sutherland, in a recent study of Harvard Law School, disputed Charles Warren's traditional argument that the delay was due to conflict with England and the embargo with its resulting economic disruption, which depressed legal business and discouraged the Harvard Corporation from starting instruction in the law. The major reason for Harvard's reticence, in Sutherland's opinion, was a conviction at the Cambridge school that legal training was not a respectable endeavor for a college. Their dilemma, Sutherland writes, was that "if education was to be practical, it would not be academically respectable; if it was to be respectably academic it must be professionally unprofitable."[1] This might partially explain why some lawyers determined to put a lawyer in the Harvard president's office in 1828, but it offers only a limited, academic perspective as a solution for a broader and more complex problem. Other historical explanations also deal with contributing factors, but they fail to discuss satisfactorily the fundamental reasons for the slow shift from experience to classroom as the preferred way to educate lawyers.[2] Nor do they touch on the causes for an absence of private law schools within the state until 1823. Responsibility for the delayed appearance of law schools lies with Massachusetts lawyers and their use of education as a means of regulating the profession as well as training law clerks.

Regulation became coupled with legal education during the middle of the eighteenth century when lawyers began organizing and structuring an autonomous profession. They did not view the student's term of study in the office of a barrister or attorney as a substitute or an alternative to a college education; a general education was expected to precede apprenticeship. The period of instruction, moreover, had to be a time when students not only acquired the technicalities of the law but also identified with their professional role. Lawyers also wanted a standard term of study that would serve as a means of controlling the number, as well as the quality, of men entering the profession.[3] These requirements necessitated a long period of close association with members of the profession and could be filled by only one contemporary institution: apprenticeship.

By the end of the century, a concept of legal education chiefly expounded by the lawyers of Suffolk County had become accepted throughout the state. Although educational prerequisites, length of study, and reading assignments might vary in some degree from county to county and lawyer to lawyer, almost all lawyers accepted a prescribed term of apprenticeship under the control of a bar association as a requirement for admission to the profession. A three-year term of study for college graduates was standard, but terms of clerkship for noncollege graduates varied between four and seven years. Some counties, such as Essex, Suffolk, and Worcester, even required oral examinations for law students—a remarkable step in an age that produced a 1791 riot at Harvard over the institution of year-end exams. The basic concept that members of a learned profession required a long period of education that would serve both as a mechanism for training and a means of control over occupational entry had been firmly established in principle in Massachusetts.[4]

Prospective lawyers faced limited opportunities for formal legal training before 1800. Attendance at the English Inns of Court was expensive and not often perceived by aspirants as an available avenue in Massachusetts. After the Revolution few Americans attended the Inns; only one person from Massachusetts attended the Middle Temple from 1783 to 1835. One notable exception is Rufus King's attempt in 1778 to ascertain the expediency of attending the Inns of Court by first passing through Spain and assumedly acquiring neutral status. The Litchfield Law School in Connecticut, a law school that was organized around a law office and emphasized the practical aspects of professional training, became a realistic alternative only after 1784. No public libraries existed to provide students with law books, and there were no law lectures in the state. The law student's most likely and usually only viable choice would have been to apprentice himself to a trained, local lawyer. The knowledge he obtained would come from law books, lawyers, and the practical experience gained while working in a law office.[5]

Dissatisfaction with the apprenticeship system arose concurrently with its evolution in the Bay province. The legal education provided under apprenticeship was undoubtedly monotonous, arduous, and often unedifying. Spending most of his time copying wills, pleadings, briefs, and other documents needed by their masters and running errands, law students often had little time left to absorb any knowledge from the few law books available in the eighteenth century. John Adams, for example, who studied law from 1756 to 1758 under a Worcester attorney, James Putnam, complained to his friends that his legal studies were tiring and that the subject matter consisted of "Old Roman Lawyers and Dutch Commentators." Their education was overwhelmingly clinical, but was it adequate?[6]

Probably the main problem was to acquire and then digest the standard law books. Because Massachusetts lawyers looked to England for their professional model and utilized a modified form of English common law, most law books in the eighteenth century were English. The average lawyer usually owned and mastered to some degree these basic works: Sir Edward Coke, *Commentaries on Littleton's Tenures* (1628); Sir John Comyns, *A Digest of the Laws of England* (1762-1767); Timothy Cunningham, *A New and Complete Law Dictionary* (1764-1765); Matthew Bacon, *New Abridgement of the Law*, 5 vols. (1736-1766); William Hawkins, *A Treatise of the Pleas of the Crown* (1762); Sir William Blackstone, *Commentaries on the Laws of England*, 4 vols. (1765-1767); John Lilly, *The Practical Register* (1734); and some brief books or notebooks on pleadings, forms, and practice.[7]

Increasingly more American lawbooks became available in the nineteenth century as professional ambition, the emergence of new fields of law such as corporations and banking, the drive to standardize the law, and the Americanization of law drove lawyers and publishers to produce their own law books. Coming in the midst of a near vacuum, such American works as James Sullivan's, *History of Land Titles in Massachusetts* (1801) Joseph Story's *A Selection of Pleadings in Civil Actions* (1805), James Kent's *Commentaries on American Law* (1826-1830), and Nathan Dane's *A General Abridgement and Digest of American Law* (1823-1829) seemed monumental. However, once the publication of law books began volumes soon overwhelmed the legal profession, and lawyers begged for a respite.[8] Young scholars wrote on the "scientific principles of law," and established lawyers and jurists refurbished their notebooks and casebooks for the public's and the profession's edification.

Before 1840 several important legal works had been produced by Massachusetts authors, among them, Story, Dane, Stearns, Parsons, Willard Phillips, Charles Jackson, Benjamin Oliver, Samuel Howe, Francis Hilliard, George T. Curtis, William Sumner, Isaac Goodwin, and Luther Cushing. Dane's *General Abridgement and Digest of American Law*, published in eight volumes between 1823 and 1829, stands out as the first systematic attempt to examine the law of the United States as peculiarly American. And Story, despite a heavy load as associate justice of the United States Supreme Court and Harvard law professor, wrote five superior books between 1832 and 1840, including *The Law of Bailments, Equity Jurisprudence, Equity Pleading*, and *Comments on Agency*.[9] But even though American legal publications had become commonplace by 1840, and optimistic lawyers proudly proclaimed the achievement of parity in legal writing with English lawyers, many apprentices, practitioners, and instructors still relied on English legal treatises and textbooks.[10]

Despite complaints about how unexciting studies were, their predicament probably did not exceed that of present-day law students, many of whom find that law school is "unmercifully dull." In fact, with the comings and goings of clients in the office and with the actual preparation of simple pleas and briefs by the apprentices, office law students may well have had a more interesting curriculum in the early nineteenth century than the present-day student isolated in classroom and study-carrel.[11]

Many law students reacted unfavorably toward the hustle and bustle of their mentor's office or their mentor's lack of concern. John Quincy Adams, despite an advantageous clerkship with a skilled and responsive lawyer, Theophilus Parsons, voiced a common criticism when he reported that Parson's office was so busy and noisy that he could not study.[12] At the same time, James Bridge, an apprentice under Pownalboro's bar association critic, John Gardiner, complained that his mentor gave him no guidance at all. Bridge claimed that Gardiner allowed him to study at home and that his only source for study was a set of Blackstone. "About once a fortnight I spend an afternoon in the family in the mode of chit-chat, cards, back-gammon etc." Bridge wrote. "This is the only kind of instruction I am here acquainted with."[13]

Another problem for the apprentice was that his connections and relations with the legal profession revolved around one man, his mentor. If disagreement occurred, the aspirant's career might be doomed from the start. John Forbes decided to relocate his clerkship because his master, John Sprague of Lancaster, after a full year of residence had not obtained the bar association's permission to accept Forbes as a student. George B. Upham, who had been a law student for four years in 1792, poised on the verge of moving to New Hampshire because his admission to the profession appeared blocked by one man who "has been busy in endeavoring to persuade some of the Gentlemen of the Law to vote against me."[14] Despite such poignant personal dilemmas, most lawyers in the state believed that the apprentice system provided the best legal instruction and that only slight adjustments might be needed.

Not all students found law studies uninteresting or unpleasant. Jonathan Mason, Jr., wrote to John Adams in 1776 that he enjoyed reading law and echoed Adams's belief that every pupil should simply read law for one or two years "before he touches at all upon the practical part." An acquaintance of John Quincy Adams claimed to find great enjoyment in legal studies even to the point of finding Blackstone "entertaining."[15] Clearly no uniformity of opinion existed, but most students did not pursue legal studies for enjoyment but for its career potential.

If dullness had been the only complaint about legal education, concerned lawyers and laymen probably would not have seen any need to change it. But often legal training depended to such a degree on young men's self-motivation and a harried practitioner's interest that it lacked the serious application necessary to produce a profession of uniformly skilled lawyers. John Adams's two years of clerkship were so unstructured that after struggling to write his first writ, he was moved to comment: "Now I feel the Disadvantages of Putnam's insensibility and neglect of me. Had he given me now and then a few hints concerning practice, I should be able to judge better at this Hour than I can now." If Adams had the best professional legal education available in mid-eighteenth-century America, as Sutherland argues, then it should be no surprise that educational reform became one of the main objects of organized lawyers.[16]

Institutions and individuals in other states at least gestured toward formal legal instruction outside of office clerkship, although it was often aimed at producing public men a la Blackstone rather than practicing lawyers.[17] Litchfield Law School, founded in 1784 by Tapping Reeve in neighboring Connecticut, provided the only place in New England where law was taught in a systematic, lecture-oriented manner. Yet William and Mary College, the University of Pennsylvania, Transylvania University, and Columbia College offered law lectures before 1800.[18] Fisher Ames, a Dedham lawyer politician, attended James Wilson's introductory law lecture at the University of Pennsylvania and became interested enough to send a copy to some Massachusetts colleagues, but he made no suggestion that the idea be copied in the Bay State. Thomas Pownall, former

Massachusetts governor and English lawyer, in 1783 hoped to endow a "law Professorship" at Harvard with land he had owned in Pownalborough, Maine. He wrote James Bowdoin that "I mean & wish to see instituted Lectures on the Science of Polity & Law-giving as derived from God & nature of man, so as to form the minds of the students to become efficient & good members of a free state." But the donated lands had been sold for taxes during the war. Three years later Isaac Royall donated a considerable amount of land to Harvard for a law professorship, but this gift lay dormant for twenty-nine years.[19] With an active, prosperous, and highly organized legal profession, Massachusetts might have been expected to foster at least one college-connected or independent institution for legal instruction. But no one made any public attempt to stimulate support for law lectures until 1815.

Law schools undoubtedly lost some of their luster and attractiveness as a model for Massachusetts because of mixed success with the lecture system and their limited acceptance by students and lawyers in other states. On the positive side, Reeve's Litchfield Law School attracted more than eight hundred students from many states over a fifty-year existence, and Samuel Howe and Theron Metcalf utilized their Litchfield experiences to form law schools in Massachusetts. But only a small percentage of the more than twenty-six hundred lawyers admitted to practice in the Bay State between 1760 and 1840 attended Litchfield. On the other hand, James Kent's law lectures at Columbia fared badly. His course's popularity dwindled from seven students and thirty-six auditors in 1794-1795 to two students in 1795-1796 and none the next year.[20] Desires for a lecture system certainly lacked universal demand among the legal profession.

As the apprenticeship system developed in Massachusetts, moreover, much more became involved in the process of training than merely schooling. One principal reason for the delayed appearance of nonapprenticeship legal education in Massachusetts was the lawyers' attempts to use education as a means of limiting professional competition. Long periods of clerkship had originally appealed to lawyers because they promised better-trained lawyers, but eventually restricting the number of lawyers became almost as important. Lawyers all too quickly perceived lengthy terms of apprenticeship and the graded system of practice as possible guarantees of high incomes and differentiated professional status based on seniority.[21]

Law students' fees may also have influenced bar leaders to prevent a few members of the profession or outside institutions from monopolizing legal education. When the average professional lawyer's income was less than $1000, the income from law clerks, not to mention their free labor, loomed very large.[22] Not for a hundred more years would secretaries, armed with typewriters and printed forms, replace much of the functional necessity for apprenticeship. Most county bar associations established standard fees for apprenticeships not only to protect the law student but also to prevent cut-rate competition for students and the concentration of available clerks in a few offices. Law students had paid as little as £10 per annum before the growth of bar associations, but these rates were rapidly escalated. After 1783 the bar associations required lawyers of Suffolk, Essex, and Middlesex counties to charge £100 for a three-year term of study, about double the prevailing per annum cost for undergraduate tuition, room, and board. Suffolk lawyers raised their rates to $150 per year in 1805 and to $500 for three years in 1810. Lawyers in Essex County charged $150 per year after 1806. Apprentices in the Maine counties paid only $150 for three years; Hampshire County practitioners required only $250 for a three-year term; and students in Bristol, Worcester, and Hampden counties had to pay $100 per year. Room and board was generally extra. Only rarely could a clerk (George N. Briggs was one) arrange to pay only $40 per year in a rural section of the state in the nineteenth century.[23] Very few lawyers were willing to sacrifice that much money and free labor for an experiment in legal education that had yet to prove itself capable of preparing qualified attorneys.

In Suffolk and Essex counties, where lawyers had become the most prosperous and numerous, a decision to allow just three clerks in a law office served four functions. It sought to aid the students by ensuring that a barrister's attention would not be too badly divided, but it limited the potential number of lawyers. It guaranteed a division of clerks' fees among a wide selection of practitioners, but it delayed the foundation of private law schools in Massachusetts until the 1820s.[24]

Lawyers in less commercially developed and less populous counties did not formally emulate their eastern brethren. Their action reflects their slim chances of attracting more than three clerks in one office in areas with poor roads and a dispersed population at the end of the eighteenth century. The absence of this regulation allowed office law schools to be launched in such counties when conditions became more favorable in the 1820s. Even though other bar associations did not follow the leadership of Suffolk and Essex counties with formal regulations, any attempts to form an office school must have been inhibited by the action of the state's leading bar associations.

Another cause contributing to the delayed founding of law schools was the requirement that students study law in the office of a barrister, counsellor, or attorney. Although this rule could be interpreted broadly enough to encompass private law schools or even college-connected law schools, the intent of the regulation discouraged candidates from studying outside of office apprenticeship.[25] When combined with later demands that prospective lawyers study in the state and county in which they sought admission, it proved to be a major impediment to the growth of law schools.

Fear and insecurity, as well as the parochial pride of county bar associations, were evidenced by lawyers' erecting exclusive barriers in response to increases in the number of active practitioners and an influx of lawyers from other states. Rules agreed to by lawyers of Suffolk, Worcester, Berkshire, and Essex counties showed a marked disdain for out-of-state attorneys. The general rules for governing the admission of attorneys spelled out by the supreme judicial court in 1810 provided that out-of-state candidates for the bar must have studied at least two years in the office of a Massachusetts counsellor. Within a few years, most county bar associations had passed similar resolutions discriminating against lawyers from other states.[26]

The appearance of a law school in Massachusetts, moreover, was probably delayed by rulings from several bar associations that before they would even recommend a candidate for admission to practice, each student should have studied for his last year in a law office in that county. A law student, for example, who spent a three-year apprenticeship in Essex County would not be eligible for a Suffolk County Bar vote of approval. Suffolk County Bar members even refused their recommendation to practice in Suffolk County to a lawyer from another county unless he provided proof of at least two years of prior practice and the support of the bar in the county where he had worked.[27] This intercounty jealousy probably discouraged educational entrepreneurs who would be dependent on attracting students from throughout the state.

A critical juncture in professional development occurred at the turn of the century as apprenticeship became less acceptable as a means of training gentlemen and professional men rather than artisans or technicians. At the same time, law was becoming more complex, and the demands of burgeoning corporations and expanding commerce required a more predictable and structured body of legal knowledge than lawyers and judges had hitherto possessed. Faced with such a conundrum, the changing concept of law appeared to offer lawyers a way out of their dilemma. By the late eighteenth century, many lawyers were predisposed to accept law as a science; by doing so, they could better impose practices that enabled them to raise their intellectual level, bolster their social status, assert control over the admission of new members, and allow them to gather legal knowledge into an understandable, standard form without altering its basic foundation. By the end of the century, the scientific ideal had led to a revolution in legal education through law schools and the case system of study that was predicated on the belief that law was a science.

The people seeking to standardize law through writing and judicial interpretation were also among the foremost exponents of systematic instruction for law students in law schools. Many of the men were also forging the law into an instrument for commercial and economic growth. Dane gave the royalties from his monumental revisionary *A General Abridgement and Digest of American Law* to provide a building and endowment for Harvard Law School. Story, the best-known exponent of the new union of commerce and law in both his judicial decisions and legal writings, was a professor of law at Harvard in its most crucial period. Isaac Parker, an early proponent of the instrumental use of law in the Massachusetts Mill cases, was the first Royall Professor of Law at Harvard. Metcalf, who founded an independent law school at Dedham, advocated innovative law from the bench and in his writings. Simon Greenleaf, a Harvard law professor, argued for the new bridge in the Charles River Bridge case. Other lawyers deeply involved in both the law school movement and the major revisions in law included John Davis, Christopher Gore, Daniel Webster, John Lowell, Charles Jackson, and Asahel Stearns.[28] These men hoped that scientifically trained lawyers would provide a uniform application of law that would allow for the smooth operation of the business world in particular and society as a whole.

The impact of the Enlightenment with its emphasis on science and systematic studies also influenced lawyers to begin applying the scientific method to law. Because advanced education or college attendance had always ranked abnormally high with professional leaders in their efforts to upgrade the legal profession, efforts to make the study of law subject to scientific systems in the nineteenth century had a solid base of an educated elite, which would find more organized, institutionalized training a plausible solution.

Law often attracted intellectually oriented people in Anglo-American society, but several factors inflated the role of a college degree in Massachusetts. Expectations of raising lawyers to the status of gentlemen demanded that candidates receive the education required in British society for that role—a college degree or at least a liberal education. Bar associations reinforced this predilection by prescribing longer periods of apprenticeship for law students without college degrees.[29] Moreover the legal practitioners' need to be well versed in Latin, Greek, and political history—skills usually honed in college—provided a realistic justification for requiring college training. An additional reason was that the rising social and economic status of the profession attracted many college graduates who previously might have become ministers, farmers, or merchants. Lawyers soon rivaled ministers as the educated elite (tables 14-17).

Of the 2,618 trained lawyers practicing in Massachusetts and Maine from 1760 to 1840, 1,859 (71 percent) held college degrees. Surprisingly the percentage for the eastern district—a largely frontier and rural area with few commercial seaports that became the state of Maine in 1820—topped that for the old Massachusetts Bay region. This phenomenon might have stemmed from the attraction of anticipated opportunities in a newly developing region. Never-

TABLE 14 OCCUPATIONAL DISTRIBUTION OF YALE GRADUATES, 1701-1815

YEARS	LAWYERS	MINISTERS	DOCTORS	OTHERS	TOTAL
1701-1745	33	242	30	178	483
1746-1763	56	186	64	199	505
1764-1778	52	154	59	219	484
1779-1792	168	129	57	189	543
1793-1805	182	109	37	212	540
1806-1815	191	108	71	231	601
Total					
1701-1792	309 (15.3%)	711 (35.3%)	210 (10.4%)	735 (39.%)	2,015
1793-1815	373 (32.7%)	217 (19.0%)	108 (9.5%)	443 (38.8%)	1,141

Source: Franklin B. Dexter, *Biographical Sketches of the Graduates of Yale College* . . .(New York, 1885-1912), 1:773, 2:786, 3:715, 4:810, 6:836; Yale University, *Catalogue of the Officers and Graduates of Yale University in New Haven, Connecticut, 1701–1910* (New Haven, 1910), 89-112.

[a]Because of limitations of the historical directory of Yale graduates, only the occupations for those graduates after 1815 who became ministers could be readily determined. Of 1,879 graduates from 1816 to 1840, there were 567 ministers (30.1 percent). When combined with the figures for 1793 to 1815, it brings a percentage of 25.9 for ministerial graduates, which is very close to the percentage of ministerial graduates registered by Dartmouth and Brown universities.

theless of 600 trained lawyers practicing from 1760 to 1840, 450 (75 percent)graduated from college. In Massachusetts itself, 1,409 or nearly 70 percent out of 2,018 practitioners held college degrees.[30]

Even more revealing is a county breakdown, which indicates that a higher percentage of college graduates admitted to the profession came in the Bay State's more urban counties of Essex and Suffolk. Between 1770 and 1807 (a period for which the bar association's records survive), the Suffolk County Bar Association accepted 91 students of law. The college status of 85 has been determined. Seventy-two (84.7 percent) possessed a college degree. In Essex County, of 184 trained lawyers admitted to practice between 1760 and 1840 whose college status is known, 160 (87 percent) had re-

TABLE 15 OCCUPATIONAL DISTRIBUTION OF BOWDOIN AND WILLIAMS GRADUATES, 1795–1835

YEARS	LAWYERS	MINISTERS	PHYSICIANS	COMMERCE	OTHERS[a]	TOTAL
1795–1805						
Williams	94	59	25	3	18	199
1806–1815						
Williams	105	100	12	3	38	258
Bowdoin	40	11	4	8	12	75
1816–1825						
Williams	45	62	20	3	20	158
Bowdoin	85	32	27	8	31	183
1826–1835						
Williams	48	116	17	7	41	229
Bowdoin	89	62	29	7	61	248

Source: H. Hall, *General Catalogue of Bowdoin College and the Medical School of Maine, 1794–1912* (Brunswick, 1912); *General Catalogue . . . of Williams College* (Boston, 1880).

a. Includes teachers, editors, farmers, and manufacturers.

TABLE 16 OCCUPATIONAL DISTRIBUTION OF BROWN AND DARTMOUTH GRADUATES, 1770–1835

YEAR		MINISTERS	DOCTORS	LAWYERS	FARMERS	COMMERCE	OTHERS	TOTAL
1770[a]	Brown	4	1	3	0	0	3	11
1780	Brown	17	9	4	1	2	16	49
	Dartmouth	48	4	5	12	5	20	94
1790	Brown	20	8	19	2	10	27	86
	Dartmouth	83	9	38	7	16	27	180
1800	Brown	49	21	53	3	14	56	196
	Dartmouth	95	31	137	8	22	56	348
1810	Brown	56	26	78	6	11	73	250
	Dartmouth	69	39	173	0	6	48	335
1820	Brown	72	26	83	4	12	77	274
	Dartmouth	116	37	138	0	6	37	334
1830	Brown	95	48	85	4	16	57	305
	Dartmouth	134	34	114	0	4	49	335
1835	Brown	35	12	24	3	9	22	105
	Dartmouth	60	15	57	1	9	25	167
Totals to 1800								
	Brown	90 (26.3%)	39 (11.4%)	79 (23.1%)	6 (1.7%)	26 (7.9%)	102 (29.6%)	342
	Dartmouth	206 (34.2%)	44 (7.3%)	180 (29.9%)	27 (4.5%)	43 (7.1%)	103 (17.0%)	603
1800–1835								
	Brown	258 (27.3%)	112 (11.8%)	270 (28.6%)	17 (1.8%)	48 (5.1%)	239 (25.3%)	944
	Dartmouth	399 (36.4%)	125 (11.4%)	482 (43.9%)	1 (0.1%)	31 (2.8%)	59 (5.4%)	1,097

Source: George T. Chapman, *Sketches of the Alumni of Dartmouth Colleges from 1771 . . .* (Cambridge, Mass., 1867), 13-281; Mary D. Vaughan, *Historical Catalogue of Brown University, 1764–1904* (Providence, 1905), 67-169.

ceived the baccalaureate. Furthermore in Essex, six of the noncollege graduates were sworn to the bar after 1836 when the revised statutes lowered formal standards.[31] Both of these counties had strong bar associations that were highly motivated to raise educational standards, and the educational level of the legal profession appears to reflect their efforts.

A comparison with counties where bar associations lacked similar authority or motivation further illustrates this point. In Bristol County, where the bar association was only sporadically active, 75 trained lawyers practiced between 1767 and 1834. College graduates numbered 53 (70.6 percent). In Worcester County, where a strong bar association existed after 1790, 172 (82 percent) of the 210 trained lawyers practicing in that region between 1760 and 1836 held college degrees. Of the 61 attorneys admitted to the court of common pleas in Worcester from 1780 to 1836, 47 (77 percent) had graduated from college. Between 1836 and 1850, however, when the bar association no longer functioned, 31 of 66 newly trained lawyers in the county held no degree.

Bar associations' role in educational standards was also important in Maine. In Kennebec County, for example, a bar association functioned only intermittently after 1814, and only 25 of the 52 attorneys admitted to the court of common pleas from 1796 to 1840, whose educational status is known, had a college degree; 27 lawyers did not. Of the 40 lawyers admitted to the rank of counsellor between 1806 and 1836, 21 lawyers held college degrees; 19 did not. Conversely in Cumberland County, where there was a consistently

TABLE 17 HARVARD GRADUATES ENTERING LAW AND RELIGION, 1761-1840

DATE	MINISTERS	LAWYERS
1761-1780	200 (23%)	108 (12.5%)
1781-1800	161 (20.7%)	185 (23.8%)
1801-1820	165 (15.8%)	252 (24.1%)
1821-1840	173 (16.3%)	214 (20.2%)

Source: Catalogue Universitatis Harvardianae, 1854 (Cambridge, Mass., 1854), 25-78.

strong bar association, of the 137 lawyers practicing in the county between 1760 and 1833 whose college education is certain, 109 (74 percent) were college graduates. Hancock County, however, even though it did not contain a strong bar association, held a high percentage of practicing lawyers who were college graduates—16 of 22 (72.2 percent). Statistical evidence suggests a high correlation between strong bar associations that required students to have a liberal education and high educational level. The realization that college graduates might independently be attracted to study or practice in the more commercial, urban areas, which also contained the strongest bar associations, tempers the force of this conclusion but does not invalidate it.

Most college-educated lawyers in Massachusetts attended Harvard College (table 18). Until 1800, over 71 percent of the lawyer graduates had matriculated at Harvard, and although this declined to 58.3 percent for the 1800-1840 period, the proportion was still overwhelming. Brown University and Williams College were the chief gainers in the post-1800 period. The dominance of Harvard graduates helps to explain why Harvard graduates often received special rulings from the bar associations. For example, the Suffolk Bar required Harvard graduates to study law for three years; all other college graduates had to study for four years. On a broader level, it partially explains how the eastern-cosmopolitan lawyers were so able to dominate professional development in Massachusetts.

The educational level of lawyers ranked between ministers and doctors and above the average for the three learned professions in Massachusetts from 1740 to 1840. A study of 3,503 ministers and doctors representing a broad cross-section of the state indicates that 62.9 percent of these groups were college graduates—84.9 percent of the 1,917 ministers and 35.3 percent of 1,576 doctors. But unlike lawyers, the other two learned professions showed a lower educational index for Maine. Ministers had 72.9 percent college graduates in Maine and 88.5 percent in Massachusetts; doctors had 16.9 percent college graduates in the eastern district and 42.9 percent in Massachusetts.[32] Ministers and lawyers emphasized the need for a college education, and physicians did not. The statistics reflect these values.

TABLE 18 COLLEGE BACKGROUNDS OF MASSACHUSETTS LAWYERS, 1760–1840

COLLEGE	TO 1760	1761–1780	1781–1800	TOTAL TO 1800	1801–1820	1821–1840	TOTAL TO 1840	TOTAL
Harvard	62 (79.5%)	108 (80.6%)	185 (64.9%)	355 (71.5%)	252 (49.9%)	214 (52.6%)	466 (51.1%)	821 (58.3%)
Brown		1 (0.8%)	23 (8.1%)	24 (4.7%)	70 (13.9%)	55 (13.5%)	125 (13.7%)	149 (10.6%)
Williams			9 (3.2%)	9 (1.8%)	60 (11.9%)	14 (3.4%)	74 (8.1%)	83 (5.9%)
Dartmouth			38 (13.3%)	38 (7.7%)	59 (11.6%)	29 (7.1%)	88 (9.7%)	126 (9.0%)
Yale	15 (19.2%)	22 (16.4%)	30 (10.5%)	67 (13.5%)	43 (8.5%)	27 (6.6%)	70 (7.7%)	137 (9.7%)
Bowdoin					7 (1.4%)	10 (2.5%)	17 (1.9%)	17 (1.2%)
Amherst						23 (5.7%)	23 (2.5%)	46 (1.6%)
Others	1 (1.3%)	3 (2.2%)		4 (0.8%)	14 (2.8%)	35 (8.6%)	49 (5.4%)	53 (3.8%)

Note: This table includes only lawyers practicing in Massachusetts proper, excluding the district of Maine.

TABLE 19 EDUCATIONAL PATTERNS OF PROFESSIONAL SCHOOLS

SCHOOLS AND DATES	COLLEGE GRADUATES	NONGRADUATES	TOTAL
Theological			
Newton, 1826-1840	99 (58.9%)	69 (41.1%)	168
Yale Divinity, 1825-1840	240 (79.5%)	62 (21.5%)	302
Andover, 1810-1840	1,172 (93.9%)	87 (6.1%)	1,259
Bangor, 1820-1840	51 (30.2%)	118 (69.8%)	169
Harvard Divinity, 1812-1840	246 (91.4%)	22 (8.6%)	268
Medical			
Yale Medical, 1814-1840	106 (23.1%)	354 (76.9%)	460
Dartmouth Medical, 1798-1840	83 (13.7%)	522 (86.3%)	605
Maine Medical, 1821-1840	93 (12.7%)	653 (87.3%)	746
Harvard Medical, 1788-1840	346 (61.5%)	217 (38.5%)	563
Law			
Harvard Law, 1820-1840	116 (73.4%)	42 (26.6%)	158
Total	2,452 (52.2%)	2,246 (47.8%)	4,698

Source: Richard D. Pierce, ed., *General Catalogue of the Newton Theological Institution, 1826–1943* (Newton Centre, Mass., 1943); *Eighth General Catalogue of the Yale Divinity School, 1822–1922* (New Haven, 1922); *General Catalogue of the Divinity School of Harvard University* (Cambridge; 1898); *General Catalogue of the Theological Seminary, Andover, Massachusetts, 1808–1908* (Boston, 1909); *Bangor Theological Seminary; Historical Catalogue, 1816–1916* (Bangor, 1916); *Catalogue of the Officers and Graduates of Yale University in New Haven, Connecticut, 1701–1910* (New Haven, 1910); *General Catalogue of Dartmouth College and the Associated Schools, 1769–1910* (Hanover, N.H., 1911); *General Catalogue of Bowdoin College and the Medical School of Maine, 1794–1912* (Brunswick, 1912); *Quinquennial Catalogue of the Officers and Graduates of Harvard University, 1636–1895* (Cambridge, 1895).

The emergence of professional schools as training grounds for lawyers, ministers, and physicians does not seem to have altered the educational pattern. Despite admission standards that were lower than the apprenticeship requirements under some bar associations, Harvard Law School attracted a student body of 73.4 percent college graduates, just slightly higher than the percentage of college graduates entering the profession from all sources. A study of ten professional schools with 4,698 students indicates that they were not attracting students with educational backgrounds that differed from those in the eighteenth-century apprenticeship system (table 19). Of professional school graduates, most ministers and lawyers had college degrees; most doctors did not.

To men already indoctrinated to classroom education through colleges, one appealing alternative to a full term of apprenticeship in Massachusetts was more institutional education. The commonwealth's courts and bar associations designed regulations to discourage the schools, but a growing number of students flocked to the law school in Litchfield until the establishment of law lectures at Harvard. Ninety-four lawyers from Massachusetts attended lectures from 1798 to 1833 and comprised one-ninth of the 805 students. Attendance from the Bay State peaked at eleven students in 1812. There were nine aspirants in 1813 and eight students in the next year, but only one in 1815. Samuel Fischer presents the student's view of why the school had become a favorite of future lawyers in the early nineteenth century: "With respect to the law school here, I have the satisfaction of being able to assure you that it answers my expectations fully. The lectures by Judge Reeve, and his associate Mr. Gould are highly valuable, & afford important assistance to a student. Generally speaking the advantages here for the study of law are certainly favorable." "I have no doubt [it is] much better for at least the first half of the time usually spent in the study before pretending to practice, than the best private office in New England," he concluded.[33] Returning law school graduates by their words and demonstrable skills provided support for lawyers and laymen who were advocating a similar system of law school instruction for Massachusetts.

Dissatisfaction with the apprenticeship system joined with the need for intensive training in the complexities of commercial and civil law to demand a more analytical approach to law. While some men proposed to codify or simplify the law to facilitate the mastery of it, others suggested better legal training. Charles P. Sumer, a

Boston attorney, urged Story in June 1815 to give a series of lectures on American statute laws, common law, and the Constitution. Ample compensation, Sumner suggested, would come from the fees of auditors, who would number at least twenty. Sumner even attempted to play on Story's nationalism with the plea that "Law Lectures & law treatises are plenty enough for an English student, but such as would be entirely useful to an American student are a very great diseratum." At first Story was amenable, but he was prepared to defer to a proposed program of lectures at Harvard. Story, who later became a Harvard law professor, reported to Sumner that "Judge Davis [John Davis, Harvard treasurer and United States district judge], however, on my last visit at Boston expressed an opinion, that public law lectures would be delivered at Cambridge, in the course of a year; and that the government had it now in contemplation."[34] The idea became reality less than two months later when the Harvard Corporation endorsed a series of law lectures.

The sale of Royall's land for $7,500 provided the occasion for this decision in August 1815. The chief sponsor of the law professorship, however, was John Lowell, a wealthy Boston lawyer and a member of the Harvard Corporation. The decision was not reached suddenly or without careful consideration. Lowell and other prominent lawyers, such as Davis, Jackson, Gore, and William Prescott, had been discussing the project for years. The stage was set as early as 1810 when the Board of Overseers was revamped to allow for the election of laymen. Lawyers quickly became a power within the Harvard governing body, to the consternation of faculty and ministerial groups. By 1815 lawyers comprised a majority of the fellows of the Harvard Corporation and held four-fifths of the seats allotted for laymen on the Board of Overseers. At the meeting of the Harvard Corporation that approved the concept of a law professorship, four of the six fellows present were sworn attorneys.[35]

Lawyers lost no significant control over legal education with the initiation of law lectures in 1815 and a law school in 1817. Although bar associations lost some of their functions, practicing lawyers remained the dominant element on law school staffs until the twentieth century. Then full-time law professors gained power, a development that many lawyers considered a move with revolutionary implications for the structure of the profession.[36] In 1815, 1817, and 1828-1829 when key decisions were made affecting the law school and legal education at Harvard, lawyers dominated the Harvard Corporation and the Board of Overseers. Evidence indicates that leading lawyers, such as Webster and Story, were instrumental in securing the appointment of Josiah Quincy, a lawyer and politician, as Harvard's first nonclerical president. Quincy subsequently played an important role in the revitalization of the law professorship and founding of the Dane Law School.[37] This continued ability to control and direct legal training undoubtedly encouraged lawyers' support for university-connected law schools and their willingness to abandon bar association controls over professional training.

Vocal support for the new law school came from lawyers and laymen throughout the state who believed that law should be systematized, much like biology, medicine, and zoology. To them the scientific study of jurisprudence was "the consideration of its origin and purposes of its particular laws philosophically and historically, so as to determine whether any case is within the scope of its authority, and if not, to be able to form a new rule by the same process and from the same elements from which, by the theory of the functions of society, all laws must necessarily have originated."[38] Proponents argued that carrying out this mission required a more complex educational system than a law office. Law now joined general educational reform to move learning from areas of experience to the classroom and to change uneven individual preparation to a standardized group course. High schools and commercial schools replaced business clerkships at the same time that law schools, medical schools, and theological seminaries became substitutes for apprenticeship. Advocates claimed that a reputable school's diploma would be a far better guarantor of competence than the approval of a bar association or medical society. Being educated at Harvard Law would be just as meaningful as being milled in Lowell or Waltham.

The case was succinctly stated by Asahel Stearns. "It was thought that the time had arrived," the new law professor said, "when the demands of the public for the means of thorough and methodical education of all engaged in the study of liberal professions, should be complied." Stearns argued that this was especially important for "those who are to administer the laws, defend the rights of their fellow citizens, and become in no inconsiderable degree the directors of public opinion, and the guardians of the public liberty and welfare."[39] Public leaders as well as lawyers, in short, should be systematically trained in the law. Both Story and Metcalf joined with Stearns in arguing that "the science of law" could best be understood in the forum of a law school.[40] Story summarized his choice between a law school and apprenticeship in the *North American Review* in 1817. Reviewing David Hoffman's *A Course of Legal Study Addressed to Students of Law in the United States* (1817), Story asserted that Hoffman's book demonstrated the necessity of the law school at Harvard: "No work can sooner dissipate the common delusion, that the law may be thoroughly acquired in the immethodical, interrupted and desultory studies of the office of a practicing counsellor."[41]

The need for clinical training was not forgotten by lawyers; even supporters of the law school plan still had an eye for the practical. Indeed, in an age when most lawyers still entered solo practice, they could not begin a career without the practical skills of the profession. The belief remained strong that at least a year of study in the office of a counsellor beyond attendance at a law school was necessary. Isaac Parker expressed this view at his inauguration as first Royall Professor of Law at Harvard in 1816. A man of broad experience as state chief justice and legal counsellor, he saw law school as a background for clerkship. "One or two years devoted to *study only*, under a capable instructor, before they shall enter into the office of a counsellor, to obtain a knowledge of practice," Parker said, "will tend greatly to improve the character of the bar of our state." Story recommended studying only one year out of the three-year term required by the bar associations at a law school. Clearly, law school training did not become "de rigeur," even for leaders of the profession, until the late nineteenth century, and apprenticeship remained the training experience of most lawyers until well into the twentieth century.[42]

Harvard Law School's growth had an important impact on the legal profession's structure and institutions. Although lawyers would be instructors in the new law schools, many practitioners sensed a threat to their control of legal education. Certainly the power of the bar associations and the regulatory aspects of the apprenticeship system would be endangered. Directors of the law schools seldom felt constrained by bar association regulations, and a law school's mere existence challenged the rule prohibiting more than three clerks in one office. For the next twenty years the questions of who and what institution would dominate legal education remained unanswered.[43]

A stalemate favored defenders of apprenticeship and bar association control, in part because they held the field. The burden of proof fell on law school advocates. Lawyers' reluctance to accept the sufficiency of a law school education directly affected the program at Harvard Law School. The school's officers consequently planned just an eighteen-month course, similar to that of the Litchfield Law School, with sufficient time within the normal three-year clerkship for an office stint.

Harvard's requirements for admission and for the granting of the degree of bachelor of laws also adhered to the rules of the Massachusetts Supreme Court and many county bar association regulations. Students who spent at least eighteen months at the university school and who then passed the remainder of their three-year or five-year term of study in the office of a counsellor of the state supreme court received a bachelor of law degree. If students had graduated from college, they could spend three years at the law school; if they were nongraduates, they could attend law school for five years and receive the same degree. Moreover Harvard's law professors were required to continue as practitioners in the supreme court.

At first the college restricted entrance to college graduates or students who had studied five years in the office of a counsellor. When this requirement proved too restrictive, standards were lowered in 1829 to allow the admittance of any student producing a recommendation of good moral character and a statement of his education. Not until 1909 did Harvard Law again require a bachelor's degree for admission. As a further incentive, tuition fees were kept at $100 per year, less than the fees required by many bar associations for study with practicing counsellors.[44] Despite these efforts to make the law school program conform to current regulations of the bar associations and courts, many lawyers still feared what they perceived as a challenge to traditional apprenticeship and local institutional control.

In 1819 Suffolk and Essex county lawyers specifically excluded graduates of the school from admission to the county court unless they had spent the last year of their term of study in the office of a counsellor in the county where they sought admission. The bar association considered Harvard Law School professors just other counsellors in the state supreme judicial court and resident practitioners of Middlesex County. Their students received no preferential treatment. Lawyers in other counties not so directly affected gradually and informally excused Harvard Law School graduates from this residency requirement. But those of Suffolk County, which contained the state's commercial and political centers, and the highest number of lawyers, remained opposed.[45]

Once Harvard College had evaded the bar associations' rulings against any counsellor having more than three clerks, several law schools, modeled on Litchfield Law School and the New Haven Law School, opened in the Bay State. Judge Samuel Howe, a graduate of the Litchfield Law School, and Elijah H. Mills, his law partner, established a law school in Northampton in 1823. With the assistance of John H. Ashmun, the school flourished with between ten and fifteen law students a year until 1829. When Howe died, Mills lost interest, Harvard College hired Ashmun as a law professor, and the school dissolved.[46]

Recruiting efforts of the Northampton Law School help reveal the influence of the scientific concept of law on innovation in legal education. In a *Hampshire Gazette* advertisement, the school boasted that "considering the progress which has been made in modern times in the science of jurisprudence, and the varied attainments necessary for distinction at the bar, the advantages of a regular system of instruction over the desultory course usually pursued, must be obvious to all who have turned their attention to the subject."[47]

Howe and Mills delivered three one-hour lectures per week. Recitations three times a week and a discussion on current cases once a week rounded out the classroom plan. Students also copied the normal writs, pleas, contracts, and varied forms that comprised the bulk of all lawyers' activities. One observer concluded that the course "combines every advantage which can arise from a term of study in the office of a counsellor with all those of an academic institution."[48] Metcalf confidently argued that private law schools and university law professorships would greatly aid young men in understanding the more intricate laws of the United States and produce a more erudite profession.[49] Advocates of classroom instruction gained ground with such appeals to intellectual elitism.

A surge of entrepreneurial activity followed this initial optimism. After the opening of Northampton Law School and the Harvard Law School, efforts were made to organize three other private law schools. The institutions of Samuel Burnside in Worcester and Samuel F. Dickinson in Amherst apparently never survived their opening announcements in 1828, a clear indication of the still limited degree of support. A former Worcester lawyer remarked to a friend, "Burnside I see by the papers here set up a school in Worcester. I do not think he is really the man—though there is no doubt I suppose but he would read a very good course of lectures." Metcalf, another graduate of Litchfield Law School, managed to found a law school in Dedham in 1828, but it survived less than two years, despite its proximity to Boston with its concentration of professional men and their commercially oriented legal practices.[50]

The failures of these law schools must be attributed to the predicament of the students who attended them rather than competition from Harvard Law School. In fact Harvard Law had declined to just two students in 1829. In Connecticut, where law schools had flourished for nearly fifty years, a college graduate could be admitted to the bar after only two years of study, the length of the program at a law school. But in Massachusetts, students found themselves trapped by residency and other requirements of the bar associations and the supreme judicial court, which called for a minimum of three years of study for college graduates and five years for noncollege graduates. Law students had to study at least one year beyond law school in the office of a counsellor. Where candidates for admission could be admitted after only two years of study, as in Virginia, Kentucky, and Connecticut, law schools could more easily attract students. In Massachusetts both lawyers and students generally preferred apprentices to enter an office for a full clerkship rather than one year, so it was usually difficult for law school graduates to find good, one-year office apprenticeships.[51]

Many lawyers and law students preferred the apprenticeship system. Such was the view of William Lincoln, son of Levi, a wealthy, influential Worcester counsellor and Thomas Jefferson's former attorney general. In a letter to Christopher Baldwin, a fellow student, Lincoln outlined the advantages of apprenticeship: "If you would root out elementary principles, there are the researches of legal sages and the long series of reporters." On the other hand, he added, "if you would attend to the practical details of business, there are the inquiring clients and the responding counsellors."[52]

The course of study also limited the law schools' attractiveness. Although lectures offered a systematic analysis of some phases of the law, particularly commerce and insurance, much of the learning process did not differ from the studies of apprentices. Apprentices and law school students read the same books and still had to master the same forms, pleas, and so forth, much of the time on their own. At Dedham Law School, Metcalf insisted that he would stress only the elementary principles of the law. Howe's lectures at Northampton and Stearns's course at Harvard emphasized the practical as much as the broad scientific aspects of the law despite contrary protestations. Both schools relied heavily on Blackstone, Littleton, Coke, Sugden, and Saunders, the standard English authorities.[53] Stearns's 1826 comment on the use of Blackstone reflects his course's conservatism. Students first read Blackstone, which Stearns felt "aids the student in fixing his attention, enables him more readily to form an acquaintance with the technical terms and language of the law, and at the same time to obtain a more distant view of that admiral outline of the science."[54] Harvard, like Northampton Law School, offered students moot courts, debating clubs, regular examinations, and written disputations.

By 1829 the Harvard Law School was in desperate straits; it had just one student and little money. Stearns attributed the decline in pupils to a diminution of law students throughout the state by nearly one-half, the establishment of similar law schools at Northampton and in Virginia, the offering of gratuitous instruction by lawyers eager for the labor of apprentices, and the lack of adequate physical facilities at Harvard.[55]

But instead of allowing its collapse, the university, with a lawyer-dominated corporation and Board of Overseers, took vigorous action to revitalize the law school. Dane's gift provided for the construction of a building and the endowment of an additional law professorship, which Dane specified should go to Story. No doubt Story, a long-time friend of Dane, welcomed the opportunity to espouse his concern for national unity and economic growth in both the verbal and written forms required by the professorship. His prolific writing and lecturing, despite his arduous court schedule, illustrate Story's determination to create and disseminate an American law of commerce. As a final measure, Harvard hired Ashmun from the Northampton Law School, thereby eliminating a major competitor and acquiring a good instructor with a coterie of students from western Massachusetts.[56] These dramatic steps saved the law school, but its future still remained uncertain.

The leading historians of Harvard Law School—Warren and Sutherland—attribute major credit for the revival of Harvard Law to the methods and reputations of professors Story and Ashmun. But just three years after their appointments as Harvard Law professors, Story expressed chagrin to his colleague at the decline of students, and he voiced hope that a new course revision and the introduction of moot courts would attract more students. He urged Ashmun to contact students at the law school at New Haven, Connecticut, where Story had just visited, to find out why their program had attracted fifty law students in 1832.[57]

The revival of Harvard Law School can be traced to the passage of the Massachusetts Revised Statutes of 1835. One section transferred institutional control over attorneys' admissions from the bar associations to the state. Candidates for the legal profession who had studied law less than three years could be sworn into practice after an examination by a member of the judiciary. Those who had studied law for three years, regardless of prior education or manner of law study, automatically were admitted to legal practice upon application.[58] This statute allowed aspirants who had completed the eighteen-month course at Harvard Law School to be admitted directly to practice in any court in the state after an examination. Moreover Harvard Law students could be admitted in the various county courts without approval by provincially minded bar committees. In short the removal of several layers of regulations not only simplified the admissions process but also removed several roadblocks to attendance at law school.[59]

Both the geographic areas from which students came and the quality of the students were affected at Harvard. In 1836 there were twenty-three students from Massachusetts and Maine at the law school, all of whom held college degrees. In 1838, only two years after the law went into effect, forty-one law students came from the same area, an increase of 78 percent. Five lacked college degrees. In the same period the school's enrollment increased 56 percent, but the students from outside Massachusetts and Maine increased from twenty-nine to thirty-seven, just 27 percent. Significant quantitative changes occurred in the degree-granting program as the number of degrees awarded jumped from thirty-six in 1836 to sixty-eight in 1838. While Harvard granted only twenty law degrees to noncollege graduates between 1820 and 1837, law degrees went to seventeen candidates without a baccalaureate in only two years, 1838 and 1839.[60] As a result, Harvard Law School became more provincially oriented and attracted a lower percentage of college graduates, but its program had gained vital support in its home state.

Harvard Corporation formally recognized the end of the three-year clerkship in 1839 by authorizing the degree of bachelor of laws for those who completed only eighteen months of study, or just one year of study if the person had already been admitted to practice. By 1845 the number of law scholars at Harvard had increased to 145, and the permanence of a Massachusetts law school seemed assured.[61]

The destruction of the county bar associations' control over entrance into the legal profession had given added impetus to Harvard Law School and paved the way for great variations in preparation for admission. Because candidates no longer needed the approval of the bar associations, they did not have to clerk with a lawyer or matriculate at a law school but could study alone. Legal knowledge demonstrated to a state judge, although generally a legally trained one, admitted a person to practice. A person's preparation, of course, did partly determine his chances for occupational success and status, but the removal of these restrictions left the courts and law schools as licensing agents in the public and professional mind.

Classroom advocates seized the opportunity to downgrade apprenticeship as a means of training lawyers, particularly those with legitimate aspirations for the profession's elite. Writing to a friend, Story voiced the position of law school enthusiasts: "In America it requires no argument to establish the importance nay necessity of a systematical and scientific study of the law. No lawyer in this country would, in the present time, deem his education at all complete without availing himself of the lectures of some Law Institution."[62] His statement was premature, but events of the 1830s made possible its fulfillment.

With Harvard Law School firmly established, proponents of a systematic course of legal study based on lectures, disputations, and books rather than experience could assume the permanence of a law school education for aspiring lawyers in the Bay State. By shifting legal education to the university, it weakened the bar associations where practicing lawyers held sway and ultimately opened the door for a new professional elite to control legal education and the direction of the profession. Ironically the professional schools became the chief defense of the exclusive nature of the profession and the main agency for the establishment of professional authority. This does not mean that all professionals saw professional schools as a means of preserving the purity and integrity of the profession. But the desire to establish high standards and the need to demonstrate professional authority to a doubting public, combined with the industrial concept that the best products are standardized, interchangeable, and subject to mass production, led reformers and entrepreneurs to establish and support professional schools. In the short run, the eighteen-month term of study at the law school provided a precedent for the discontinuance of the traditional three- and five-year terms of study. Not until 1871 did Harvard extend the requirements for an LL.B to two years of study, and in 1899 it raised them to three years.[63] The opposition of many legal educators to the clerkship system and the apathy of other lawyers eroded support for the apprenticeship system and bar association control of legal training. The profession's corporate nature was weakened by the internal dispute over legal education. But lawyers' community standing grew from the extension of their power to the university while the profession retained its control of legal training, albeit in a more modern institution. In Massachusetts apprenticeship and the power of the bar associations grew strong together, and together they fell into disrepute.

NOTES

1. Arthur E. Sutherland, *The Law at Harvard: A History of Ideas and Men, 1817–1967* (Cambridge, Mass., 1967), 43-45; Charles Warren, *A History of Harvard Law School and of Early Legal Conditions in America* (New York, 1908), 1:285.

2. Samuel E. Morison, *Three Centuries of Harvard, 1636–1936* (Cambridge, Mass., 1936), 238-239 offers the defense that Harvard could not obtain the legacy of Isaac Royall for thirty years. Josiah Quincy, *The History of Harvard University* (Boston, 1860), 2:317-319, offers no explanation for the delay in the appearance of the law school. Alfred A. Reed, *Training for the Public Profession of the Law* (New York, 1921), 128, 134-135 touches on the basic reason when he argues that English tradition and the Suffolk County Bar rule of 1783 prohibiting barristers from training more than three apprentices at a time stifled the growth of law schools, but his view is too narrow. Anton-Hermann Chroust, *The Rise of the Legal Profession in America* (Norman, 1965), 1:191-202, attempts no explanation for the delay.

3. Among the best discussions of the role of professional education are Everett Hughes, *Men and Their Work* (Glencoe, Ill., 1958), and Roy Lubove, *The Professional Altruist: The Emergence of Social Work as a Career, 1880–1930* (Cambridge, Mass., 1965); Burton Bledstein, *The Culture of Professionalism: The Middle Class and the Development of Higher Education in America* (New York, 1976). Paul M. Hamlin's *Legal Education in Colonial New York* (New York, 1939) is a good study of legal education in early America. For a perceptive but one-faceted interpretation of professional training in the colonies, see Daniel Boorstin, *The Americans: The Colonial Experience* (New York, 1958), 199-239. With the decline of the Inns of Court, legal training in England was also almost solely through apprenticeship. William Holdsworth, *A History of English Law* (London, 1938), 12, 15-18, 22-27, 77-88, 100. For a detailed view of English legal education, see Edwin Freshfield, ed., *The Records of the Society of Gentlemen Practisers in the Courts of Law and Equity Called the Law Society* (London, 1897); William J. Reader, *Professional Men: The Rise of the Professional Classes in Nineteenth Century England* (London, 1966); Robert Robson, *The Attorney in Eighteenth Century England* (Cambridge, Mass., 1959).

4. For further information on the various apprenticeship terms, see chap. 1-3, and Oscar Handlin and Mary Handlin, *Facing Life: Youth and the Family in American History* (Boston, 1971), 127-128.

5. Rufus King to ?, December 20, 1778, MB; Dwight C. Kilbourn, *The Bench and Bar of Litchfield County, Connecticut, 1709–1901* (Litchfield, 1909); Warren, *Harvard Law*, 1:131-133; Simeon E. Baldwin, *The American Judiciary* (New York, 1905), 350. At least 120 Americans attended

the Middle Temple before the Revolution but only 20 did from 1784 to 1835. C. E. A. Bedwell, "American Middle Templars," *American Historical Review* 25 (July 1920): 680-689.

6. Probably Johannes Van Muyden, *Compendium Institutionum Justani Tractatio in Usum Collegeiorum*, an abridgement of *Justinian's Institutes* published in 1694. John Adams to John Wentworth, to Tristram Dalton, and to Samuel Quincy, October-November 1758, in Lyman H. Butterfield, ed., *The Earliest Diary of John Adams* (New York, 1964), 62-63. Recent complaints center around a lack of clinical experience in law school. Reformers of the 1970s are coping with the same problems. Legal education, they say, is too rigid, too uniform, too repetitious, and too long. Reformers today want to include more practical experience, while those of two centuries ago wanted to introduce more theory in legal education. Barrie Thorne, "Professional Education in Law," *Education for the Professions of Medicine, Law, Theology, and Social Welfare* (New York, 1973), 101-102.

7. Charles Warren, *A History of the American Bar*, 3d ed. (New York, 1966), 172; James Bridge to John Q. Adams, September 28, 1787, in "Diary of John Q. Adams," Massachusetts Historical Society *Proceedings*, 2d ser. 16 (1902): 435; Benjamin Brown to George Thacher, June 4, 1789, Greenough Papers, MHi; Jonathan Mason to John Adams, August 12, 1776, and Nathaniel Freeman to John Q. Adams, January 5, 1788, Adams Papers, MHi.

8. Anonymous, "Review of Joseph Story's Commentaries on the Conflict of Laws, Foreign and Domestic in Regard to Rights and Remedies . . .," *American Jurist and Law Magazine* 11 (April 1834): 366.

9. For the publication of law books, see book reviews and lists of new publications in the *North American Review* and *American Jurist and Law Magazine* for the appropriate years. For a fuller discussion of the growth of the publication of American law books and journals, see Gerard W. Gawalt, "Massachusetts Lawyers: An Historical Analysis of the Process of Professionalization, 1760-1840" (Ph.D. diss., Clark University, 1969), chap. 5.

10. G. S. Hilliard, "Review of David Hoffman's *A Course of Legal Study* . . . ," *North American Review* 46 (January 1838): 72.

11. Alexander Hamilton to Edwin Conant, October 19, 1830, Conant Papers, MWA; Thomas F. Bergin, "The Law Teacher: A Man Divided Against Himself," *Virginia Law Review* 54 (1968): 649; Robert Stevens, "Two Cheers for 1870: The American Law School," in Donald Fleming and Bernard Bailyn, eds., *Law in American History* (Boston, 1971), 529-548.

12. Warren, *History of the American Bar*, 172; Simeon Baldwin, "The Study of Elementary Law: The Proper Beginning of a Legal Education," *Yale Law Review* 13 (October 1930): 3n; James Bridge to John Q. Adams,

September 26, 1787, in "Diary of John Q. Adams," 435; Benjamin Brown to George Thacher, June 4, 1789, Greenough Papers, MHi; Journal of Dwight Foster, January 1777-September 1778, MWA.

13. James Bridge to John Q. Adams, September 28, 1787, "John Q. Adams Diary," 435. William Thomas to Issac Goodwin, August 27, 1809, Goodwin Papers, MWA, reveals the same attitude, as does an exchange of letters between Joseph Story and his mentor Samuel Sewall, 1799-1800, quoted in James McClellan, *Joseph Story and the American Constitution* (Norman, 1971), 12-14. A distinct lack of enthusiasm is also shown in Lemuel Shaw to John Shaw, February 19, 1800, Shaw Papers, MHi; memorandum in lawyers ledger, 1823-1833, of Sumner Bastow and Ira M. Barton, MWA; Essex County Bar, *Rules, 1819*, 16, as to November term, 1814. Joseph G. Kendall to Willard Phillips, February 10, 1811, and Phillips to Edmund Story, January 24, 1811, Phillips Papers, MHi.

14. John Forbes to Dorothy Forbes, January 19, 1789, and George B. Upham to John Forbes, July 26, 1792, Forbes Papers, MHi.

15. Jonathan Mason, Jr., to John Adams, August 12, 1776, Nathaniel Freeman to John Q. Adams, January 15, 1788, Adams Papers, MHi; John Forbes to Dorothy Forbes, January 19, 1789, Forbes Papers, MHi.

16. John Adams, *Diary and Autobiography of John Adams*, ed. L. H. Butterfield et al. (New York, 1964), 1: 62-63; Sutherland, *Law at Harvard*, 15.

17. For a full discussion of the American application of Blackstone's plan to design law lectures for public men rather than simply practicing lawyers, see Gerard W. Gawalt, "The Historical Background to Law Schools' Schizophrenia," *Journal of Legal Education* (forthcoming).

18. Timothy Dwight, *Travels in New England and New York: 1801–1802* (New Haven, 1922), 4:306; Baldwin, *American Judiciary*, 348-349; James Thayer, "The Teaching of English Law at Universities," *Harvard Law Review* 9 (October 1894): 170-171; Reed, *Training*, 118, 128-130.

19. Fisher Ames to Thomas Dwight, January 6, 1791, Ames Papers, Dedham Historical Society; Thomas Pownall to James Bowdoin, February 28, December 9, 1783, January 11, 1784, and James Bowdoin to Thomas Pownall, November 20, 1783, "Bowdoin-Temple Papers," MHS, *Collections*, 7th ser. 6 (Boston, 1907): 1-6, 21-27, 30-32; Morison, *Three Centuries of Harvard*, 238-239.

20. Samuel H. Fisher, *The Litchfield Law School, 1775–1833* (New Haven, 1933); Frederick C. Hicks, "James Kent," *Dictionary of American Biography*.

21. See chap. 1-3 for the development of these rules.

22. See chaps. 2 and 3.

23. Clifford Shipton and J. L. Sibley, *Biographical Sketches of Those Who Attended Harvard College* (Boston, 1873-1975), 15:278-281; George

Dexter, ed., "Record Book of the Suffolk Bar," MHS, *Proceedings* 19 (December 1881):152-155; Beverly McAnear, "The Selection of an Alma Mater by Pre-Revolutionary Students," *Pennsylvania Magazine of History and Biography* 73 (October 1949): 431-433. Suffolk Bar, *Rules, 1805*, 8; Worcester Bar Rules, 1809, Lincoln Papers, MWA; James D. Hopkins, *An Address to the Members of the Cumberland Bar . . . 1833* (Portland, 1833), 30; Hollis Bailey, *Attorneys and Their Admission to the Bar in Massachusetts* (Boston, 1907), 36-37; Essex Bar, *Rules, 1806*, 9; Suffolk Bar, *Rules, 1810*, 14; Hampden Bar, *Rules, 1816*, 4; Bristol Bar, *Rules, 1817*, 12; Suffolk Bar, *Rules, 1819*, 17; Essex Bar, *Rules, 1819*, 8-9; Worcester Bar, *Rules, 1816*, 5; George N. Briggs to Rufus Briggs, October 15, 1813, in William C. Richards, *Great in Goodness: A Memoir of George N. Briggs* (Boston, 1866), 40-41.

24. Dexter, "Record Book," 157; Suffolk Bar, *Rules, 1805*, 11; Essex Bar, *Rules, 1806*, 11-12; Suffolk Bar, *Rules, 1819*, 20; Essex Bar, *Rules, 1819*, 10. In 1800 of approximately 200 trained lawyers in the state, 33 lived in Suffolk County and 14 in Essex County. By 1820, of 489 trained lawyers in the state, 135 practiced in Suffolk County and 41 in Essex County. See table 7.

25. Adams, *Diary*, 1:316; Dexter, "Record Book," 149; Essex County Bar Rules, 1768, in Dexter, "Record Book," 149; Bailey, *Attorneys*, 32-33; rules of the Berkshire Bar, 1792, Sedgwick Papers, MHi; Suffolk Bar, *Rules, 1805,* 11; Essex County Bar, *Rules, 1806,* 11-21. "Rules of the Supreme Judicial Court, 1810," in Dudley A. Tyng, *Reports of Cases Argued and Determined in the Supreme Judicial Court of Massachusetts, 1806–1822* (Boston, 1808-1823), 382; Worcester County Bar, *Rules, 1816*, 7.

26. Berkshire County Bar Rules, 1792, Sedgwick Papers, MHi; Dexter, "Record Books," 174; Bailey, *Attorneys*, 35-37; Essex County Bar, *Rules, 1806*, 13; Tyng, *Reports, 1806–07*, 74; Tyng, *Reports, 1808-10*, 383; Hampden County Bar, *Rules, 1816*, 2-4; Suffolk County Bar, *Rules, 1805*, 4-5; Worcester County Bar Rules, 1809, Lincoln Papers, MWA. Increasing opportunities for legal talent also helped stimulate a call for law schools.

27. Dexter, "Record Book," 167; William Willis, "Thomas Rice," *Maine Historical and Genealogical Recorder* 9 (May 1894): 130; Suffolk County Bar, *Rules, 1805*, 11-12; Essex County Bar, *Rules, 1806*, 13; Worcester County Bar, *Rules, 1816*, 7; Hampden County Bar, *Rules, 1816*, 2-3; Suffolk County Bar, *Rules, 1819*, 18; Essex County Bar, *Rules, 1819*, 11, 14-15; Suffolk County Bar, *Rules, 1814*, 16.

28. Some of the particular instances of these men's innovative actions and commercial orientation in law can be found in Morton Horwitz, *The Transformation of American Law, 1780–1860* (Cambridge, Mass., 1977),

38-39, 49, 57-58, 81-82, 87-88, 181-200. The emphasis of law school courses on commercial law as well as natural law and political philosophy can be seen in Story's published works, for which his lectures served as a basis; Stearns's law lectures, *The Law of Real Actions*; and Howe's Northampton law lectures, *The Practice of Civil Actions.*

29. Reader, *Professional Men*, 9-11, 45-47; Suffolk Bar, *Rules, 1805*, 11-12; Bristol County Bar, *Rules, 1817*, 12; Essex County Bar, *Rules, 1806*, 13.

30. The high percentage of college graduates in the legal profession for this period becomes even more startling when compared to recent figures. In 1909, for example, only 8 percent of those entering the legal profession in the United States were college graduates. And as late as the 1960s, the national legal profession had not attained the record of the Massachusetts lawyers in the last century. A 1963 study of American lawyers reveals that only 62.6 percent had college degrees, but 85.6 percent had attended college. Massachusetts in the late 1960s was still only one of five states to require a college degree as a prerequisite for taking the bar examination. Quintin Johnstone and Dan Hopson, Jr., *Lawyers and Their Work: An Analysis of the Legal Profession in the United States and England* (New York, 1967), 20n; Jerold S. Auerbach, "Enmity and Amity: Law Teachers and Practitioners, 1900-1922," in Fleming and Bailyn, eds., *Law in American History*, 574; *The Bar Examiners Handbook* (Chicago, 1968), 312.

31. These statistics were compiled from county bar records and published lists of college graduates.

32. See table 28.

33. Kilbourn, *Bench and Bar of Litchfield*, 195-214; Samuel Fisher to Willard Phillips, February 3, 1811, Phillips Papers, MHi; see also Joseph Willard to Theodore Willard, October 12, 1819, in Susan Willard, ed., "Letters of Rev. Joseph Willard," Cambridge Historical Society, *Proceedings* 11 (October 1916): 21.

34. Charles P. Sumner to Joseph Story, June 27, 1815, MHS, *Proceedings*, 2d ser. 15 (1901): 202-204; Joseph Story to Charles P. Sumner, June 30, 1815, Warren, *Harvard Law*, 1:290.

35. Morison, *Three Centuries of Harvard*, 238-239; Warren, *Harvard Law*, 1:285-292; John Lowell to Joseph Story, October 4, 1834, Story Papers, DLC.

36. The achievement of professional schools' control over training ultimately had two important consequences. First, the theoretical aspects of professional education were emphasized to the point that graduates of professional schools required a period of on-the-job clinical training or apprenticeship before they could practice, preach, or plead on their own. Simultaneously professional school instructors were becoming full-time

teachers and not part-time instructors with regular professional practices. This change reinforced the theoretical aspects of instruction because the teachers now had little or no practical experience to impart to their students. And the first consequence also stimulated the second because clinicians could not spend enough time mastering the mysteries of professional theoretical knowledge. On this point also see Auerbach, "Enmity and Amity," 551-565.

37. Sutherland, *Law at Harvard*, 45, 92-102; Daniel Webster to Joseph Story, April 18, 1828, Story Papers, DLC.

38. Anonymous, "Origins of Customary Law," *American Jurist and Law Magazine* 2 (July 1830): 33.

39. Asahel Stearns' Report to the Corporation, 1825, in Warren, *Harvard Law*, 1:304.

40. Theron Metcalf, "Notice of James Kent's Commentaries on American Law," *United States Review and Literary Gazette* (May 1827): 81-83; Joseph Story, "Review," 77. The same view was expressed in Isaac Parker, "Inaugural Address Delivered in the Chapel of Harvard University . . . ," *North American Review* 3 (May 1816): 15-19.

41. Story, "Review," 77.

42. Parker, "Inaugural Address," 25; Story, "Review," 77. Asahel Stearns recommended the same course of action to Ira Barton in a letter, February 6, 1828, Ira Barton Papers, MWA; Stevens, "Two Cheers for 1870," 426-427.

43. Constructive criticism of legal education was afoot in England also, but reformers there achieved more limited results. Disgruntled attorneys and solicitors founded the Law Society in 1825 and sponsored twice-weekly law lectures after 1833. Then in 1836 the common law judges, at the urging of the Law Society, set up an examining board—the first serious qualifying exams for any branch of the legal profession in England. Reader, *Professional Men*, 55-56.

44. *Boston Daily Advertiser*, July 28, 1817; Sutherland, *Law at Harvard*, 54, 57, 123-124; Harvard College catalogs, 1825-1839, MWA; Essex County Bar, *Rules, 1806*, 9; Suffolk County Bar, *Rules, 1805*, 8; Worcester County Bar, *Rules, 1816*, 5; Stevens, "Two Cheers for 1870," 426-427.

45. Suffolk County Bar, *Rules, 1819*, 18; Essex County Bar, *Rules, 1819*, 11; Joseph Story to Suffolk Law Association, 1830, in Warren, *Harvard Law*, 2:161.

46. *Hampshire Gazette* (Northampton), July 2, 1823, June 17, September 9, 1829; Lawrence E. Wikander et al., eds., *The Northampton Book . . . 1644–1954* (Northampton, 1954), 290; Chroust, *Rise of the Legal Profession*, 2:217-218; William Lincoln, *History of Worcester* (Worcester,

1862), 211; Joel Parker, *The Law School at Harvard College* (New York, 1871), 10-11, 13; Sutherland, *Law at Harvard*, 99.

47. *Hampshire Gazette*, July 2, 1823. The emphasis on a systematic course of study can be seen in the lectures of Howe published in 1834 as Samuel Howe, *The Practice on Civil Actions and Proceedings at Law in Massachusetts* (Boston, 1834).

48. "The Law School at Northampton," *New York Review and Atheneum* 1 (September 1825): 322-324.

49. Metcalf, "Notice of Kent's Commentaries," 81-83.

50. Peter C. Bacon to Ira M. Barton, March 19, 1828, Barton Papers, MWA; "Prospectus of Samuel F. Dickinson's Law School," *American Jurist and Law Magazine* 1 (July 1829): 192-193; Reed, *Training*, 431; Chroust, *Rise of the Legal Profession*, 2:219-220; "Metcalf's Law School at Dedham," *American Jurist and Law Magazine* 1 (April 1929): 378-80; Anonymous, "The Litchfield Law School," *Albany Law Journal* 20 (1879): 73.

51. Sutherland, *Law at Harvard*, 79; Frederick C. Hicks, *Yale Law School* (New Haven, 1936), 2-3, 20-31; Kilbourn, *Bench and Bar,* 195-214; Reed, *Training*, 83-84, 450.

52. William Lincoln to Christopher Baldwin, June 1, 1823, Lincoln Papers, MWA.

53. Reading lists of Harvard Law School students in Warren, *Harvard Law*, 1:333-334, 355-356; Morison, *Three Centuries of Harvard*, 238-241; Samuel Howe, *The Practice of Civil Actions and Proceedings at Law, in Massachusetts* (Boston, 1834); "Metcalf's Law School at Dedham," 378-380. Asahel Stearns' law lectures at Harvard were published in 1826 as *The Law of Real Actions* (Boston, 1826). Harvard College catalogs, 1829-1830, MWA; Asahel Stearns to the Board of Overseers, January 9, 1826, in Warren, *Harvard Law*, 1:334; Joseph Story to John Ashmun, May 14, 17, December 2, 1831, Story Papers, MHi.

54. Asahel Stearns to Board of Overseers, 1826, Warren, *Harvard Law*, 1:333.

55. Warren, *Harvard Law*, 1:365-370.

56. Ibid., 413-433. James McClellan, *Joseph Story and the American Constitution* (Norman, 1971), 50-52, 251-262; Gerald Dunne, *Justice Joseph Story and the Rise of the Supreme Court* (New York, 1970), 101-102, 386-387; Quincy, *History of Harvard*, 2:378-381.

57. Warren, *History of the American Bar*, 365; Warren, *Harvard Law*, 1:431-434; Sutherland, *Law at Harvard*, 92-139. Joseph Story to John H. Ashmun, January 17, 19, 1832, Story Papers, MHi. Story gave credit to an advertising campaign for a sudden increase in students in 1836. Story to

Harvard Treasurer, September 24, 1836, in Warren, *Harvard Law*, 1:505.

58. The many reasons for the state's assertion of control over the legal profession in 1835 are fully explored in chapter 5. The legal studies program at Harvard Law School had also influenced the passage of the 1835 statutory regulations of the profession. One traditional argument of lawyers had been that three years represented the minimum time necessary to train attorneys. This reason was demonstrably weakened by an 1834 decision of Harvard College. At first three years of study and apprenticeship had been required for a bachelor of law degree, even though the lecture course consisted of just three terms, or eighteen months. The Harvard Corporation, however, decided in 1834 that a degree would be conferred on students who completed the school's course and the "remainder of the time necessary for bar admission" of the state in which they intended to practice. This decision undercut early recommendations of the Commissioners of the Revised Statutes to retain the traditional standards for admission to legal practice when they were challenged by the reform-minded members of the general court in 1835. *The Revised Statutes of Massachusetts* (Boston, 1836), pt. III, title I, chap. 88, 541-542.

59. Doctors and ministers, who favored professional school education, were also able to capitalize on the breakdown of licensing regulations by medical associations, examining boards, and consociations. Medical spokesmen such as Daniel Drake strongly urged that a medical school diploma be the sole criterion for admission to practice. At the same time that state governments were ending bar association and medical society controls over admission to practice, professional schools were opening at a rapid rate. The schools had been fighting to secure independent licensing or admissions authority, and now, with the help of their opponents, they had it thrust upon them. The spurt in professional schools that followed is no coincidence. Nine medical schools were established between 1820 and 1830, eleven before 1840, and eighteen by 1850—almost forty in all. Law schools, which had previously flourished only in states with low admissions standards such as Kentucky, Virginia, and Connecticut, now achieved success in other states, including Massachusetts. And between 1818 and 1840, at least twenty-five theological seminaries were founded by Protestant sects. This overall theme is more fully discussed in Gerard W. Gawalt, "Professionalization and Polarization in American Society, 1740-1850" (paper delivered at Social Science History Conference, Ann Arbor, Michigan, 1977). Daniel Drake, *Practical Essays on Medical Education and the Medical Profession in the United States* (Cincinnati, 1831), 92; Abraham Flexner, *Medical Education in the United States and Canada: A Report to the Carnegie Foundation for the Advancement of Teaching* (New York, 1910), 6-8;

William W. Sweet, *Religion in the Development of American Culture, 1765–1840* (New York, 1952), 178-183.

60. Both Maine and Massachusetts are used because many law students from Maine settled in Massachusetts. Harvard College catalog, 1836, 1838, MWA; *Harvard University: Quinquennial Catalogue*, Law School Graduates, 1820-1845; Parker, *Law School*, 14; Warren, *Harvard Law*, 2:91; Harvard College Catalog, 1836-1845, MWA.

61. *Harvard University: Quinquennial Catalogue.*

62. Joseph Story to James Wilkinson, August 25, 1832, in Story, *Life*, 2:108. For similar views, see Josiah Quincy, "President Quincy's Address on the Occasion of the Dedication of Dane Law College," *American Jurist and Law Magazine* 5 (January 1833): 48-66; Anonymous, "Review of the Daniel Mayes' Introductory Lecture at Transylvania University," *American Jurist and Law Magazine* 7 (April 1832): 349-352; James Gould, "Preface of Gould's Treatise on the Principles of Pleading in Civil Actions," *American Jurist and Law Magazine* 7 (April 1832): 3; Lemuel Shaw, "Extracts of Lemuel Shaw's Address to the Suffolk Bar, 1827," *American Jurist and Law Magazine* 7 (January 1832): 68.

63. Stevens, "Two Cheers for 1870," 427.

5

The Modern Profession Emerges

The traditional goal of a legally recognized, locally controlled corporate profession was achieved by 1810. But conservative bar leaders discovered they faced a frustrating paradox because neither society at large nor an increasing part of the profession would accept it. Within thirty years the more cosmopolitan and politically minded lawyers triumphed over professional purists and parochial members of the legal profession. When antielitist Democrats rushed in to crush the bar associations in the 1830s, they had cornered a red herring. The profession as a whole did not suffer a setback. In fact the curtailment of bar associations helped the profession continue its quantitative, economic, and political expansion, while its quality was protected by lawyers' control of law schools and the judiciary. By 1840 the profession's real power had reached a level that was almost immune to frontal attacks, but the traditional ideal of a unitary, corporate legal profession had withered away.

Internal divisions and long-term professional developments rather than societal pressures culminated in the vast changes of the profession in the 1830s. Throughout the eighteenth century and into the early nineteenth century, the limited number of lawyers made it possible to rely upon personal acquaintance and voluntary consent on professional aims. But as the profession proliferated and spread geographically, lawyers became increasingly divided. This numerical increase also led to the decline of circuit riding by 1800, thus undermining the foundation for the corporate, professional guild system. In occupational terms, lawyers were divided as they handled different clientele or specialized in certain areas of law. Lawyers in coastal regions, for example, were more apt to handle admiralty law or commercial insurance cases than were rural inland lawyers. Lawyers in rural Maine were more likely to argue squatter sovereignty cases than were urban attorneys. The more commercially oriented lawyers now sought to avoid litigation and thus diminished the traditional advocacy role of lawyers. Controlled stability rather than sudden seizures was their goal. They were divided also by their failure to arrive at some consensual system of regulating legal training and admitting new lawyers into the profession. The reputation of a candidate's mentor rather than the prospective lawyer's qualifications often determined his fitness for membership. Some alternative to personal acquaintance had to be found as a means to ascertain ability to function within a growing and diversifying profession.

Some lawyers suggested that law schools, the state legislature, and the judicial system might serve as effective institutions to administer a statewide system of professional regulation. As the nineteenth century progressed without major institutional changes occurring in either the legal profession or the system of justice, certain radical lawyers and some laymen reintroduced plans that theoretically would have abolished a regulated legal profession. One of their proposals was to abandon almost all formal qualifications for admission to the practice of law, placing the burden of selection upon the client's shoulders. In a kind of Gresham's law, it was assumed that the competent lawyers would eliminate the bad. In the 1830s these three groups—traditional lawyers, commercial-cosmopolitan lawyers and laymen who sought to broaden the power and institutions of the legal profession, and radical reformers—clashed in their conflicting efforts to mold the practice of law to their own design.

Few lawyers showed overt concern about dangers to the autonomy of the legal profession and the maintenance of traditional rules and institutions even as the threat from democratic forces of society became increasingly serious in the 1820s and 1830s. An undercurrent of discontent with the legal profession had rumbled through the populace as part of Anglo-American folk culture. In times of stress, it surfaced with almost volcanic force. After 1810 protests against the legal profession assumed broader implications for society when they became intertwined with an increasingly virulent assault on the common-law system. The combined opposition produced a clamor for change that transformed the profession's traditional regulations and institutions, undermined as they were by apathy on the part of most lawyers, the disunity of moderates and conservatives, and the hostility of reformers among concerned professionals.

Lawyers were outspoken on behalf of radical, moderate, and conservative positions in the legal reform controversy. The opposition of most of the legal profession to radical reform of the common-law system, however, added impetus to a growing sentiment against the privileges of lawyers. Critics claimed that authority and precedent guided lawyers in their practice of law and that this situation "accounts for the opposition of lawyers to any which may disturb the accustomed routine and savor of innovation."[1]

Much of the critique of the legal profession continued along familiar lines. Practitioners were castigated for retaining outmoded forms of practice, for encouraging debt, for perverting the course of justice, and for excessive fees. Such standard accusations brought stock rebuttals. Lawyers responded, publicly and privately, that the profession was a necessity in a society founded on law, that the prejudice stemmed from the ignorant and vulgar elements of society, and that lawyers were undoubtedly among the most honest people.[2] But the repetitiveness of these arguments had eroded much of their power and value for both lawyers and their critics.

The growing prominence of a professional class in the nineteenth century, however, gave the antilawyer sentiment of the 1830s more vitality. Admissions systems and other regulatory devices undoubtedly contributed to these exclusionary developments, and contemporary critics and historians have focused on these institutional systems. But statistical studies of more than six thousand lawyers, doctors, and ministers reveal the restrictive nature of several less formal but equally powerful forces of selectivity for professional classes: education, paternal occupation, and marriage patterns. And it was the presence of this professional class that aroused intense opposition from antielitist laymen and politicians, making professionals an exposed target in this age of egalitarianism. Ironically it was also the solidification of this professional elite that probably helped give lawyers the confidence to abandon local bar associations as sources of professional autonomy.

For the purposes of this study, statistical data were gathered for 2,618 lawyers, 1,917 ministers, and 1,576 doctors who practiced in Massachusetts between 1740 and 1840. My chief concern is with the 2,618 lawyers who practiced in Massachusetts and the district of Maine between 1760 and 1840, but an overview of the three learned professions makes possible a more realistic analysis.[3]

The high educational level of members of the legal profession has already been established. Evidence that about 71 percent were college graduates reflects the striking measure of success that members of the legal profession had in recruiting college graduates. Moreover at this point, the professional schools probably were not avenues of vertical mobility for the uneducated. Indeed studies of ten professional schools in New England indicate that more than half of their students had college degrees and that 73.4 percent of the students at Harvard Law School between 1820 and 1840 were collegate graduates.

Education, then as now, provided opportunities for some members of lower economic strata to enter the professional class.[4] Most members, however, apparently were born into it. Most lawyers were the sons of professional men. During the period from 1760 to 1840, they increasingly represented the sons of lawyers and judges. The majority of college-educated lawyers in Massachusetts and the counties of Maine were the children of lawyers, judges, doctors, or ministers (table 20). Of the noncollege graduates, a majority of the paternal occupations were in this category in Massachusetts, but this fell to less than 50 percent for the district of Maine.

A more detailed examination of the paternal occupations of lawyers makes the presence of an interwoven professional class even more vivid. Statistics for lawyers who were college graduates in Massachusetts, exclusive of the Maine counties, indicate that their fathers increasingly tended to be either judges and/or lawyers. Of the 185 lawyers who represent the sample for this aspect of the study and who were admitted to the bar before 1810, only 71 (38.3 percent) were the sons of lawyers and judges. After 1810, however, 109 (54.8 percent) of the 199 lawyers examined were the offspring of lawyers or judges. Conversely the descendants of members of

TABLE 20 PATERNAL OCCUPATION OF LAWYERS, 1760–1840

FATHER'S OCCUPATION	MASSACHUSETTS LAWYERS, COLLEGE GRADUATES 1760–1809	1810–1840	MAINE LAWYERS, COLLEGE GRADUATES 1760–1809	1810–1840	MASSACHUSETTS LAWYERS, NONGRADUATES 1760–1809	1810–1840	MAINE LAWYERS, NONGRADUATES 1760–1809	1810–1840
Lawyer or judge	38.2%	54.5%	25.0%	68.0%	52.4%	62.7%	22.2%	35.2%
Doctor or minister	34.9	20.5	38.6	12.7	14.3	11.9	22.2	5.8
Small farmer	9.7	6.0	20.4	10.6	9.5	13.7	11.1	35.2
Gentleman farmer	7.0	1.0	2.2	0	0	3.9	5.5	5.8
Artisan	1.6	0.5	0	0	0	1.9	0	5.8
Innkeeper	0.5	0	0	0	0	0	0	0
Sea captain	0	4.5	0	0	4.8	1.9	5.5	0
Shopkeeper	0	1.0	0	0	0	0	0	0
Teacher	0	0	0	0	4.8	0	11.1	5.8
Merchant	8.1	9.5	11.3	8.4	14.2	3.9	22.2	0
Manufacturer	0	1.5	0	0	0	0	0	5.8
Other	0	1.5	0	0	0	0	0	5.8

other professions such as medicine and the ministry showed a declining tendency to enter the legal profession. Before 1810, 35 percent (65) of the lawyers were the sons of doctors and ministers; after that date, only 20.6 percent (41) of the trained practitioners were the children of such professional men.

Over this same period the sons of merchants, manufacturers, and sea captains entered the profession in increasing numbers, while those of farmers and tradesmen fell. One sign that the legal profession declined as a vehicle for upward mobility in Massachusetts, except for the district of Maine, was the drop in the number of farmers' sons entering the profession. The number fell from eighteen (9.7 percent) before 1810 to twelve (6 percent) after 1810. Moreover the sons of prosperous farmers entering the practice of law fell even more sharply from thirteen men (7 percent) before 1810 to two (1 percent) after 1810. Although there was some slippage in the number of sons of fathers from nonprofessional groups entering the legal profession after 1810, this in itself does not indicate that the legal profession discriminated against lower-class men. Statistics do indicate, however, that after 1810 college-educated lawyers in the present geographic area of Massachusetts tended to be second-generation lawyers, sons of professionals and, increasingly, the sons of members of upper economic status: merchants, manufacturers, and sea captains.

A study of the college-educated lawyers who practiced in the eastern district of Massachusetts, which became the state of Maine in 1820, reveals some radical differences. Of the lawyers admitted to practice before 1810, only eleven (25 percent) were the sons of lawyers or judges. But of those admitted to the bar in 1810 or after, thirty-two (68 percent) were the sons of judges or lawyers. The number whose fathers were doctors or ministers declined more precipitously than in the developed part of Massachusetts from seventeen (38.6 percent) before 1810 to six (12.7 percent) after that date. The percentage of lawyers whose fathers were farmers, however, shifted even more dramatically in the eastern district than in Massachusetts. Nine lawyers (20.4 percent) were descended from farmers before 1810, but only five (10.6 percent) were the sons of husbandmen after 1810. Children of tradesmen did not appear in the sampling. These findings indicate that before 1810, lawyers with lower-status or less-well-connected fathers sought opportunities in the frontier region of the state. Separate studies of noncollege graduates in Massachusetts and the eastern district of Maine indicate that the same developments occurred, with the notable exception of an increasing percentage of the sons of farmers entering the legal profession after 1810.

An examination of the marriage patterns of lawyers indicates the same continued formation of a professional class in society. Lawyers increasingly married the daughters of lawyers, doctors, and ministers. The major effect of this development for the social status of lawyers was that their social position relative to other occupational groups became solidified. Clearly not all professionals were of equal status, so that mobility within the professional class was a factor that has not been measured. Not only does this point to a peaking of social mobility through the professions, but it also indicates the increasingly self-perpetuating nature of the legal profession and the other learned professions as well.

This interpretation is supported by an examination of the family background of lawyers' wives. The occupations of the fathers-in-law of 113 college-educated lawyers admitted to the profession in Massachusetts before 1810 and of 91 for the years 1810 to 1840 were examined. Seventy-three (64.6 percent) of the wives were the daughters of lawyers, doctors, and ministers before 1810; after 1810, 61 (67 percent) were. Other classifications showed a corresponding decline. The daughters of merchants married to lawyers fell from 14 percent (16) before 1810 to 12 percent (11) after 1810. The number of wives whose fathers were farmers dropped precipitously from 14.1 percent (16) before 1810 to 8.7 percent (8) after 1810.

A similar pattern emerged for the district of Maine. The only exception was that a higher percentage of wives were the daughters of lawyers, doctors, or ministers—86.6 percent (13) to 1810 and 72 percent (13) after 1810. Significantly more lawyers in the eastern district tended to move up in economic status for wives after 1810 than before. While no daughter of merchants appeared in the sampling before 1810, 4 (21 percent) wives were from mercantile families after 1810. The breakdown for other occupational groups was: 1 farmer, and 1 wealthy landowner before 1810; 1 publisher and 1 soldier after 1810.

TABLE 21 MARRIAGE PATTERNS OF LAWYERS, 1760–1840

OCCUPATION OF FATHER-IN-LAW	MASSACHUSETTS LAWYERS		MAINE LAWYERS	
	1760–1809	1810–1840	1760–1809	1810–1840
Lawyer, doctor, or minister	64.6%	68.5%	86.6%	68.0%
Merchant	14.1	12.0	0	21.0
Farmer	14.1	8.9	6.6	0
Artisan	14.9	1.1	0	0
Banker	0.9	1.1	0	0
Sea captain	2.6	5.5	0	0
Manufacturer	0	0	0	5.2
Tavern keeper	0.9	0	0	0
Other	1.8	2.2	6.6	5.2

Note: All lawyers were college graduates.

The studies of noncollege-educated lawyers proved inconclusive because of the lack of necessary information. For Massachusetts, relevant data for noncollege graduates were found for only seven wives before 1810 and ten wives after 1810. The occupations of their fathers followed the same pattern. One lawyer, three merchants, and three farmers were the fathers of wives of lawyers before 1810. For the period after 1810, their occupations were six professionals—doctors, lawyers, and ministers—one merchant, one farmer, one prosperous farmer, and one sea captain. Noncollege graduates in the district of Maine before 1810 married wives whose fathers were four professionals, three farmers, and one sea captain. After 1810 they chose the daughters of six professionals, one merchant, and one gentleman farmer. Even with this small sampling, the trends revealed for the marriage patterns of college graduates remained basically the same for noncollege graduates.

Studies of ministers and doctors strengthen this concept of the professional class (tables 29-34). Ministers less often than lawyers and doctors, however, were the offspring of professionals. For example, only 36.6 percent of the college-educated ministers before 1800 in Massachusetts proper were the sons of professionals, compared to 51.8 percent of the doctors. In the post-1800 period ministers continued to be the least inbred; 55 percent of the college graduates and one-fourth of the nongraduates were professionals' children. Surprisingly ministers most often married the children of professionals. From 1740 to 1799, 67.4 percent of the wives of college graduate ministers in Massachusetts were the children of professionals; 72 percent were in the post-1800 period. Doctors least often married daughters of other professionals, and this may be evidence of their low status within the professional class. We do not know if other occupational groups were so tightly inbred. A recent study of Massachusetts Normal School students in 1859 indicates that only 4.2 percent were the offspring of professionals.[5] But there appears to have been ample justification for critics of the legal profession and proponents of social mobility to rail against the restrictive natue of the professions in the 1830s.

The economic power of the legal profession—an old object of laymen's displeasure—entered the new and broader commercial and industrial boom and thereby attracted additional hostility. In the eighteenth century, lawyers had been concerned largely with legal fees and land speculation and it was their minimum fee schedules that attracted political and popular anger. But toward the end of that century and increasingly in the nineteenth century, lawyers plunged into the new industrial age with a vigor matched by few other occupational groups. This new economic interest combined with judicial willingness to pursue the public welfare brought new power to law and its interpreters. It was at this point, according to Morton Horwitz, that business leaders, reassured by their alliance with commercially oriented urban lawyers, accepted judicial interpretation of commercial law and thus were able to turn legal actions and law to their economic advantage. Conversely this converging of interests among men of law and business increased the legal profession's impact on society. Moreover it offered new opportunities for entrepreneurial-minded lawyers. As early as 1819, Warren Dutton, who later was a counsel in the Charles River Bridge case, recognized the importance of this new business orientation: "In this country, there is little or no division of labour in the profession. All are attornies, conveyancers, proctors, barristers and counsellors. . . . It is this habit of practical labour, this general knowledge of business, which connects the professional man in this country with all classes of the community, and gives him an influence, which pervades all.''[6]

Many legal practitioners ventured into these newer opportunities. Canals, banks, railroads, and manufacturing attracted many practitioners. Although neither lawyers nor members of any other profession provided the chief sources of capital for the rising corporations, lawyers nevertheless devoted large portions of their cash and skills.[7] Their legal knowledge and often their political connections held more attraction than their money for ambitious entrepreneurs.

Few lawyers became as deeply involved as quickly in corporations as James Sullivan. While simultaneously president of the Middlesex Canal Company and of the Boston Aqueduct Corporation, Sullivan also invested in the Massachusetts Mutual Fire Inc. and the West Boston Bridge Company. Sullivan, like fellow lawyers William Tudor and Perez Morton, was also a proprietor of the Amoskeag Canal in New Hampshire.[8] William Cranch, a young attorney in Haverhill, found the cash to purchase $700 in shares in the Haverhill Bridge Company for Abigail Adams and himself. Boston attorney Tudor also owned twenty shares in the Boston South-Bridge Corporation, for which he paid an assessment of $4,600 in 1804, and seventy-two shares of the South Boston Associates, a real estate development corporation, worth $720.[9]

Lawyers in central as well as eastern Massachusetts also became deeply involved in industry, banking, and transportation. After only sixteen years of practice in Worcester, Thomas Kinnicutt in 1839 possessed $83,879.47 in various corporate investments and placed his net worth at $29,870.53. Isaac Davis, another Worcester counsellor, served variously as president of the Quinsigamond Bank (1835-1845, 1854-1879), president of the Mechanics Savings Bank (1851-1855), a director of the Providence and Worcester Railroad (1857-1878), and president of the Worcester and Nashua Railroad (1848-1853, 1874-1879).[10] A survey of the directors and officers of banks and corporations in Massachusetts from 1800 to 1840, however, shows that lawyers held a minority of the offices and that most lawyers did not reach such positions of commercial influence.[11] Entrepreneurial lawyers, nevertheless, had gained access to the upper echelons of economic power.

In the nineteenth century an increasing number of lawyers left

TABLE 22 LAWYERS LEAVING THE PROFESSION

	MINISTRY	FARMING	BANKING	RAILROADS	COMMERCE[a]	OTHERS[b]
Massachusetts College Graduates						
1760–1809	2	5	0	0	7	6
1810–1840	7	16	18	9	40	46
Maine College Graduates						
1760–1809	0	0	0	0	0	0
1810–1840	8	5	5	4	10	7
Massachusetts Noncollege Graduates						
1760–1809	1	1	0	0	0	1
1810–1840	2	1	1	1	5	2
Maine Noncollege Graduates						
1760–1809	0	0	0	0	1	1
1810–1840	2	1	0	2	4	1

Source: Compiled from my lawyer file. The sampling for this study was 1,188 of 2,018 lawyers in Massachusetts and 427 of 600 lawyers in the district of Maine.

a. Includes manufacturing and industrial endeavors.

b. Includes insurance agents, editors, teachers, and land speculators.

private practice to become officers in railroads, banks, and other industrial or commercial corporations (table 22). Before 1810, only seven lawyers abandoned office practice for commerce or industry in Massachusetts, but between 1810 and 1840, this study shows that more than seventy lawyers entered banking, railroad, or commercial enterprises. And although lawyers in private practice seldom were as wealthy as the commercial and banking magnates, their close association in business as well as in litigation strengthened their economic power.[12] Their business associations also reinforced the popular view of lawyers as agents of society's well-to-do. Although the economic and social gap between the professionals or their wealthy clients and the subsistence farmer or laborer or displaced artisan was not subject to rapid political revisions, the privileges of the professions were.

The anti-Masonic and nascent union movements in the 1830s reinvigorated one traditional complaint against the legal profession: that it was a privileged monopoly. Critics compared the bar associations with the Masonic order as monopolistic conspiracies against the rights and liberties of the people by a "secret, powerful, organized fraternity." In actuality, however, the bar associations continued to exhibit an inability to enforce many of their regulations, particularly of an ethical nature.[13] Even more dangerous to the profession's privileged position was the opposition to the rising unions as conspiracies to restrain trade through collective combinations of men.

The long-standing use of the English common law to oppose workmen's unions in their quests to improve wages or working conditions increased procodification and antilawyer sentiment. English law since the 1349 State of Labourers had punished workers' collective action and the application of the common-law crime of conspiracy became an additional trap for union organizers. Thus spokesmen for the Workingmen's party, such as Frederick Robinson, an unsworn attorney and Marblehead representative to the general court, Robert Rantoul, Jr., a Democratic state legislator and lawyer, and J. S. Kimball, a union lawyer, supported both codification and the curtailment of the lawyers' monopoly. The Workingmen's Party of the eastern seaport towns, which grew out of demands by carpenters and ship caulkers for a ten-hour day, soon began to denounce imprisonment for debt and excessive lawyers' fees.[14]

Lawyers, particularly in Suffolk and Essex counties, may have been induced to abandon willingly the bar associations and their restrictive rules and regulations, in part, by the combined conservative law-business community's view of unions as illegal conspiracies to restrain trade. Lawyers may have also felt uncomfortable defending what was becoming a working-class device for occupational improvement. After Robinson, Rantoul, and other union spokesmen raised the issue in the early 1830s, leading lawyers may have feared that bar associations would be considered illegal or criminal conspiracies. This is precisely what later happened in the Boston bootmakers' trial in 1840 when Samuel D. Parker, the Suffolk County prosecuting attorney, argued that "it was anti-republican and grossly tyranical for a society of men to undertake to prevent a man for working lawfully, as he pleases, and for whome he pleases, and at what prices he pleases, and that such interference was an invasion of the liberty of the subject." Parker then resorted to a stronger argument: "Such a Society, and power amounted to a government within a government, and when Trades' Union Societies began to be in vogue in Massachusetts, the Association of the Suffolk Bar set the good example of abolishing their bar rules regulating fees etc."[15]

In an ironic twist Rantoul and Kimball, attorneys for the Boston bootmakers, countered Parker's arguments by claiming that the Bootmaker's Society was legal and pointed to similar combinations "among members of the *legal* and *medical* profession . . . to regulate prices." Rantoul attempted to call Parker as a defense witness to testify about the Suffolk Bar Association but settled for Edward Blake, the bar association secretary, who produced the rules of the Suffolk Bar signed by nearly all Boston lawyers that required attorneys not to charge less than the minimum fee schedules and not to associate in business with anyone who "shall not have subscribed to these rules."[16] It is difficult to calculate the effect of Rantoul's argument on the course of the trial; but the ongoing criticism of bar associations and the legal profession by labor leaders and Democrats when combined with the condemnations of trades unions as criminal conspiracies helps to explain why some lawyers so readily abandoned the bar associations after 1835.

The antimonopolistic attitude of members of the Massachusetts Democratic party also increased the pressure against the exclusiveness of the legal profession. Lawyers were prime subjects for attacks because of their key public role as political leaders, their exclusivity, and their occupational roles as interpreters and applicators of the law and spokesmen for commercial interests. Critics resented this dominant role, but they focused on the traditional efforts of lawyers to restrict entrance into the profession and their attempts to prevent nonlawyers from exercising any occupational role within the legal system. As Robinson said: "And although you have left no means unattempted to give you the appearance of *Officers*, you are still nothing more than followers of a trade or calling like other men, to get a living, and your trade like other employments, ought to be left open to competition. What right have you to form associations for the purpose of preventing others from competing with you, more than the followers of any other trade." Some lawyers, who were advocating increased economic competition through changes in commercial law and in court and in print, probably felt uneasy supporting restrictions on competition in their own profession.[17]

Physicians and clerics came under similar attacks. Opponents denounced ministers and doctors for their professional training and the artificial requirements established by medical societies for licensing and by ministerial associations for ordination. These, critics said, led to monopoly officeholding. Ministers and religion as well as lawyers were often castigated as instruments of upper-class tyranny and tools of the "wise and good." Economically dislocated people saw churchmen as both buttresses and beneficiaries of special privileges. For the ordained ministers, this meant more impetus to the rapidly declining permanency of office and more short-term contracts. Doctors were castigated for their licensing privileges and their fee schedules. Unlimited opportunities were to replace privilege and exclusion, according to the antielitist reformers and dissatisfied practitioners.[18]

The legislative destruction of the profession's seniority system and the bar associations' autonomous regulatory power was occasioned by the revision of state statutes under the auspices of Republican governor and Worcester counsellor Levi Lincoln, Jr. But the change itself grew out of the conflict between men of the radical stamp of Rantoul and Robinson and moderate reformers within the profession.

Since the turn of the century, the codification movement had been a rallying point for radical reformers of the law. These men, who were among the Jeffersonian and Jacksonian leaders in Massachusetts, wanted to reduce judge-made law by substituting written legal codes for the common law. To these lawyers and laymen, already critical of the privileges of the legal profession, the issue was simple: "Written standing laws are the legislative voice of the people. Common law is the stretch of power of the judges." Lawyers were badly divided by the codification issue. Writing in the *North American Review*, William H. Gardiner, a Boston counsellor, predicted that within the profession, codifiers and anticodifiers would wage "a fierce and interminable war." Yet despite this professional split, the conservative stance of many powerfully placed lawyers and judges became just one more grievance against the legal profession and one more reason for destroying its privileged position.[19]

In response to mounting popular and political pressure for codification, the Massachusetts legislature in 1832 sought to escape the trauma of codification of the common law by authorizing Lincoln to appoint a commission to systematize and codify statute law and to suggest means of correcting contradictions or omissions. The general court's moderation and the preeminent role that moderate spokesmen for the legal profession played in the revisionary movement could be seen in the commission membership. Three professionally respected counsellors, Jackson, Stearns, and Ashmun—two professors of law and a former judge of the Massachusetts Supreme Court—received the original appointments, with John Pickering, a Boston lawyer and politician, later filling the spot vacated on Ashmun's death.[20]

The commissioners' draft report sustained the prevailing role of the courts and trained lawyers in regulating the legal profession. By authorizing the courts to establish the rules and regulations for attorneys and counsellors, the commissioners acknowledged their support for the status quo. They stated bluntly in their report that the powers granted to the courts to regulate the legal profession had always been exercised by those institutions and that the two sections were proposed "merely to prevent any inference that the provisions of this chapter are intended to take away or impair those powers."[21] Supporters of the bar associations and a corporate autonomous profession could not have hoped for more.

Between the time the commissioners' report was made public and the passage of the Revised Statutes by the legislature, powerful pressure was apparently brought to bear behind the scenes. Defenders of the common law, such as Shaw and Story, and moderate reformers, like Jackson, Stearns, and Pickering, may have feared that the retention of the legal profession's privileged autonomy might produce severe repercussions against the common-law system by further antagonizing codification proponents, who had succeeded in having a committee appointed to study codification of the common law. At the same time, supporters of Harvard Law School and other law-school-oriented legal educators may have seen advantages for their training program in the declining power of the bar associations. Moreover lawyers who had gained a broad perspective of the political, social, and economic powers of the legal profession saw no advantages in local autonomy for professional institutions. They did not fear state regulation because they expected to control it.

Finally a compromise evolved between Robinson's plan and the traditional stance enunciated by the commissioners. When the section regulating lawyers came before the house—where lawyers comprised 10.2 percent of the membership but controlled the important Judiciary Committee—Robinson moved to amend the commissioners' plan. Undoubtedly angered by his recent exclusion from court practice by the bar of Essex County, Robinson probably sought vengeance as well as reform when he proposed that anyone should have the unchallenged right to appear as an attorney, counsellor, or barrister in any court in the state. Rantoul, although a Jacksonian Democrat like Robinson, moved to commit the entire issue to a special committee.[22] The three-man committee was composed of two lawyers, Rantoul and Robert C. Winthrop, a political supporter of Governor Edward Everett, and Charles E. Billings, a representative from Conway in rural western Massachusetts and a relative of William Billings, Conway's lawyer. Given the composition of this committee—one ardent proponent of reform of the legal system and legal profession, one political manager and moderate reformer, and one rural representative—it should have been able to agree on some modifications of standing practices.[23]

After two weeks of discussion, the committee headed by Rantoul failed to reach agreement on modifying Robinson's proposal for lawyers. In an effort to break the stalemate, Rantoul then independently proposed that anyone twenty-one years of age and of good moral character should be admitted to the bar. Anyone found guilty of misconduct, however, would be permanently disbarred. Rantoul's motion first passed on October 27, but professional, protectionist lawyers and their allies rallied and defeated the plan upon reconsideration on October 30. Before radicals could recover from that defeat, moderates brought out their compromise plan that three years of law study or the passing of an examination administered by the judiciary be required.[24]

Rantoul considered this compromise a defeat for the radical reformers. He correctly feared the extension of lawyers' power because principles that had been only sanctioned by bar regulations and court rules now had the approval and weight of statute law.[25] Rantoul probably placed too much importance on statutory sanction, but a further examination of the regulations shows how little the legal profession lost.

The compromise ended the local autonomy of bar associations, eliminated the seniority system within the profession, and returned control of admission to the legislature and the courts. Rather than allow the courts to establish rules and regulations, as the commissioners originally proposed, the revised statutes established new admission standards. Any candidate who studied law in a school or in the office of an attorney in the state for three years was to be automatically admitted to the bar upon his application to the supreme court or the court of common pleas. If a person believed he could qualify after fewer than three years of study, then he could apply to the judges of the supreme court or the court of common pleas for an examination. Every attorney admitted to practice in any court could practice in all courts in the state. The various ranks of attorney and counsellor were abolished.[26] The basis for much of the complex system of bar association rules and regulations was thus formally eliminated.

Yet power had not been taken away from the legal profession; it had only been transferred to other institutions that were controlled or greatly influenced by lawyers. This transmission of power had the open and tacit support of many leaders of the bar. Professional lawyers held most of the judicial posts in the state, thus ensuring that the examinations given to candidates who had not studied law for three years would at least meet the profession's minimum expectations. And lawyers controlled the law school at Harvard, which remained the chief alternative to law office apprenticeship in the state. Even in retrospect, the guarantees to uphold the legal profession's standards seem adequate.

The profession's seniority system, usually termed the graded profession, with its regimented status and economic allocation system, was eliminated by the law. The entire profession was theoretically open to competition to determine the allocation of legal business, but there is no evidence that this led to economic equalization or even equal economic opportunities for members of the bar. Competition within the profession was also stimulated, although a clear advantage was given to dominant lawyers when the Revised Statutes eliminated the limitation on the number of lawyers that a client could retain for a court appearance. Since 1786 clients had legally been restrained from hiring more than two lawyers per case. But a thorough study of the court reports indicates that clients, lawyers, and judges had largely ignored this regulation. More than a hundred instances of clients' retaining more than two lawyers are reported in the supreme judicial court after 1800. Lawyers continued to be differentiated by economic opportunities and achievements as they had in the past, even though one formal, even artificial, system of allocation had been abolished.[27]

The loss of autonomy of the bar associations and the reduced admission standards have been attributed solely to the democratic forces of the time by most scholars, and consequently the importance of this legislative action has been misinterpreted.[28] Historians have viewed this action as a defeat for the legal profession and as evidence of the victory of democratic forces over conservative and monopolistic special interest groups. Instead it signaled a victory for moderate-reform elements in the legal profession and the legislature. In the process of their examination, scholars have overlooked real intellectual, political, and socioeconomic divisions within the legal profession. The allegiance of several leading lawyers, such as Lincoln, Rantoul, Davis, Cushing, and Winthrop, to political and reform philosophies that opposed privileged elements in society is only one illustrative case. Moreover the apathetic reaction of most lawyers to the reorientation of power, and the prior sterility of bar associations, precluded any effective countermeasures by conservatives or local-power brokers within the legal profession.

What might have spurred a strenuous counterattack just twenty years before brought compliance in 1835. The highly individualized, specialized, and competitive profession of the 1830s had little or no sympathy for the corporate and rigid seniority system of the guild-based bar associations. Like other formal institutions from the colonial era, the bar organization seemed starkly out of place in an altered society.[29] The institutional form had to be recast so that the profession could grow unimpeded. The legal profession pledged its allegiance to the American act of faith that what expands is good and what limits growth is bad. Rituals of competition replaced forms of restraint, as the Massachusetts legal profession accepted its loss of local organizational autonomy with scarcely a backward glance.

Instead of organizing the bar associations to reverse or destroy the effectiveness of these legislative measures—as lawyers had done with other "antilawyer" laws of 1785, 1786, and 1790—they either embraced or acquiesced in the program. The Suffolk County Bar Association was reorganized by members as a voluntary fraternity of lawyers. It had no control over legal education, admission to practice, or the deportment of its members, but it probably retained a fee schedule. As a result, the association soon fell into obscurity. The Essex County Bar Association, with over fifty members, dissolved upon the passage of the bill. Not until 1856 was a voluntary bar association reorganized for that county. The Franklin County Bar also disbanded in 1835.[30]

The Worcester County Bar wavered between fighting for its traditional role and surrendering to the legislative plan. It appointed a special committee to consider the expediency of dissolving the bar association. After a long written argument on the need of an association to work for the improvement of the profession and a prediction of the dire effects that the new law would have on the quality of the profession, the committee recommended its dissolution. The Worcester lawyers evidently admired tradition, order, seniority, and deference: "Let the Law thus, have its full force and full effects, alike unaided and unembarrassed by bar interference. Let the Profession give way to the demands of popular feeling. Their own honor demands of them no resistance to the will of the government," they wrote. "As the purpose of the Association are superceded [*sic*] by the Law, let them submit with deference to its authority. The Committee see no inducement, under present circumstances to continuing the organization of the Association and they recommend its dissolution."[31] Vigor had fled the profession's local institutions.

There was some individual willingness to retain aspects of the corporate profession. A few lawyers continued to address each other as "brother lawyers," but this sign of fraternal spirit became increasingly scarce. Worcester County lawyers decided to retain the county law library, even though the state no longer gave it the excise tax on new admissions to support it. Lawyers in Suffolk County made futile attempts to obtain a state subsidy for the Boston Social Law Library.[32] But attorneys on the whole no longer exhibited interest in the traditions and institutions of the restricted corporate profession.

Reform of the legal profession in Massachusetts was not an isolated incident. It was part of a broad movement in the United States and Great Britain. In both countries the profession's connections with the state and its reputation for liberal learning made law an occupation fit for gentlemen only, and for that reason it was particularly attractive to the rising middle class. Demands for equal opportunity from the ever-growing number of aspirants to the professional class increased the pressure to reform exclusive, traditional practices.

Reformers of the English legal profession, as in Massachusetts, came from within the profession, as well as from the ranks of laymen. Written examinations for candidates became the rallying point for reform. Attorneys and solicitors in the newly founded Law Society applied most of the pressure for professional improvement. At the urging of the Law Society, common-law judges set up the first examining board for legal candidates in 1836, the first serious qualifying test for any branch of the legal profession in England. By 1854 four solicitors and a master of one of the courts of common law sat as examiners for each term, a system remarkably close to that established by the Massachusetts Supreme Court in 1806. The Inns of Court declined to hold any real qualifying examinations until 1872 on the grounds that a barrister who is not qualified "will get no business, and if he is qualified he will get business." Unlike in Massachusetts, the distinction between barrister and solicitor survived the reformers in Great Britain.[33] Despite the superficially opposing aims of raising entrance standards in Britain and ostensibly lowering them in Massachusetts, reformers in both countries hoped to open the legal profession to a greater number of aspirants and to broaden the path of social and economic advancement.

In the United States the legal profession quickly lost much of its autonomous regulatory power in its traditional forms. Examinations, hailed as a cure for the restricted and allegedly incompetent profession in England, had been tried and found lacking as a means of providing an open profession in many states. As legislative reform became prevalent, many state governments applied the principle of equal opportunity much more indiscriminately than in the Bay State. In 1838 the New Hampshire legislature wrested control from the state federation of bar associations and authorized any citizen of the state, aged twenty-one and of good moral character, to petition for an examination by the supreme court upon the recommendation of any attorney in the state. A required period for preparation had already been abolished in Georgia, Tennessee, South Carolina, Louisiana, Mississippi, and Arkansas. Yet the neighboring states of Vermont, Rhode Island, and Connecticut maintained their pre-Jacksonian standards for admission, which required only two years of preparation for admission and permitted a lawyer to practice in all courts once he was admitted to one. Massachusetts, however, never lowered its standards to those of New Hampshire, Maine (1843), and New York (1846), where any resident over twenty-one years of age could automatically be admitted to the practice of law upon application and without examination.[34]

In the Bay State a complex interaction between opponents of privileged elements in society, reform-minded lawyers, apathetic lawyers, and lawyers who wanted to broaden the power base of the legal profession produced radical changes in the institutions, organizational structure, and regulations of the legal profession. The profession's eighteenth-century institutions and regulations, modeled on the English legal profession with its artificial barriers designed to eliminate external competition and control internal rivalries, failed to survive. The British corporate bar gave way to a highly individualistic and competitive American profession. But Jacksonian Democrats failed to destroy the power of lawyers in Massachusetts.

The legal profession emerged from the crucible of the Jacksonian era with its modern outlook and form essentially in place. Admission to the profession was no longer controlled by local bar associations, and preparation for practice was not limited to the personal training system of apprenticeship. The legislature and the judiciary retained an important role in regulating the profession, but the way was open for law schools to become the essential institution for training lawyers and regulating entrance into the profession.

More important for the development of the profession, lawyers now dominated the judiciary and played key roles in the executive and legislative branches of government. The new breed of lawyer did not fear the impingement of state government or the judiciary on professional autonomy. They seized state power and used it to mold their version of the public and professional good.

So too the alliance of lawyers and businessmen, which throughout the eighteenth century was on unsteady ground, became solidified during the decades of industrial and commercial growth after the turn of the century. Law became an instrument for entrepreneurial expansion. Lawyers and businessmen became partners, economically and psychologically, working together to exploit the vast opportunities and natural resources in Massachusetts and the United States. Lawyers, in a sense, moved from the backroom to the boardroom, serving as corporation presidents, directors, counsels, and managers, as well as legal advocates and bill collectors. In rural Massachusetts the lawyer had been viewed as the agent of the gentleman farmer and the merchant. Now he became the agent of commerce and industry.

Competition within the profession was no longer institutionally restrained by the county bar associations. An aggressive individual's drive for achievement did not face artificial, corporate obstructions and ethical limitations in the form of fee schedules, artificial geographic barriers to practice, a vertically graded professional structure, and restrictions on business associates. Contingency fees, retainers, referrals, group practice, negotiated settlements, cocounsel agreements, corporate counsels, interstate practices, and occupational specialties were coming to the fore as circuit riding, court-fixed fees, solo practitioners, and the primacy of the advocacy role began to slide downward on the professional scale.

Patterns of education, marriage, and occupation selectivity had reinforced the lawyers' position in society to such an extent that they were able to abandon the institutional props of exclusivity. Indeed this professional class became nearly self-perpetuating and almost immune to efforts to democratize the professions. With a secure social status, a powerful political position, and rising economic power, the legal profession by 1830 was ready to abandon its traditional training and regulatory agencies—apprenticeship, local bar associations, and the graded system of professional advancement. Many lawyers had come to view them as too restrictive and conservative. Law schools, statewide legislative and judicial regulations, and occupational competitiveness were not only acceptable but welcome. These developments were seen as more flexible, more innovative, and more powerful avenues for personal and professional advancement.

The Massachusetts legal profession, despite its early affinity for an Anglicized professional structure, does not appear to have been strikingly different from the profession in other areas of the country in 1840. Perhaps it was more highly educated (although the studies for comparison are lacking), more exclusive, more powerful politically, or more economically entrenched. But the available studies indicate that the legal profession was developing along similar broad lines throughout the country. The profession was numerically strong. Two decades into the nineteenth century Massachusetts had 710 (1 to 1,159 people) trained lawyers, but New York had at least 1,248 (1 to 1,137) and Connecticut 242 (1 to 1,137).[35] The emergence of a professional class based on education, paternal occupation, and marriage patterns does not appear to have been parochial, although the studies have been very limited. Gary Nash has found that the Philadelphia bar was overwhelmingly upper and middle class. Between 1800 and 1805, 72 percent of the lawyers admitted to the bar came from upper-class backgrounds, with 16 percent from the middle and only 12 percent from the lower class. And in 1860-1861 the lawyers admitted to the profession in Philadelphia still came from the same class: 44 percent from the upper class, 44 percent from the middle class, and 12 percent from the lower class. In a small random national survey, Maxwell Bloomfield found that more than 50 percent of the lawyers were sons of professionals.[36] Just as the fraternal and cohesive corporate profession declined in Massachusetts with the deterioration of circuit riding, the same development was found to be true in Tennessee.[37] From these studies of geographically distant areas, it is possible to conclude that this was probably part of the developmental cycle of the profession throughout the country.

Lawyers in other areas of the country had experimented with the lecture system of professional education much sooner than in Massachusetts, but once Bay State lawyers engaged in law-school training, their interest challenged the most avid advocates of classroom education. Connecticut's New Haven Law School (Yale University), Virginia's law lectures at William and Mary College and the law program at the University of Virginia, Kentucky's legal program at the University of Transylvania, and law lectures in New York and Philadelphia established the pattern of university-connected legal training. Massachusetts did not enter this area until 1815, largely because of the inhibiting regulations of the bar associations and the success of the combined college-apprenticeship system of education. It was not until the legislative elimination of bar association regulations and the graded profession that the permanency of law school education was assured in the Bay State. By 1840 the outline of legal education as it appears in the United States today, with its strengths and weaknesses, was clearly in place in Massachusetts, Virginia, Kentucky, and Connecticut. The best place for legal training had been judged by the profession's leaders to be a university-connected law school designed in the tradition of Blackstone to produce attorneys who were also gentlemen of the law and men of public affairs.[38]

The autonomy of the profession's institutions in Massachusetts was severely limited by 1840, bringing it in line with the rest of the country. The bar association system had been strongest in the Northeast, although there is evidence of bar association activity in such disparate places as Mississippi, South Carolina, and Michigan. Legislative and judicial control of the profession was standard in virtually all states of the South and Northwest. Michigan, Ohio, Illinois, Indiana, South Carolina, Virginia, Georgia, and North Carolina, for example, had well-established records of formal legislative control of legal training, admission to practice, and professional activities, although in most cases it is not known how these laws were actually administered.[39] After 1835 Massachusetts lawyers were simply operating on what had become the normal plane of professional regulation. It is not known whether the political and judicial power of the profession in Massachusetts was unique. It almost certainly was not, but the factual studies have not been done to substantiate this conclusion.[40] It is clear, nevertheless, that the legal profession in Massachusetts was not only in the mainstream of professional development but was helping to establish the intellectual and institutional framework of the modern American legal profession.

NOTES

1. Anonymous, "Proposed Involvency Laws of Massachusetts," *American Jurist and Law Magazine* 5 (July 1831): 128; See also a Member of the Massachusetts Bar, "Legal Reform," *New Clerks Magazine*, 2d ed. (Boston, 1833), vii.

2. George Watterston, *The Lawyer or Man as He Ought Not to Be* (Charlestown, 1829); Asa Greene, "The Writ," *Berkshire American* (North Adams), January 23, 1828; "Querus," *Jurisprudent* (Boston), November 6, 1830; "Learning a Trade," *Essex Register* (Salem), March 16, 1835; George Bliss, Jr., *An Address to the Members of the Bar of the Counties of Hampshire, Franklin and Hampden . . . 1826* (Springfield, 1827), 5; James D. Hopkins, *An Address to Members of the Cumberland Bar . . . 1833* (Portland, 1833), 41; *Jurisprudent*, July 30, November 13, 1830; John Pickering, "A Lecture on the Alleged Uncertainty of the Law," *American Jurist and Law Magazine* 8 (October 1832): 287; *Pittsfield Sun*, December 26, 1821, January 2, 1822; William Sullivan, *Address to the Members of the Bar of Suffolk . . . 1824* (Boston, 1825), 12-13.

3. For the purposes of these statistical studies, a professional is defined as one who was specially trained either through apprenticeship or professional classroom education in the fields of law, medicine, or religion; practiced his occupational specialty on a regular, full-time basis; and was recognized by other professionals as a member of their peer group through formal measures, such as licensing or ordination, or through informal means, such as membership in a professional society or bar association. The breakpoint dates for these studies—1760, 1810 (1800 for doctors and ministers), and 1840—are somewhat arbitrary, but there is some rationale for them. The year 1760 was chosen because the number of trained lawyers practicing in Massachusetts before then was very small; 1800 is not only the start of a century but also a watershed in American political and economic development; 1810 marks the achievement of professional autonomy for lawyers; and 1840 signifies the approximate end of the era of Jacksonian democracy. The professional groups were then divided into the categories of college and noncollege graduates both in Massachusetts and the Maine counties. Education, geographic residence, and the year of either ordination or admission to practice by a licensing agency or court were the factors determining to which group a particular professional was assigned.

These studies can only suggest tentative conclusions when taken by themselves. They are not definitive because of the lack of detailed information necessary to make them scientifically or mathematically exact. There are too many professionals about whom I know too little. Women and blacks were excluded from the legal profession in Massachusetts before 1840. And although some women and blacks did practice medicine or preach, they were not considered professionals by contemporaries.

The information is taken from sources with definite limitations on accuracy and comprehensiveness—college records, college catalogs, genealogies, directories, local histories, diaries, society and court records, and so forth. The objection that these reflect only the more visible people and not the whole professional population immediately springs to mind. This objection has some validity, but these people were also the most visible in the 1740-1840 period. They were the men most people identified as members of the professional class, and within this context, these statistics become a historically valid tool. For specific pagination citations to sources for the studies of Massachusetts lawyers, see Gerard W. Gawalt, "Massachusetts Lawyers: A Historical Analysis of the Process of Professionalization, 1760-1840" (Ph.D. diss., Clark University, 1969), appendix 1.

4. This was particularly true for ministers but least true for lawyers. See David F. Allmendinger, Jr., *Paupers and Scholars: The Transformation of Student Life in Nineteenth Century New England* (New York, 1975), and

Burton J. Bledstein, *The Culture of Professionalism: The Middle Class and the Development of Higher Education in America* (New York, 1976).

5. Richard M. Bernard and Maris A. Vinovskis, "The Female School Teacher in Ante-Bellum Massachusetts," *Journal of Social History* 10 (March 1977): 336, table 1. A more thorough study of the impact of a professional class on the development of the legal, medical, and ministerial professions in the nineteenth century is Gerard W. Gawalt, "Professions and the Polarization of Society, 1740-1850" (paper presented to the Social Science History Conference, Ann Arbor, Michigan, October 1977).

6. Morton Horwitz, *The Transformation of American Law, 1780–1860* (Cambridge, Mass., 1977), 140-159; Warren Dutton, *An Address Delivered to the Members of the Bar of Suffolk . . . 1819* (Boston, 1819), 6-7.

7. Joseph S. Davis, *Eighteenth Century Business Corporations in the United States* (Cambridge, Mass., 1917), 298.

8. Ibid., 69, 171, 237, 251; proprietors of Amoskeag Canal, Samuel Blodgett Papers, DLC.

9. William Cranch to Richard Cranch, February 20, 1794, Cranch Papers, MHi; receipt of October 24, December 19, 1804, and August 9, 1805, Tudor Papers, MHi.

10. Account book of Thomas Kinnicutt, 1833-1840, Kinnicutt Papers, MWA; William Lincoln, *History of Worcester, Massachusetts, from Its Earliest Settlements to September, 1836* (Worcester, 1862), 209; Mary D. Vaughan, ed., *Historical Catalogue of Brown University* (Providence, 1905), 134.

11. *The Massachusetts Register and United States Calendar* (Boston, 1800-1840).

12. Edward Pessen, "The Egalitarian Myth and the American Social Reality: Wealth, Mobility, and Equality in the 'Era of the Common Man,'" *American Historical Review* 76 (October 1971): 995, 998-999, 1016, 1021. See numerous business papers in Merrick, Haven, and Lincoln Papers, MWA; Lemuel Shaw and Harrison Gray Otis Papers, MHi; account book of Christopher Gore and cash book of Elias Gray Loring, MHB; Caleb Cushing Papers, DLC.

13. Frederick Robinson, *Letter to the Hon. Rufus Choate Containing a Brief Exposure of Law Craft, and Some of the Encroachments of the Bar upon the Rights and Liberties of the People* (1832), 3-4. For example, the Worcester County Bar failed to take action on the four violations of rules reported between 1824 and 1833. Records of the Society of Attorneys, 1824-1833, Lincoln Papers, MWA. As late as 1832 Benjamin R. Curtis was allowed to practice law for six months while still a student. Benjamin R. Curtis to George W. Phillips, February 11, 1832, quoted in Curtis, *A*

Memoir of Benjamin Robbins Curtis, ed. Benjamin R. Curtis, Jr. (Boston, 1879), 1: 54-55.

14. Arthur B. Darling, *Political Changes in Massachusetts 1824-48: A Study of Liberal Movements in Politics* (New Haven, 1925), 98-99; Daniel J. Boorstin, *The Americans: The National Experience* (Garden City, N.Y., 1965), 46-48; *Boston Morning Post*, October 21, 1840.

15. *Boston Morning Post*, October 21, 1840; Walter Nelles, "Commonwealth v. Hunt," *Columbia Law Review* 32 (November 1932): 1146; Mark DeWolfe Howe, *Readings in American Legal History* (Cambridge, Mass., 1949), 459n; Leonard W. Levy, *The Law of the Commonwealth and Chief Justice Shaw* (Cambridge, Mass., 1957), 138-206.

16. *Boston Morning Post*, October 21, 1840.

17. Robinson, *Letter to Rufus Choate*, 14-15; Horwitz, *Transformation of American Law*, 109-139.

18. Daniel H. Calhoun, *Professional Lives in America: Structure and Aspirations, 1750-1850* (Cambridge, Mass., 1965), 88-177; Michael B. Katz, *The Irony of Early School Reform* (Cambridge, Mass., 1967), 31; Anonymous Doctor, "Character and Abuses of the Medical Profession . . . ," *North American Review* 32 (April 1831): 367-368; Bertram Wyatt-Brown, "Prelude to Abolitionism: Sabbatarian Politics and the Rise of the Second Party System," *Journal of American History* 58 (September 1971): 321, 335-336; New York Physicians' Petition, quoted in Joseph Kett, *The Formation of the American Medical Profession: The Role of Institutions, 1780–1860* (New Haven, 1968), 41-42.

19. L. F. Greene, ed., *The Writings of the Late Elder John Leland* (New York, 1845), 733; William H. Gardiner, "Review of the Report from the Commissioners Appointed to Revise the Statute Laws of the State of New York," *North American Review* 24 (January 1827): 194. For a fuller discussion of the codification movement in Massachusetts, see Gawalt, "Massachusetts Lawyers," 159-188.

20. "Revision of the Laws of Massachusetts," *American Jurist and Law Magazine* 16 (1835): 351-352.

21. *Report of the Commissioners to Revise the Statutes* (Boston, 1835), 59; pt. III, chap. 88, sec. 19-32, 56-57, contain all laws regulating the legal profession.

22. Journal of the Massachusetts House, September-November 1835, 103-104, 106, 109, 181, 200; Journal of the Massachusetts Senate, 1835, 70, 76, 158, 160, M-Ar; table 8.

23. Journal of the Massachusetts House, September-November 1835, 93, 103-104, M-Ar.

24. Ibid., Robert D. Bulkley, "Robert Rantoul, Jr., 1805-1852, Politics

and Reform in Antebellum Massachusetts'' (Ph.D. diss., Princeton University, 1971), 169-170.

25. Bulkley, ''Rantoul,'' 170.

26. *The Revised Statutes of Massachusetts* (Boston, 1836), 541-542.

27. Marvin Mayer, *The Lawyers* (New York, 1966), 13-14, 16. See, for example, Pickering, *Reports*, 4:64-65, 105, 5:244-248, 285-291, 469-475, 10:1-4, 21, 195-197, 11:59-61, 70-73.

28. This is the basic position of these scholars: Alfred A. Reed, *Training for the Public Profession of the Law* (New York, 1921), 68-73; W. Raymond Blackard, ''The Demoralization of the Legal Profession in Nineteenth Century America,'' *Tennessee Law Review* 16 (April 1940): 314-315; James W. Hurst, *The Growth of American Law* (Boston, 1950), 278; Roscoe Pound, ''The Lay Tradition as to the Lawyer,'' *Michigan Law Review* 12 (June 1914): 631; Anton-Hermann Chroust, *The Rise of the Legal Profession in America* (Norman, 1965), 2:231-32. Donald P. Kommers, ''Reflections on Professor Chroust's *The Rise of the Legal Profession in America*,'' *American Journal of Legal History* 10 (July 1966): 209, questions whether the decline of local bar associations was due to Jacksonian democracy but offers no answer. One recent exception is the work of Maxwell Bloomfield, who in several articles and papers, and most recently in *American Lawyers*, has argued that the quality of the bar did not suffer in the pre-1850 period.

29. In the next century lawyers and laymen turned to voluntary bar associations as a means of policing professional ethics and reimposing minimum fees.

30. Chroust, *Rise of the Legal Profession*, 2:136-137, 140; Northend, *Address*, 50-51; *Boston Morning Post*, October 12, 1840; Nelles, ''Commonwealth v. Hunt,'' 1146.

31. Report of the Committee of the Worcester County Bar on the Expediency of Dissolving the Bar Association, 1-6, Lincoln Papers, MWA.

32. ''Review of the Sixth Report of the Common Law Commissioners on the Inns of Court,'' *North American Review* 42 (April 1836): 549; James Richardson, ''Extracts from an Address Delivered before the Norfolk Bar . . . 1837,'' *American Jurist and Law Magazine* 18 (April 1838): 49-51, 69, 72; Emory Washburn, *Sketches of the Judicial History of Massachusetts from 1630 to the Revolution in 1775* (Boston, 1840), 398; Robert C. Winthrop to Edward Everett, June 22, 1836, Everett Papers, MHi; John Davis to Ira Barton, January 2, 1835, Davis Papers, MWA; *Columbian Centinel*, March 14, 21, April 5, 1836; *Boston Advertiser*, April 12, 1836.

33. William J. Reader, *Professional Men* (London, 1966), 55-56; William Holdsworth, *A History of English Law* (London, 1938), 6:444.

34. ''Legislation,'' *Law Reporter* 1 (October 1838): 175; ''New Hamp-

shire Legislation,'' *American Jurist and Law Magazine* 19 (October 1838): 193; *The Revised Statutes of the State of Vermont* (Burlington, 1840), 161; Reed, *Training*, 86-87; Calhoun, *Professional Lives*, 180-183. Medical licensing laws, which were strongly opposed by some medical sects, such as Thomsonians and osteopaths, were also largely swept away during this period. By 1843 ten states had abolished laws penalizing medical practice by nonlicentiates, and by 1849 the American Medical Association reported that only New Jersey and the District of Columbia had laws regulating the practice of medicine. Henry B. Shafer, *The American Medical Profession, 1783–1850* (New York, 1936), 214.

35. By way of comparison, the United States in 1960 had one lawyer in private practice for each 900 people. *The Connecticut Register . . . 1820* (New London, 1820); *The New York Annual Register . . . 1820* (New York, 1820); Paul A. Freund, ''The Legal Profession,'' in Kenneth S. Lynn, ed., *The Professions in America* (Boston, 1963), 36.

36. For 1800-1805, Nash found these figures for lawyers' fathers' occupation: 29.5 percent merchants, bankers, or manufacturers; 34 percent professional; 29.5 percent farmer-landowner; 5 percent small business; 2 percent worker. For 1860-1861, he found: 21.5 percent large business; 30.5 percent professional, 15 percent farmer-landowner; 27 percent small business or officeworker; 6 percent worker. Gary Nash, ''The Philadelphia Bench and Bar, 1800-1861,'' *Comparative Studies in Society and History* 7 (January 1965): 214-219; Maxwell H. Bloomfield, *American Lawyers in a Changing Society, 1776–1876* (Cambridge, Mass., 1976), 147.

37. Calhoun, *Professional Lives*, 59-87.

38. Gerard Gawalt, ''The Historical Background to Law Schools' Schizoprenia,'' *Journal of Legal Education* (forthcoming).

39. Chroust, *Legal Profession*, 2:224-280.

40. A study of Wisconsin shows that lawyers predominated in the political and judicial offices in that state. Howard Feiginbaum, ''The Lawyers in Wisconsin, 1836-1860: A Profile,'' *Wisconsin Magazine of History* 55 (Winter 1971-1972): 100-106.

Appendix

TABLE 23 PROFESSIONS' NUMERICAL STRENGTH, 1740–1840

DATE	LAWYERS	MINISTERS	DOCTORS	TOTAL
1740	15	254	96	364
	(10,349:1)	(596:1)	(1,579:1)	(416:1)
1770	71[a]	327	252	630
	(9,349:1)	(816:1)	(1,058:1)	(423:1)
1800	200	503	411	1,114
	(2,872:1)	(1,142:1)	(1,398:1)	(515:1)
1840	640	1,004	644	2,288
	(1,153:1)	(735:1)	(1,145:1)	(321:1)

Source and Note: Figures compiled from my files of trained ministers, doctors, and lawyers in conjunction with the *Massachusetts Register.* Some trained professionals may not have been encompassed in this counting procedure, and therefore these figures may be an underrepresentation of actual numbers. The ratio of population to professionals (in parentheses) is based on figures from U.S. Bureau of the Census, *Historical Statistics of the United States, Colonial Times to 1957* (Washington, D.C., 1960), 13, 756.
[a]This figure is for 1775.

TABLE 24 MOBILITY IN MASSACHUSETTS: MINISTERS, 1740-1840

GEOGRAPHIC LOCATIONS	COLLEGE GRADUATES, 1740-1799[a]	COLLEGE GRADUATES, 1800-1840[b]	NONCOLLEGE GRADUATES, 1740-1799[c]	NONCOLLEGE GRADUATES, 1800-1840[d]
Practiced in native town	38 (5.9%)	16 (2.3%)	2 (8%)	3 (2.1%)
Practiced in one town	571 (89.9%)	408 (60.3%)	18 (72%)	85 (58.6%)
Practiced in two towns	53 (8.3%)	189 (27.9%)	2 (8%)	31 (21.4%)
Practiced in three or more towns	11 (1.8%)	80 (11.8%)	5 (20%)	29 (20%)
Moved out of state	72 (11.3%)	259 (38.2%)	7 (28%)	51 (35.1%)
Moved into state	132 (20.8%)	237 (35%)	7 (28%)	66 (45.5%)

a. 635 ministers in this category.
b. 677 ministers in this category.
c. 25 ministers in this category.
d. 145 ministers in this category.

TABLE 25 MOBILITY IN MASSACHUSETTS: DOCTORS, 1740-1840

GEOGRAPHIC LOCATIONS	COLLEGE GRADUATES, 1740-1799[a]	COLLEGE GRADUATES, 1800-1840[b]	NONCOLLEGE GRADUATES, 1740-1799[c]	NONCOLLEGE GRADUATES, 1800-1840[d]
Practiced in native town	88 (39.1%)	80 (30.8%)	116 (29.1%)	50 (20.1%)
Practiced in one town	184 (81.8%)	194 (74.6%)	337 (84.5%)	187 (75.4%)
Practiced in two towns	36 (16%)	50 (19.3%)	54 (13.5%)	49 (19.7%)
Practiced in three or more towns	5 (2.2%)	16 (6.1%)	8 (2%)	12 (4.9%)
Moved out of state	24 (10.6%)	41 (15.8%)	47 (11.7%)	32 (12.9%)
Moved into state	11 (4%)	41 (15.8%)	39 (9.7%)	73 (29.4%)

a. 225 doctors in this category.
b. 260 doctors in this category.
c. 399 doctors in this category.
d. 248 doctors in this category.

TABLE 26 MOBILITY IN THE DISTRICT OF MAINE: MINISTERS, 1740-1840

GEOGRAPHIC LOCATIONS	COLLEGE GRADUATES, 1740-1799[a]	COLLEGE GRADUATES, 1800-1840[b]	NONCOLLEGE GRADUATES, 1740-1799[c]	NONCOLLEGE GRADUATES, 1800-1840[d]
Practiced in native town	0	4 (1.8%)	0	3 (2.6%)
Practiced in one town	89 (86.4%)	138 (64.6%)	3 (100%)	63 (54.8%)
Practiced in two towns	8 (7.8%)	42 (19.6%)	0	20 (17.4%)
Practiced in three or more towns	6 (5.8%)	34 (15.9%)	0	32 (27.8%)
Moved out of state	14 (13.6%)	106 (49.5%)	1 (33.3%)	38 (33%)
Moved into state	88 (85.4%)	154 (71.9%)	3 (100%)	59 (51.3%)

a. 103 ministers in this category.
b. 214 ministers in this category.
c. 3 ministers in this category.
d. 115 ministers in this category.

TABLE 27 MOBILITY IN THE DISTRICT OF MAINE: DOCTORS, 1740-1840

GEOGRAPHIC LOCATIONS	COLLEGE GRADUATES, 1740-1799[a]	COLLEGE GRADUATES, 1800-1840[b]	NONCOLLEGE GRADUATES, 1740-1799[c]	NONCOLLEGE GRADUATES, 1800-1840[d]
Practiced in native town	0	9 (14.5%)	2 (2.1%)	41 (14.8%)
Practiced in one town	11 (91.7%)	46 (74.2%)	65 (69.1%)	187 (67.4%)
Practiced in two towns	1 (8.3%)	16 (25.8%)	24 (25.6%)	63 (22.8%)
Practiced in three or more towns	0	0	5 (5.3%)	26 (9.8%)
Moved out of state	2 (16.6%)	17 (27.4%)	4 (4.2%)	43 (15.5%)
Moved into state	8 (66.6%)	28 (45.2%)	67 (71.3%)	62 (22.4%)

a. 12 doctors in this category.
b. 62 doctors in this category.
c. 94 doctors in this category.
d. 276 doctors in this category.

TABLE 28 LEVEL OF EDUCATION OF MINISTERS AND DOCTORS, 1740-1840

		MINISTERS		DOCTORS	
College graduates					
Maine:	1740-1799	103[a]	97.2[b]	12[a]	11.3[b]
	1800-1840	214	65.0	62	18.3
	Total	317	72.9	74	16.9
Massachusetts:	1740-1799	635	96.2	225	36.1
	1800-1840	677	82.4	260	51.2
	Total	1,312	88.5	485	42.9
Noncollege graduates					
Maine:	1740-1799	3	2.8	94	88.7
	1800-1840	115	35.0	276	81.7
	Total	118	17.1	370	83.1
Massachusetts:	1740-1799	25	3.2	399	63.9
	1800-1840	145	17.6	248	48.8
	Total	170	11.5	647	57.1
Totals					
	1740-1799	766	96.2[c]	730	32.5[c]
	1800-1840	1,151	77.4	846	38.1
	Total	1,917	84.5	1576	35.5
Total ministers and doctors:		3,503	62.9		
Total ministers, doctors, and lawyers:[d]		6,121	66.1		

a. Absolute numbers.

b. Percentage of total in this category.

c. Percentage that were graduates of college.

d. Of 2,618 trained lawyers in Massachusetts and the district of Maine, 1760-1840, there were 1,879 (71.4 percent) college graduates.

TABLE 29 PATERNAL OCCUPATION OF MASSACHUSETTS MINISTERS, 1740–1840

FATHER'S OCCUPATION	COLLEGE GRADUATES, 1740–1799		COLLEGE GRADUATES, 1800–1840		NONCOLLEGE GRADUATES, 1740–1799		NONCOLLEGE GRADUATES, 1800–1840		PROFESSIONAL SCHOOL, 1800–1840	
	(No.)	*(%)*	*(No.)*	*(%)*	*(No.)*	*(%)*	*(No.)*	*(%)*	*(No.)*	*(%)*
Doctor	6	1.9	16	10.7	0	0	0	7.1	2	13.3
Minister	109	34.1	50	33.6	2	16.6	4	14.3	6	40.0
Lawyer	2	0.6	13	8.7	0	0	1	3.6	3	20.0
Farmer	76	23.7	29	19.5	4	33.3	12	42.8	2	13.3
Gentleman farmer	5	1.6	2	1.4	1	8.3	0	0	0	0
Merchant	23	7.2	16	10.7	1	8.3	3	10.7	0	0
Artisan	65	20.3	10	6.7	4	33.3	5	17.8	1	6.7
Sea captain	8	2.5	5	3.3	0	0	0	0	0	0
Manufacturer	3	0.9	2	1.4	0	0	0	0	0	0
Innkeeper	10	3.1	1	0.6	0	0	0	0	0	0
Teacher	4	1.2	2	1.4	0	0	0	0	0	0
Other	9	2.5	3	2.0	0	0	1	3.6	1	6.7
Totals	320		149		12		28		15	

TABLE 30 PATERNAL OCCUPATION OF MASSACHUSETTS DOCTORS, 1740–1840

FATHER'S OCCUPATION	COLLEGE GRADUATES, 1740–1799		COLLEGE GRADUATES, 1800–1840		NONCOLLEGE GRADUATES, 1740–1799		NONCOLLEGE GRADUATES, 1800–1840		PROFESSIONAL SCHOOL 1800–1840	
	(No.)	*(%)*	*(No.)*	*(%)*	*(No.)*	*(%)*	*(No.)*	*(%)*	*(No.)*	*(%)*
Doctor	37	30.9	56	47.1	62	44.6	30	45.5	28	51.9
Minister	25	20.9	20	16.8	22	15.8	11	16.7	9	16.7
Lawyer	0	0	6	5.0	1	0.7	3	4.5	1	1.8
Farmer	18	15.0	13	10.9	39	28.1	16	24.3	9	16.7
Gentlemen farmer	6	5.0	0	0	2	1.4	1	1.5	0	0
Merchant	12	10.0	16	13.5	2	1.4	1	1.5	5	9.3
Artisan	12	10.0	3	2.5	7	5.1	2	3.0	1	1.8
Sea captain	5	4.2	3	2.5	2	1.4	1	1.5	0	0
Manufacturer	2	1.6	1	0.8	0	0	1	1.5	0	0
Innkeeper	2	1.6	1	0.8	1	0.7	0	0	0	0
Teacher	1	0.8	0	0	0	0	0	0	0	0
Other	0	0	0	0	0	0	0	0	0	0
Total	120		119		139		66		54	

TABLE 31 PATERNAL OCCUPATION OF MAINE MINISTERS AND DOCTORS, 1740–1840

FATHER'S OCCUPATION	MINISTERS COLLEGE GRADUATES 1740–1799		MINISTERS COLLEGE GRADUATES 1800–1840		DOCTORS NONGRADUATES 1740–1799		DOCTORS NONGRADUATES 1800–1840		DOCTORS PROFESSIONAL SCHOOL 1800–1840	
	(No.)	*(%)*	*(No.)*	*(%)*	*(No.)*	*(%)*	*(No.)*	*(%)*	*(No.)*	*(%)*
Doctor	0	0	4	8.7	12	40.0	13	24.1	13	43.4
Minister	13	32.5	16	34.8	2	6.7	7	12.9	5	16.7
Lawyer	0	0	2	4.3	1	3.3	0	0	0	0
Farmer	13	32.5	13	28.3	9	30.0	25	46.2	7	23.3
Gentleman farmer	2	5.0	4	8.7	0	0	1	1.9	3	10.0
Merchant	1	2.5	1	2.2	3	10.0	1	1.9	1	3.3
Artisan	8	20.0	5	10.8	3	10.0	7	13.0	1	3.3
Sea captain	0	0	1	2.2	0	0	0	0	0	0
Manufacturer	0	0	0	0	0	0	0	0	0	0
Innkeeper	1	2.5	0	0	0	0	0	0	0	0
Teacher	1	2.5	0	0	0	0	0	0	0	0
Other	1	2.5	0	0	0	0	0	0	0	0
Total	40		46		30		54		30	

TABLE 32 MARRIAGE PATTERNS OF MASSACHUSETTS MINISTERS, 1740–1840

OCCUPATION OF FATHER-IN-LAW	COLLEGE GRADUATES, 1740–1799		COLLEGE GRADUATES, 1800–1840		NONCOLLEGE GRADUATES, 1740–1799		NONCOLLEGE GRADUATES, 1800–1840		PROFESSIONAL SCHOOL 1800–1840	
	(No.)	*(%)*	*(No.)*	*(%)*	*(No.)*	*(%)*	*(No.)*	*(%)*	*(No.)*	*(%)*
Doctor	21	6.8	27	17.7	1	7.1	1	6.6	1	14.3
Minister	180	58.3	63	41.2	4	28.6	1	6.6	3	42.8
Lawyer	7	2.3	20	13.1	0	0	1	6.6	1	14.3
Farmer	38	12.3	9	5.9	4	28.6	4	26.7	1	14.3
Gentleman farmer	17	5.5	3	2.0	0	0	0	0	0	0
Merchant	30	9.7	17	11.1	4	28.6	3	20.0	1	14.3
Artisan	3	0.9	2	1.3	1	7.1	4	26.7	0	0
See captain	4	1.4	7	4.6	0	0	0	0	0	0
Manufacturer	0	0	1	0.7	0	0	1	6.6	0	0
Innkeeper	3	0.9	0	0	0	0	0	0	0	0
Teacher	0	0	2	1.3	0	0	0	0	0	0
Other	6	1.9	2	1.3	0	0	0	0	0	0
Total	309		153		14		15		6	

TABLE 33 MARRIAGE PATTERNS OF MASSACHUSETTS DOCTORS, 1740–1840

OCCUPATION OF FATHER-IN-LAW	COLLEGE GRADUATES, 1740–1799		COLLEGE GRADUATES, 1800–1840		NONCOLLEGE GRADUATES, 1740–1799		NONCOLLEGE GRADUATES, 1800–1840		PROFESSIONAL SCHOOL 1800–1840	
	(No.)	*(%)*	*(No.)*	*(%)*	*(No.)*	*(%)*	*(No.)*	*(%)*	*(No.)*	*(%)*
Doctor	8	11.4	14	21.2	17	18.7	9	28.1	12	40
Minister	17	24.3	9	13.6	19	20.9	4	12.5	4	16.6
Lawyer	5	7.1	13	19.7	3	3.3	3	9.4	4	16.6
Farmer	12	17.2	3	4.5	25	27.4	7	21.8	1	3.3
Gentleman farmer	5	7.1	4	6.1	8	8.8	1	3.1	2	6.7
Merchant	19	27.2	12	18.2	8	8.8	5	15.6	2	6.7
Artisan	1	1.4	2	3.1	1	1.1	2	6.2	2	6.7
Sea captain	3	4.3	5	7.6	7	7.7	0	0	2	6.7
Manufacturer	0	0	1	1.5	0	0	0	0	0	0
Innkeeper	0	0	0	0	1	1.1	1	3.1	0	0
Teacher	0	0	0	0	0	0	0	0	0	0
Other	0	0	3	4.5	2	2.2	0	0	0	0
Totals	70		66		91		32		30	

TABLE 34 MARRIAGE PATTERNS OF MAINE MINISTERS AND DOCTORS, 1740–1840

OCCUPATION OF FATHER-IN-LAW	MINISTERS COLLEGE GRADUATES 1740–1799 (No.)	(%)	1800–1840 (No.)	(%)	DOCTORS NONCOLLEGE GRADUATES 1740–1799 (No.)	(%)	1800–1840 (No.)	(%)
Doctor	2	7.1	11	24.5	2	10.5	1	5.5
Minister	12	42.8	21	46.7	6	31.6	0	0
Lawyer	1	3.5	6	13.3	0	0	0	0
Farmer	5	17.8	1	2.2	4	21.0	11	61.1
Gentleman farmer	4	14.6	0	0	0	0	1	5.5
Merchant	3	10.7	2	4.4	4	21.0	1	5.5
Artisan	0	0	1	2.2	0	0	1	5.5
Sea captain	0	0	2	4.4	2	10.5	2	11.0
Manufacturer	0	0	0	0	0	0	0	0
Innkeeper	1	3.5	0	0	0	0	0	0
Teacher	0	0	0	0	0	0	0	0
Other	0	0	1	2.2	1	5.3	1	5.5
Totals	28		45		19		18	

Outline of Massachusetts Court System

Superior Court of Judicature replaced in 1782 by the Supreme Judicial Court

Inferior Court of Common Pleas replaced in 1782 by County Courts of Common Pleas, replaced in 1811 by Circuit Court of Common Pleas; replaced in 1821 by Commonwealth Court of Common Pleas

Judges of Probate; replaced in 1784 by County Courts of Probate

Judges of General Sessions of the Peace; replaced in 1807 by General Courts of Sessions; abolished in 1828. (1809-1819 duties assumed by the County Courts of Common Pleas and Circuit Court of Common Pleas)

Boston Court of Common Pleas established in 1814

Boston Police Court established in 1822

District Courts of Admiralty (superseded by the federal court system in 1789)

Abbreviations

AAS, *Proceedings* *Proceedings of the American Antiquarian Society*
AHR *American Historical Review*
AJLH *American Journal of Legal History*
AJLM *American Jurist and Law Magazine*
EIHC *Essex Institute Historical Collections*
DLC Library of Congress, Washington, D.C.
MAr Massachusetts State Archives, Boston, Massachusetts
MHB Baker Library, Harvard University, Cambridge, Massachusetts
MHi Massachusetts Historical Society, Boston, Massachusetts
MHS, *Collections* *Collections of the Massachusetts Historical Society*
MHS, *Proceedings* *Proceedings of the Massachusetts Historical Society*
MLQ *Massachusetts Law Quarterly*
MWA American Antiquarian Society, Worcester, Massachusetts
NAR *North American Review*
NEHGR *New England Historical and Genealogical Register*
NEQ *New England Quarterly*
NN New-York Historical Society, New York, New York
PMHB *Pennsylvania Magazine of History and Biography*
WMQ *William and Mary Quarterly*
YLJ *Yale Law Journal*

Bibliography

PRIMARY SOURCE MATERIAL

PERSONAL MANUSCRIPTS

John Adams Papers, MHi
Samuel Adams Papers, New York Public Library
Charles Allen Papers, MWA
Fisher Ames Papers, MWA
Ames Papers, Dedham (Massachusetts) Historical Society
Christopher C. Baldwin Papers, MWA
Edward D. Bangs Papers, 1785-1838, MWA
Ira M. Barton Papers, MWA
Francis Bernard Papers, DLC
Abijah Bigelow Papers, MWA
Francis Blake Papers, MWA
George Blake Papers, MWA
Samuel Blodgett Papers, DLC
Boston Association of Booksellers Records, 1801-1820, MWA
Elias Boudinot Papers, DLC
Samuel Burnside Papers, MWA
Chamberlain Collection, Boston Public Library
Edwin Conant Papers, MWA
Andrew Craige Papers, 1717-1815, MWA
Cranch Family Papers, DLC
Christopher Cranch Papers, MHi
Richard Cranch Papers, MHi
Jabez M. Curry Papers, DLC
Cushing Papers, MHi
Caleb Cushing Papers, DLC
Dana Papers, MHi
Davis Papers, MHi
Isaac Davis Papers, MWA
John Davis Papers, MWA
Legal Records of Dukes County, Force Papers, DLC

Edward Everett Papers, MHi
Everett-Peabody Papers, MHi
John Fell Diary, DLC
Forbes Papers, MHB, DLC
Dwight Foster Journal, MWA
Elbridge Gerry Papers, Knox College, MHi, DLC
Isaac Goodwin Papers, MWA
Gore Papers, MHB
Greenough Papers, MHi
Hancock Papers, MHB
Samuel Holten Papers, DLC
Samuel Haven Papers, MWA
Estes Howe Papers, MWA
James Kent Papers, DLC
Thomas Kinnicutt Papers, MWA
Henry Knox Papers, MHi
Enoch Lincoln Papers, MWA
Lincoln Papers, MWA
William Lincoln Papers, MWA
Loring Papers, MHB
John Lowell Papers, MHi
Massachusetts Records, Force Papers, DLC
Pliny Merrick Papers, MWA
Miscellaneous Manuscript, Copley Library, La Jolla, California
Rejoice Newton Papers, MWA
Old Bar Record Book, Harvard Law Library
Harrison Gray Otis Papers, MHi
Nathaniel Paine Papers, MHi
Robert T. Paine Papers, MHi
Willard Phillips Papers, MHi
Pickering Papers, MHi
William Plumer Papers, DLC
Saltonstall Papers, MHi
Theodore Sedgwick Papers, MHi
Sewall Family Papers, MWA
Lemuel Shaw Papers, MHi
Shays's Rebellion Collection, MWA
Joseph Story Papers, MHi, DLC
James Sullivan Papers, MWA
Increase Sumner Papers, MHi
Henry Taft Papers, MHi
Tudor Papers, MHi

Washburn Collection, MHi
John E. Worcester Papers, MHi
Worcester County Collection, MWA
Worcester Papers, MWA

PUBLISHED PERSONAL PAPERS

Adams, John. "John Adams to Charles Cushing, April 1, 1756." MHS, *Proceedings* 32 (1912-1913): 410-412.

———. *The Earliest Diary of John Adams: June, 1753-April 1754, Sept. 1758-January, 1759.* Edited by L. H. Butterfield, Cambridge, Mass., 1966.

———. *Diary and Autobiography of John Adams.* Edited by L. H. Butterfield et al. 4 vols. New York, 1964.

———. *Adams Family Correspondence.* Edited by L. H. Butterfield. 2 vols. New York, 1965.

———. *Legal Papers of John Adams.* Edited by L. Kinvin Wroth and Hiller B. Zoebel. 3 vols. Cambridge, Mass., 1965.

Adams, John Q. "Diary of John Q. Adams." MHS, *Proceedings* 36 (November 1902): 295-464.

———. *Writings of John Quincy Adams.* Edited by Worthington C. Ford. New York, 1913.

Ames, Fisher. *Works, with a Selection from His Speeches and Correspondence.* Edited by Seth Ames. 2 vols. Boston, 1854.

Baldwin, Christopher. *Diary of Christopher C. Baldwin, Librarian of the American Antiquarian Society, 1829–1835.* Worcester, 1901.

Bentley, William. *The Diary of William Bentley.* 4 vols. Gloucester, 1962.

Bigelow, Abijah. "Letters of Abijah Bigelow, Member of Congress, to His Wife, 1810-1815." AAS, *Proceedings* 16 (October 1903): 305-403.

"Bowdoin-Temple Papers." MHS, *Collections* 7th ser. 6 (1907).

Chipman, Ward. "Ward Chipman's Diary: A Loyalist's Return to New England in 1783." *EIHC* 87 (July 1951): 211-241.

Colden, Cadwallader. The Colden Letter Books: 1760-1775. NYHS, *Collections.* 2 vols. New York, 1876-1877.

Curtis, Benjamin R. *A Memoir of Benjamin Robbins Curtis.* Edited by Benjamin R. Curtis, Jr. 2 vols. Boston, 1879.

"Cushing Letters." MHS, *Proceedings* 44 (March 1911): 524-528.

Dana, Richard H. Jr. *The Journal of Richard Henry Dana, Jr.* Edited by Robert F. Lucid. 2 vols. Cambridge, Mass., 1968.

Douglas, William. "Letters from Dr. William Douglas." MHS, *Collections* 4th ser. 2 (1854): 188-189.

Fairfield, John. *The Letters of John Fairfield.* Edited by Arthur G. Staples. Lewiston, Maine, 1922.

Kent, James. *Memoirs and Letters of James Kent.* Edited by William Kent. Boston, 1898.

King, Charles R. *Life and Correspondence of Rufus King.* 2 vols. New York, 1894.

Leland, John. *The Writings of the Late Elder John Leland.* Edited by L. F. Greene. New York, 1845.

Lynde, Benjamin. *The Diaries of Benjamin Lynde and Benjamin Lynde, Jr.* Boston, 1880.

Mills, Elijah H. "Extracts from the Familiar Correspondence of the Hon. E. H. Mills." Edited by Henry C. Lodge. MHS, *Proceedings* 19 (September 1881): 12-53.

Phelps, Elizabeth. "Diary of Elizabeth Phelps." Edited by Thomas E. Andrew. *NEHGR* 119 (July 1965): 205-223.

Price, Ezekiel. "Diary of Ezekiel Price." MHS, *Proceedings* 7 (November 1863): 185-262.

Pynchon, William. *The Diary of William Pynchon of Salem.* Edited by Fitch E. Oliver. Boston, 1890.

Rantoul, Robert. *Memoirs, Speeches and Writings of Robert Rantoul, Jr.* Edited by Luther Hamilton. Boston, 1854.

Richards, William C. *Great in Goodness: Memoir of George N. Briggs, Governor of the Commonwealth of Massachusetts 1844–1851.* Boston, 1866.

Rowe, John. "Extracts from the Diary of John Rowe, 1764-1779." Edited by Edward L. Pierce. MHS, *Proceedings* 30 (March 1885): 41-107.

The Saltonstall Papers, 1607–1815. Edited by Robert E. Moody. 2 vols. Boston, 1972-1974.

Savage, James. *Letters of James Savage to His Family.* Boston, 1906.

Sewall, Jonathan. "Letters of Jonathan Sewall." Edited by Henry Lee. MHS, *Proceedings* 30 (January 1896): 407-426.

Story, Joseph. "Letters Between James Kent and Joseph Story, 1819-1846." Edited by Charles C. Smith. MHS, *Proceedings* 34 (January 1901): 398-413.

———, and Webster, Daniel. "Letters of Daniel Webster to Joseph Story, 1816-1846." Edited by Charles C. Smith. MHS, *Proceedings* 34 (January 1901): 398-413.

Story, William W., ed. *Life and Letters of Joseph Story.* 2 vols. Boston, 1851.

Sullivan, James. *Life of James Sullivan with Selections from His Writings.* Edited by Thomas C. Amory. 2 vols. Boston, 1859.

Tudor, William. "Memoir of Hon. William Tudor." MHS, *Collections* 2d ser. 7 (1826): 285-325.

Warren, Charles. *Jacobin and Junto; or Early American Politics as Viewed in the Diary of Dr. Nathaniel Ames, 1758–1822.* Cambridge, Mass., 1931.

Warren-Adams Letters: Being Chiefly a Correspondence Among John Adams, Samuel Adams and James Warren, 1743–1814. MHS, *Collections* 72-73 (1917 and 1925).

Willard, Susan ed. "Letters of Rev. Joseph Willard." Cambridge Historical Society, *Proceedings* 11 (October 1916): 11-32.

NEWSPAPERS

American Herald (Boston)
Berkshire American and Adams Manufacturer (North Adams)
Berkshire Chronicle and the Massachusetts Intelligencer (Pittsfield)
Boston Daily Advertiser
Boston Gazette and Country Journal
Columbian Centinel (Boston)
Columbian Register (New Haven)
Connecticut Journal (New Haven)
Cumberland Gazette (Portland)
Eastern Argus (Portland)
Essex Journal & New Hampshire Packet (Newburyport)
Essex Register (Salem)
Evening Mercantile Journal (Boston)
Greenfield Gazette and Franklin Herald
Hampshire Gazette (Northampton)
Herald of Freedom and the Federal Advertiser (Boston)
Impartial Register (Salem)
Independent Chronicle and the Universal Advertiser (Boston)
Jurisprudent (Boston)
Kennebec Daily Journal (Augusta)
Massachusetts Centinel (Boston)
Massachusetts Eagle (Lenox)
Massachusetts Gazette and Newsletter (Boston)
Massachusetts Spy (Worcester)
Pittsfield Sun
Salem Gazette
Western Star (Stockbridge)

PUBLISHED PRIMARY

American Jurist and Law Magazine 26 vols. Boston, 1829-1843.

American Law Journal and Miscellaneous Repertory. 6 vols. Philadelphia, 1808-1810, 1813-1814, 1817.

Anonymous. "Character and Abuses of the Medical Profession: Rules and Regulations of the Boston Medical Association." *NAR* 32 (April 1831): 367-386.

———. "Review of Joseph Story's Commentaries on the Law of Bailments." *AJLM* 7 (January 1832): 128-202.

———. "Review of the Sixth Report of the Common Law Commissioners on the Inns of Court: London, 1834." *NAR* 42 (April 1836): 513-549.

———. "Review of Dudley A. Tyng's, Reports of Cases . . . in the Supreme Judicial Court of Massachusetts . . . 1806," *AMJMR* 1 (1809): 361-374.

———. "Review of Nathan Dane's *A General Abridgement and Digest of American Laws.*" *AJLM* 4 (July 1830): 63-86.

Anthon, John. *American Precedents of Declarations . . . of Chief Justice Parsons and Other Accomplished Pleaders.* Boston, 1802.

Bancroft, George. "Review of Kent's Commentaries." *American Quarterly Review* 1 (March 1827): 162-185.

Blackstone, William. *Commentaries on the Laws of England.* 2d ed. Oxford, 1766.

Bliss, George Jr. *An Address to the Members of the Bar of the Counties of Hampshire, Franklin and Hampden . . . 1826.* Springfield, 1827.

Bristol County Bar. *Rules and Regulations of the Bar in the County of Bristol.* Taunton, Massachusetts, 1817.

Commission to Consider and Report upon the Practicality and Expediency of Reducing to a Written and Systematic Code, the Common Law of Massachusetts. *Reports.* Boston, 1837.

Commissioners to Revise the Statutes. *Report.* Boston, 1835.

Cushing, Caleb. "Review of Reports Made to the General Assembly of the State of Louisiana, of the Plan of the Penal Code . . . by Edward Livingston," *NAR* 17 (October 1823): 242-268.

Cushing, Luther S. "Review of a Report of a Special Committee of the House of Representatives as Relates to . . . Codifying the Common Law." *AJLM* 15 (April 1836): 121-128.

Dexter, George, ed. "Record Book of the Suffolk Bar." MHS, *Proceedings* 19 (December 1881): 141-178.

Drake, Daniel. *Practical Essays on Medical Education and the Medical Profession in the United States.* Cincinnati, 1831.

Dutton, Warren. *An Address Delivered to the Members of the Bar of Suffolk . . . 1819.* Boston, 1819.

Dwight, Timothy. *Travels in New England and New York: 1821-1822.* 4 vols. New Haven, 1822.

Essex County Bar. *Rules and Regulations of the Bar in the County of Essex . . . 1806.* Salem, 1806.

Everett, Edward. "Essay on Code Napoleon." *NAR* 20 (April 1825): 393-417.

Freshfield, Edwin, ed. *Records of the Society of Gentlemen Practisers in the Courts of Law and Equity Called the Law Society.* London, 1897.

Gardiner, William H. "Review of Report from the Commissioners Appointed to Revise the Statute Law of the State of New York." *NAR* 24 (January 1827): 193-209.

Hampden County Bar. *Rules for the Regulation of the Gentlemen Practicing at the Bar . . . in the County of Hampden.* 1816.

Handlin, Oscar, ed. *This Was America.* Cambridge, Mass., 1949.

Haven, N. "Review of Simon Greenleaf's Reports on Cases Argued . . . in the Supreme Judicial Court of *Maine . . .*" *NAR* 22 (January 1826): 27-34.

Hilliard, G. S. "Review of David Hoffman's *A Course of Legal Study . . . .*" *NAR* 46 (January 1838): 72-82.

Holmes, Abraham. *Address Before the Bar of the County of Bristol . . . 1834.* New Bedford, 1834.

Hopkins, James D. *An Address to the Members of the Cumberland Bar . . . 1833.* Portland, Maine, 1833.

Howe, Samuel. *The Practice in Civil Actions and Proceedings at Law, in Massachusetts.* Boston, 1834.

Law Reporter. 3 vols. Boston, 1838-1840.

Manning, William. *The Key of Liberty: Shewing the Causes Why a Free Government Has Always Failed, and a Remedy Against It, 1798.* Edited by Samuel E. Morison. Billerica, 1922.

Metcalf, Theron. "Notice of James Kent's *Commentaries on American Law.*" United States Review and Literary Gazette 2 (May 1827): 81-83.

———. "Review of Dudley A. Tyng's *Reports of Cases. . . .*" *NAR* 7 (July 1818): 184-197.

Miller, Perry, ed. *The Legal Mind in America from Independence to the Civil War.* Garden City, N.Y. 1962.

Parker, Isaac. "Inaugural Address Delivered in the Chapel of Harvard University . . . Chief Justice of Massachusetts and Royal Professor of Law." *NAR* 3 (May 1816): 11-27.

Pickering, John. "A Lecture on the Alleged Uncertainty of the Law . . . 1830," *AJLM* 12 (October 1834): 285-311.

Quincy, Josiah, Jr. *Reports of Cases Argued and Adjudged in the Superior Court of Judicature of the Province of Massachusetts Bay . . . 1761-1772.* Edited by Samuel Quincy. Boston, 1865.

"Record of the Transactions of the Annual Convocation of Ministers in the Province of New Hampshire, begun July 28, 1747." New Hampshire Historical Society, *Collections* 9 (1889): 1-67.

Richardson, James. "Extracts from an Address Delivered before the Members of the Norfolk Bar . . . 1837." *AJLM* 18 (April, July 1837): 44-80, 477-482.

Robinson, Frederick. *Letter to the Hon. Rufus Choate Containing a Brief Exposure of the Law Craft, and Some of the Encroachments of the Bar Upon the Rights and Liberties of the People.* 1832.

Sedgwick, Henry D. "The Common Law: Review of William Sampson's *An Anniversary Discourse*" *NAR 19 (October 1824): 411-439.*

Shaw, Lemuel. "Extracts of Lemuel Shaw's Address to the Suffolk Bar, 1827." *AJLM* 7 (January 1832): 56-70.

Story, Joseph. *A Selection of Pleadings in Civil Actions. . . .* Salem, Massachusetts, 1805.

———. "An Address Delivered Before the Members of the Suffolk Bar . . . 1821." *AJLM* 1 (January 1829): 1-34.

———. "Review of David Hoffman's Courses of Legal Study." *NAR* 6 (November 1817): 45-77.

———. "Review of William Johnson's Reports of Cases Adjudged in the Court of Chancery in New York." *NAR* 11 (July 1820): 140-66.

Suffolk County Bar. *Rules and Regulations of the Bar in the County of Suffolk. . . .* Boston, 1805, 1810, 1819.

Sullivan, William. *An Address to the Members of the Bar of Suffolk County . . . 1824.* Boston, 1825.

———. *Familiar Letters on Public Characters. . . .* Boston, 1834.

Thatcher, Peter O. "Extracts from His Address to the Suffolk Bar . . . 1831." *AJLM* 5 (April 1831): 397-399.

Wait, T. B. *Rules of the Supreme Judicial Court of Massachusetts and Regulation of Attornies.* Portland, Maine, 1806.

Walker, Timothy. "Legal Reform." *AJLM* 9 (April 1833): 289-304.

Washburn, Emory. "Parts of an Address Before the Bar of the County of Worcester . . . 1836 on the Occasion of the Dissolving of Their Association." *AJLM* 19 (April 1838): 49-73.

———. *Sketches of the Judicial History of Massachusetts from 1630 to the Revolution in 1775.* Boston, 1840.

Watterston, George, *The Lawyer, or Man as He Ought Not to Be: A Tale.* Charlestown, 1829.

Webster, Daniel. "Review of Henry Wheaton's *Reports. . . .*" *NAR* 8 (December 1818): 63-71.

———. *The Works of Daniel Webster.* 6 vols. Boston, 1854.

Willard, Joseph. *An Address to the Members of the Bar of Worcester County . . . 1829.* Lancaster, 1830.

———, et al. *Addresses Before the Members of the Bar of Worcester County.* Worcester, 1879.

Williamson, William D. *The History of the State of Maine.* 2 vols. Hallowell, Maine, 1832.

Willis, William. "Notes of the Early Jurisprudence of Maine." *Law Reporter* 3 (May, June, August 1840): 31-35, 41-51, 121-127.

Worcester County Bar. *Bar Rules of the County of Worcester.* Worcester, 1816.

———. *Rules of the Bar of the County of Worcester.* Worcester, 1828.

PUBLIC DOCUMENTS

American State Papers, Miscellaneous. Washington, D.C., 1834.

Chaffee, Zachariah, Jr., and Morison, Samuel, eds. *Records of the Suffolk County Court, 1671-1680. Publications of the Colonial Society of Massachusetts.* 2 vols. Boston, 1933.

Docket Books. Kennebec County Court of Common Pleas, 1799-1839. MS, Augusta, Maine.

———. Worcester County Court of Common Pleas, 1780-1836. MS, Worcester, Massachusetts.

———. Massachusetts Superior Court of Judicature, 1760-1782. Microfilm, MHi.

———. Supreme Judicial Court of Massachusetts and Maine, Kennebec County, 1799-1840. MS, Augusta, Maine.

———. Supreme Judicial Court of Massachusetts, 1783-1800. Microfilm, MHi.

———. Supreme Judicial Court of Massachusetts, Worcester County. MS, 1783-1840, Worcester, Massachusetts.

Fairfield, John. *Reports of Cases Argued and Determined in the Supreme Judicial Court of the State of Maine, 1833–1835.* 3 vols. Hallowell, 1835-1837.

Greenleaf, Simon. *Reports of Cases Argued and Determined in the Supreme Judicial Court of the State of Maine, 1820–1832.* 9 vols. Hallowell, 1822, 1824, Portland, 1826-1835.

Hall, Junius, ed. *The Act to Amend Some of the Proceedings, Practice and Rules of Evidence of this Commonwealth, Passed 1851.* Boston, 1851.

Maine, State of. *Acts and Resolves Passed by the Twenty-third Legislature of the State of Maine, 1819–20.* Augusta, 1894.

———. *Debates and Journal of the Constitutional Convention of the State of Maine, 1819–20.* Augusta, 1894.

———. *Laws of Maine . . . 1821.* Brunswick, 1821.

———. *Laws of the State of Maine . . . 1822.* Portland, 1822.

———. *Laws of Maine, 1822–1831.* Portland, 1831.

———. *Public Acts of the State of Maine . . . 1837.* Augusta, 1837.

———. *Resolves of the State of Maine from 1820–1835.* 2 vols. Portland, 1835.
———. *The Revised Statutes of the State of Maine, Passed October 22, 1840.* Augusta, 1841.
Massachusetts General Court. House and Senate Journals, 1780-1840. MAr.
———. *Report of the Committee on Judicial Reform.* Boston, 1798.
Massachusetts, State of. *Acts and Resolves, Public and Private, of the Province of Massachusetts Bay . . . 1692–1780.* 5 vols. Boston, 1869, 1874.
———, *Acts and Resolves, Public and Private of the Province of the Massachusetts Bay, 1779-1780.* Boston, 1922.
———. *Acts and Laws of the Commonwealth of Massachusetts: 1780–1781.* Boston, 1890.
———. *Acts and Laws of the Commonwealth of Massachusetts, 1782–1787.* Boston, 1890.
———. *Acts and Laws of . . . Massachusetts, 1784-1787.* Boston, 1893.
———. *Acts and Laws of the Commonwealth of Massachusetts, 1788–89.* Boston, 1890.
———. *Acts and Laws of the Commonwealth of Massachusetts, 1796.* Boston, 1896.
———. *The Charters and General Laws of the Colony and Province of Massachusetts Bay.* Boston, 1914.
———. *Debates and Proceedings in the Convention of the Commonwealth of Massachusetts . . . 1788. . . .* Boston, 1836.
———. *Documents . . . of the Commonwealth of Massachusetts, During the Session of the General Court, 1836.* Boston, 1836.
———. *Journal of the Convention for Framing a Constitution of Government for the State of Massachusetts Bay from . . . 1779 to . . . 1780.* Boston, 1853.
———. *Journal of the Debates and Proceedings in the Convention of Delegates Chosen to Revise the Constitution of Massachusetts . . . 1820–1821.* Boston, 1853.
———. *The Laws of the Commonwealth . . . 1780–1807. . . .* 2 vols. Boston, 1807.
———. *The Laws of the Commonwealth of Massachusetts . . . 1812 to 1818.* Boston, 1818.
———. *The Laws of the Commonwealth . . . 1822–1825.* Boston, 1825.
———. *Pamphlett Laws of Massachusetts, 1834–1836.* Boston, 1836.
———. *Private and Special Statutes of the Commonwealth . . . 1814–1822.* Boston, 1823.
———. *Resolves of the General Court of the Commonwealth of Massachusetts, 1784–1787.* 4 vols. Boston, 1784-1787.

———. *Resolves of the General Court of the Commonwealth . . . 1835–1836.* Boston, 1836.

———. *The Revised Statutes of the Commonwealth of Massachusetts, Passed November 4, 1835.* Boston, 1836.

———. *Rules of the Court of Common Pleas, 1823.* Boston, 1823.

———. *Rules of the Supreme Judicial Court of Massachusetts, 1836.* Boston, 1836.

Pickering, Octavius. *Reports of Cases Argued and Determined in the Supreme Judicial Court of Massachusetts, 1822–1839.* 23 vols. Boston, 1824-1864.

Shepley, John. *Reports of Cases Argued and Determined in the Supreme Judicial Court of the State of Maine, 1836–1840.* 6 vols. Hallowell, 1838-1841.

Shurtleff, Nathaniel E. *Records of Governor and Company of Massachusetts Bay in New England.* 4 vols. Boston, 1853-1854.

Tyng, Dudley A. *Reports of Cases Argued and Determined in the Supreme Judicial Court of Massachusetts, 1806–1822.* 18 vols. Boston, 1808-1823, Newburyport, 1809-1816.

United States. Bureau of the Census, *Historical Statistics of the United States, Colonial Times to 1957.* Washington, D.C., 1960.

———. Tax Records, 1815. 15th Congressional District, Worcester County. MS, MWA.

Vermont. *The Revised Statutes of the State of Vermont.* Burlington, 1840.

Walton, E. P., ed., *Records of the Governor and Council of the State of Vermont.* Montpelier, 1875.

Williams, Ephraim. *Reports of Cases Argued and Determined in the Supreme Judicial Court of Massachusetts, 1804–1805.* Northampton, 1805.

Worcester County. Assessors List. 1798 and 1834, MWA.

SECONDARY SOURCES

ARTICLES

Adams, Donald R. Jr. "Some Evidence of English and American Wage Rates, 1790-1830." *Journal of Economic History* 30 (September 1970): 499-520.

Ames, Ellis. "Indictment Against Two Judges of the Supreme Judicial Court for Traveling on the Lord's Day." MHS, *Proceedings* 19 (March 1882): 252-255.

Anonymous. "Reform in Legal Education." *American Law Review* 10 (July 1876): 626-641.

———. "The Litchfield Law School." *Albany Law Journal* 20 (1879): 72-73.

Auerbach, Jerold S. "Enmity and Amity: Law Teachers and Practitioners, 1900-1922." In *Law in American History,* edited by Donald Fleming and Bernard Bailyn, 551-604. Boston, 1971.

Baldwin, Simeon E. "The Study of Elementary Law: The Proper Beginning of a Legal Education." *YLJ* 13 (October 1903): 1-15.

Barber, Bernard. "Some Problems in the Sociology of the Professions." In Kenneth Lynn, ed. *The Professions in America,* 15-34. Boston, 1965.

Bedwell, C. E. A., "American Middle Templars." *AHR* 25 (July 1920): 680-689.

Blackard, W. Raymond. "Requirements for Admission to the Bar in Revolutionary America." *Tennessee Law Review* 15 (February 1938): 116-127.

———. "The Demoralization of the Legal Profession in Nineteenth Century America." *Tennessee Law Review* 16 (April 1940): 314-323.

Bloomfield, Maxwell. "William A. Sampson and the Codifiers: The Roots of American Legal Reform, 1820-1830." *AJLH* 11 (July 1967): 424-436.

Brown, Charles L. "The Genesis of the Negro Lawyer in New England." *Negro History Bulletin* 22 (April 1959): 147-152.

Brown, E. Francis. "The Law Career of Major Joseph Hawley." *NEQ* 4 (July 1931): 482-508.

Brown, Richard D. "The Emergence of Urban Society in Rural Massachusetts, 1760-1820." *JAH* 56 (June 1974): 29-51.

Chroust, Anton-Hermann. "The Dilemma of the American Lawyer in the Post-Revolutionary Era." *Notre Dame Lawyer* 25 (December 1959): 48-76.

Corwin, Edward S. "The Progress of the Constitutional Theory Between the Declaration of Independence and the Meeting of the Philadelphia Convention." *AHR* 30 (April 1925): 511-536.

Cushing, John D. "The Judiciary and Public Opinion in Revolutionary Massachusetts." In George A. Billias, ed., *Law and Authority in Colonial America,* 168-186. Barre, 1965.

David, Richard B. "The Early American Lawyers and the Profession of Letters." *The Huntington Library Quarterly* 12 (February 1949): 191-205.

Day, Alan, and Day, Katherine. "Another Look at the Boston Caucus." *Journal of American Studies* 5 (April 1971): 19-42.

Dowd, Morgan D. "Justice Story and the Politics of Appointment." *AJLH* 9 (October 1965): 265-285.

Dunne, Gerald T. "The Story-Livingston Correspondence (1812-1822)." *AJLH* 10 (July 1966): 224-36.

Farnsworth, Albert. "Shays' Rebellion." *MLQ* 12 (February 1927): 29-43.

Feiginbaum, Howard. "The Lawyers in Wisconsin, 1836-1860: A Profile." *Wisconsin Magazine of History* 55 (Winter 1971-1972): 100-106.

Freund, Paul A. "The Legal Profession." In Kenneth Lynn, ed., *The Professions in America,* 35-46. Boston, 1965.

Gawalt, Gerard W. "Massachusetts Legal Education in Transition, 1766-1840." *AJLH* 17 (January 1973): 27-50.

———. "Professionalization and Polarization in American Society, 1740-1850." Paper delivered at Social Science History Conference, Ann Arbor, Mich., 1977.

———. "Sources of Anti-Lawyer Sentiment in Massachusetts, 1740-1840." *AJLH* 14 (October 1970): 283-307.

———. "The Historical Background to Law Schools' Schizophrenia." *The Journal of Legal Education* (forthcoming).

Grinnell, Frank W. "The Bench and Bar in Colony and Province (1630-1776)." In Albert B. Hart, ed., *Commonwealth History of Massachusetts.* 2:156-191. New York, 1928.

———. "The Judicial System and the Bar (1820-1861)." In Albert B. Hart, ed., *Commonwealth History of Massachusetts,* 4:35-73. New York, 1928.

———. "The Constitutional History of the Supreme Judicial Court of Massachusetts from the Revolution to 1813." *MLQ* 2 (May 1917): 329-352.

Hallam, Oscar. "Early Courts and Lawyers." *YLR* 25 (March 1916): 386-396.

"Hancock County Lawyers." *Bangor Historical Magazine* 2 (March 1887): 173-176.

Harno, Albert J. "American Legal Education." *American Bar Association Journal* 46 (August 1960): 845-851.

Harris, P. M. G. "The Social Origins of American Leaders: The Demographic Foundation." *Perspectives in American History* 3 (1969): 159-344.

Herbst, Jurgen. "The American Revolution and the American University." *Perspectives in American History* 10 (1976): 279-354.

Hornblower, William B. "A Century of Judge-Made Law." *Columbia Law Review* 7 (November 1907): 453-475.

Horwitz, Morton. "The Emergence of an Instrumental Conception of American Law, 1780-1820." In *Law in American History*, edited by Donald Fleming and Bernard Bailyn, 287-326. Boston, 1971.

Howe, Mark DeWolfe. "The Creative Period in the Law of Massachusetts."

MHS, *Proceedings* 69 (1947-1950): 232-251.

Ingersoll, Henry H. "Attorneys and Counsellors." *YLJ* 16 (June 1907): 577-584.

Klein, Milton, M. "The Rise of the New York Bar: The Legal Career of William Livingston." *WMQ* 15 (July 1958): 334-358.

———. "Prelude to Revolution in New York: Jury Trials and Judicial Tenure." *WMQ* 17 (October 1960): 439-462.

Kommers, Donald P. "Reflections on Professor Chroust's *The Rise of the Legal Profession in America.*" *AJLH* 10 (July 1966): 201-213.

Lloyd, William H., Jr. "The Courts from the Revolution to the Revision of the Civil Code." *University of Pennsylvania Law Review and American law Register* 56 (February 1908): 88-115.

Mason, Albert. "Judicial History Prior to 1780." *MLQ* 2 (November 1916): 82-100.

McAnear, Beverly. "The Selection of an Alma Mater by Pre-Revolutionary Students." *PMHB* 73 (October 1949): 429-440.

Morris, Richard B. "Insurrection in Massachusetts." In Daniel Aaron, ed., *America in Crisis*, 21-49. New York, 1952.

———. "Legalism versus Revolutionary Doctrine in New England." *NEQ* 4 (April 1931): 195-215.

Morse, John T. "The Bench and Bar in Boston." In Justin Winsor, ed., *The Memorial History of Boston*, 3:571-606. Boston, 1881.

Murin, John M. "The Legal Transformation: The Bench and Bar in Eighteenth Century Massachusetts." In Stanley Katz, ed., *Colonial America: Essays in Politics and Social Development,* 415-449. Boston, 1971.

Nash, Gary. "The Philadelphia Bench and Bar, 1800-1860." *Comparative Studies in Society and History* 7 (January 1965): 203-220.

Nelles, Walter. "Commonwealth vs. Hunt." *Columbia Law Review* 32 (November 1932): 1128-1169.

Newmeyer, R. Kent. "A Note on the Whig Politics of Justice Joseph Story." *Mississippi Valley Historical Review* 48 (December 1961): 480-491.

Noble, John. "A Few Notes on Shays Rebellion." AAS *Proceedings* 14 (October 1902): 200-232.

Pessen, Edward. "The Egalitarian Myth and the American Social Reality: Wealth, Mobility, and Equality in the 'Era of the Common Man.'" *AHR* 76 (October 1971): 989-1034.

Pound, Roscoe. "Judge Story in the Making of American Law." Cambridge Historical Society, *Proceedings* 7 (January 1912): 33-56.

———. "The Legal Profession in America." *Notre Dame Lawyer* 19 (June 1944): 334-354.

———. "The Place of Judge Story in the Making of American Law." *MLQ* 1 (May 1916): 121-140.

———. "The Lay Tradition as to the Lawyer." *Michigan Law Review* 12 (June 1914): 627-638.

Sedgwick, H. D. "The Sedgwicks of Berkshire." Berkshire Historical and Scientific Society, *Collections* 3 (1899): 91-106.

Smith, Frank S. "Admission to the Bar in New York." *YLJ* 16 (May 1907): 514-522.

Stevens, Robert. "Two Cheers for 1870: The American Law School." In *Law in American History*, edited by Donald Fleming and Bernard Bailyn, 405-548. Boston, 1971.

Taft, Henry W. "Judicial History of Berkshire," Berkshire Historical Society, *Collections* 1 (1892): 89-115.

Thorne, Barrie. "Professional Education in Law." *Education for the Professions of Medicine, Law, and Social Welfare*, 101-168. New York, 1973.

Vinovskis, Maris, and Bernard, Richard M. "The Female School Teacher in Ante-Bellum Massachusetts." *Journal of Social History* 10 (March 1977): 332-345.

Waters, John J., and Schutz, John A. "Patterns of Massachusetts Colonial Politics: The Writs of Assistance and the Rivalry Between the Otis and Hutchinson Families." *WMQ* 24 (October 1967): 543-567.

Welch, Richard E., Jr. "The Parsons-Sedgwick Feud and the Reform of the Massachusetts Judiciary." *Essex Institute Historical Collections* 92 (April 1956): 171-187.

Willis, William. "Thomas Ricc." *Mainc Historic and Genealogical Recorder* 9 (May 1898): 129-132.

Wyatt-Brown, Bertram. "Prelude to Abolitionism: Sabbatarian Politics and the Rise of the Second Party System." *Journal of American History* 58 (September 1971): 316-341.

BOOKS AND DISSERTATIONS

Adams, Charles F. *Three Episodes of Massachusetts History.* 2d ed. 2 vols. Boston, 1903.

Amory, Francis. *Catalogue of the Library of the Hon. Theophilus Parsons* . . . Boston, 1814.

Allmendinger, David. "Indigent Students and Their Institutions, 1800-1840." Ph.D. dissertation, University of Wisconsin, 1968.

———. *Paupers and Scholars: The Transformation of Student Life in Nineteenth Century New England.* New York, 1975.

Aronson, Sidney H. *Status and Kinship in the Higher Civil Service.* Cambridge, Mass., 1964.

Bailey, Hollis R. *Attorneys and Their Admission to the Bar in Massachusetts.* Boston, 1907.

Bailyn, Bernard. *The New England Merchant in the Seventeenth Century.* New York, 1964.

———. *The Ordeal of Thomas Hutchinson.* Cambridge, Mass., 1974.

Baldwin, Simeon E. *The American Judiciary.* New York, 1905.

Banks, Ronald F. *Maine Becomes a State: The Movement to Separate Maine from Massachusetts 1785–1860.* Middletown, 1970.

Banner, James M., Jr. *To the Hartford Convention: The Federalists and the Origin of Party Politics in Massachusetts, 1789–1815.* New York, 1970.

Bates, Ralph S. *Scientific Societies in the United States.* 2d ed. New York, 1958.

Baxter, Maurice G. *Daniel Webster and the Supreme Court.* Amherst, 1966.

Bernhard, Winfred E. *Fisher Ames: Federalist and Statesman, 1758–1808.* Chapel Hill, 1965.

Bertoff, Rowland. *An Unsettled People: Social Order and Disorder in American History.* New York, 1971.

Billias, George, ed. *Law and Authority in Colonial America.* Barre, 1965.

Biographical Directory of the American Congress, 1774–1961. Washington, D.C., 1961.

Birdsall, Richard D. *Berkshire County: A Cultural History.* New Haven, 1959.

Blau, Peter N., and Duncan, Otis D. *The American Occupational Structure.* New York, 1967.

Bledstein, Burton J. *The Culture of Professionalism: The Middle Class and the Development of Higher Education in America.* New York, 1976.

Bloom, Murray Teigh. *The Trouble with Lawyers.* New York, 1968.

Bloomfield, Maxwell. *American Lawyers in a Changing Society, 1776–1876.* Cambridge, Mass., 1976.

Boorstin, Daniel J. *The Americans: The Colonial Experience.* New York, 1958.

———. *The Americans: The National Experience.* Garden City, 1965.

Brennan, Ellen. *Plural Office-holding in Massachusetts, 1760–1780.* Chapel Hill, 1945.

Brown, E. Francis. *Joseph Hawley: Colonial Radical.* New York, 1931.

Brown, Elizabeth G. *British Statutes in American Law, 1776–1836.* Ann Arbor, 1964.

Brown, Samuel. *The Life of Rufus Choate.* Boston, 1870.

Brown, Wallace. *The King's Friends: The Composition and Motives of the American Loyalist Claimants.* Providence, 1965.

Bulkley, Robert D. "Robert Rantoul Jr. 1805-1852. Politics and Reform in Antebellum Massachusetts." Ph.D. dissertation, Princeton University, 1971.

Burrage, Walter L. *A History of the Massachusetts Medical Society, 1781–1922.* Norwood, 1923.

Calhoun, Daniel H. *Professional Lives in America: Structure and Aspirations, 1750–1850.* Cambridge, Mass. 1965.

Carpenter, E. W., and Morehouse, C. F. *The History of the Town of Amherst.* Amherst, 1896.

Cary, John J. *Joseph Warren, Physician, Politician, Patriot.* Urbana, 1961.

Chroust, Anton-Hermann, *The Rise of the Legal Profession in America.* 2 vols. Norman, 1965.

Cushing, John D. "A Revolutionary Conservative: The Public Life of William Cushing, 1732-1810" (Ph.D. Dissertation, Clark University, 1960).

Darling, Arthur. *Political Changes in Massachusetts, 1824–1848: A Study of Liberal Movements in Politics.* New Haven, 1925.

Davis, Joseph S. *Eighteenth Century Business Corporations in the United States.* Cambridge, Mass. 1917.

Davis, William T. *Bench and Bar of the Commonwealth of Massachusetts.* 2 vols. Boston, 1895.

———. *History of the Judiciary of Massachusetts* . . . Boston, 1900.

Davol, Ralph. *Two Men of Taunton.* Taunton, 1912.

Drake, Samuel A. *A History of Middlesex County.* 2 vols. Boston, 1880.

Dunn, Richard S. *Puritans and Yankees, The Winthrop Dynasty of New England, 1630–1717.* Princeton, 1962.

Dunne, Gerald T. *Justice Story and the Rise of the Supreme Court.* New York, 1970.

East, Robert A. *Business Enterprise in the American Revolutionary Era.* New York, 1938.

Ehrenfried, Albert. *A Chronicle of Boston Jewry from the Colonial Settlement to 1900.* 1963.

Ekirch, Arthur A. *The Idea of Progress in America, 1815–1860.* New York, 1944.

Elliott, Philip. *The Sociology of the Professions.* New York, 1972.

Ellis, Richard E. *The Jeffersonian Crisis: Courts and Politics in the Young Republic.* New York, 1971.

Essex Bar Association. *A Catalogue of the Essex County Law Library.* Salem, 1872.

Eulau, Heinz, and Sprague, John D. *Lawyers in Politics: A Study in Professional Convergence.* New York, 1964.

Fischer, David H. *The Revolution of American Conservatism: The Federalist Party in the Era of Jeffersonian Democracy.* New York, 1965.

Fish, Carl R. *The Rise of the Common Man.* New York, 1927.

Fisher, Samuel H. *The Litchfield Law School, 1775–1833.* New Haven, 1933.

Flexner, Abraham. *Medical Education in the United States and Canada: A Report to the Carnegie Foundation for the Advancement of Teaching.* New York, 1910.

Gambrell, Mary L. *Ministerial Training in Eighteenth Century New England.* New York, 1937.

Gawalt, Gerard W. "Massachusetts Lawyers: A Historical Analysis of the Process of Professionalization, 1760-1840." Ph.D. dissertation, Clark University, 1969.

Goebel, Julius, Jr. *Cases and Materials on the Development of Legal Institutions.* New York, 1931.

Goodman, Paul. *The Democratic-Republicans of Massachusetts: Politics in a Young Republic.* Cambridge, Mass., 1964.

Griswold, Erwin N. *Law and Lawyers in the United States.* Cambridge, Mass., 1965.

Groce, George C. Jr. *William Samuel Johnson: A Maker of the Constitution.* New York, 1937.

Hall, Van Beck. "The Commonwealth in the New Nation: Massachusetts, 1780-1790." Ph.D. dissertation, University of Wisconsin, 1964.

———. *Politics Without Parties: Massachusetts, 1780–1791.* Pittsburgh, 1972.

Hamlin, Paul M. *Legal Education in Colonial New York.* New York, 1939.

Handlin, Oscar. *Boston Immigrants, 1790–1865: A Study in Acculturation.* Cambridge, Mass., 1941.

Handlin, Oscar, ed. *This Was America.* Cambridge, Mass., 1949.

———. *Facing Life: Youth and the Family in American History.* Boston, 1971.

———, and Handlin, Mary. *Commonwealth: A Study of the Role of Government in the American Economy: Massachusetts, 1774–1861.* New York, 1947.

Harno, Albert J. *Legal Education in the United States.* San Francisco, 1953.

Haskell, Thomas L. *The Emergence of Professional Social Science: The American Social Science Association and the Nineteenth Century Crisis of Authority.* Urbana, 1977.

Haskins, George L. *Law and Authority in Early Massachusetts: A Study in Tradition and Design.* New York, 1960.

Henretta, James A. *The Evolution of American Society, 1700–1815: An Interdisciplinary Analysis.* Lexington, 1973.

Hicks, Frederick C. *Yale Law School.* New Haven, 1936.

Holdsworth, William. *A History of English Law.* vol. 12. London, 1938.

Horton, John. *James Kent: A Study in Conservatism, 1763–1847.* New York, 1969.

Horwitz, Morton, J. *The Transformation of American Law, 1780–1860.* Cambridge, Mass., 1977.

Howe, Mark DeWolfe. *Readings in American Legal History.* Cambridge, Mass., 1949.

Hughes, Everett C. *Men and Their Work.* Glencoe, 1958.

Hurd, Hamilton, ed. *History of Worcester County.* 2 vols. Philadelphia, 1889.

Hurst, James W. *The Growth of American Law: The Law Makers.* Boston, 1950.

Hutchinson, Thomas. *The History of the Province of Massachusetts Bay, From 1749 to 1774.* Edited by John Hutchinson. 3 vols. London, 1828.

Jackson, Francis. *History of the Early Settlement of Newton, 1639–1800.* Boston, 1854.

Johnstone, Quintin, and Hopson, Dan, Jr., *Lawyers and Their Work: An Analysis of the Legal Profession in the United States and England.* New York, 1967.

Jones, E. Alfred. *American Members of the Inns of Court.* London, 1924.

Katz, Michael B. *The Irony of Early School Reform: Educational Innovation in Mid-Nineteenth Century Massachusetts.* Cambridge, Mass., 1968.

Kilbourn, Dwight C. *The Bench and Bar of Litchfield County, Connecticut, 1709–1901.* Litchfield, 1909.

Kohn, Hans. *American Nationalism.* New York, 1957.

Kraus, Michael. *Intercolonial Aspects of American Culture on the Eve of the Revolution.* New York, 1964.

Krause, Elliot A. *The Sociology of Occupations.* Boston, 1971.

Labaree, Benjamin. *Patriots and Partisans: The Merchants of Newburyport, 1764–1815.* Cambridge, Mass., 1962.

Levy, Leonard W. *The Law of the Commonwealth and Chief Justice Shaw.* Cambridge, Mass., 1957.

Lewis, Alonzo, and Newhall, James R. *History of Lynn, Essex County, Massachusetts.* Boston, 1865.

Lincoln, William. *History of Worcester, Massachusetts, from Its Earliest Settlements to September, 1836.* Worcester, 1862.

Lipset, Seymour, and Bendix, Reinhard. *Social Mobility in Industrial*

Society. Los Angeles, 1959.

Livermore, Shaw, Jr. *The Twilight of Federalism: The Disintegration of the Federalist Party, 1815–1830.* Princeton, 1962.

Lubove, Roy. *The Professional Altruist: The Emergence of Social Work as a Career, 1880–1930.* Cambridge, Mass., 1965.

Lynn, Kenneth, ed. *The Professions in America.* Boston, 1963.

McClellan, James. *Joseph Story and the American Constitution.* Norman, 1971.

McCormick, Richard P. *Experiment in Independence New Jersey in the Critical Period, 1781–1789.* New Brunswick, 1950.

McDonald, Forrest. *E Pluribus Unum: The Formation of the American Republic, 1776–1790.* Boston, 1965.

———. *We The People.* Chicago, 1958.

McKirdy, Charles. "Lawyers in Crisis: The Massachusetts Legal Profession, 1760-1790." Ph.D. dissertation, University of Wisconsin, 1969.

Main, Jackson T. *Political Parties Before the Constitution.* Chapel Hill, 1973.

———. *The Social Structure of Revolutionary America.* Princeton, 1965.

Mann, Herman. *Historical Annals of Dedham, from Its Settlement in 1635 to 1847.* Dedham, 1847.

Massachusetts Bar Association. *Minimum Fee Schedule: Adopted September 13, 1967.*

Mayer, Marvin. *The Lawyers.* New York, 1966.

Morgan, Edmund S. *Puritan Dilemma: The Story of John Winthrop.* Boston, 1958.

——— and Morgan, Helen M. *The Stamp Act Crisis: Prologue to Revolution.* Chapel Hill, 1953.

Morison, Samuel E. *Intellectual Life of Colonial New England.* 2d ed. Ithaca, 1963.

———. *The Life and Letters of Harrison Gray Otis: Federalist, 1765–1848.* Boston, 1913.

———. *Three Centuries of Harvard, 1636–1936.* Cambridge, Mass., 1936.

Morris, Richard D. *Studies in the History of American Law.* 2d ed. New York, 1963.

Mott, Frank L. *A History of American Magazines, 1741–1850.* New York, 1930.

Nelson, William E. *Americanization of the Common Law.* Cambridge, Mass., 1975.

Newcomer, Lee N. *The Embattled Farmers: A Massachusetts Countryside in the American Revolution.* 2d ed. New York, 1971.

Northend, William D. *Address Before the Essex Bar Association, December 8, 1885.* Salem, 1885.

Nye, Russel B. *The Cultural Life of the New Nation, 1776–1830.* New

York, 1960.

Parker, Joel. *The Law School of Hårvard College.* New York, 1871.

Parsons, Theophilus, Jr. *Memoir of Theophilus Parsons. . . .* Boston, 1859.

Plymton and Marett. *To Be Sold at Public Auction . . . the Library of the Late Ebenezer Rockwood.* Boston, 1815.

Polishook, Irwin H. *Rhode Island and the Union.* Evanston, Illinois, 1969.

Pound, Roscoe. *Readings on the History and System of the Common Law.* 2d ed. Boston, 1913.

———. *The Formative Era of American Law.* New York, 1950.

———. *The Lawyer from Antiquity to Modern Times.* St. Paul, 1956.

Quincy, Josiah. *Memoir of Josiah Quincy Jr.* Boston, 1825.

———. *The History of Harvard University.* 2 vols. Boston, 1860.

Reader, William J. *Professional Men: The Rise of the Professional Classes in Nineteenth Century England.* London, 1966.

Reed, Alfred A. *Training for the Public Profession of the Law.* New York, 1921.

Robson, Robert. *The Attorney in Eighteenth Century England.* Cambridge, Mass., 1959.

Rudolph, Frederick. *The American College and University.* New York, 1962.

Shafer, Henry B. *The American Medical Profession, 1783–1850.* New York, 1936.

Smith, Alan. "Virginia Lawyers, 1680-1776: The Birth of an American Profession." Ph.D. dissertation, John Hopkins University, 1967.

Smith, Brian Abel, and Stevens, Robert. *Lawyers and the Courts: A Sociological Study of the English Legal System, 1750–1965.* Cambridge, Mass., 1967.

Smith, Charles Page. *James Wilson: Founding Father, 1742–1796.* Chapel Hill, 1956.

Smith, Frank. *A History of Dedham, Massachusetts.* Boston, 1936.

Smith, J. E. *The History of Pittsfield, Massachusetts.* 2 vols. Boston, 1869-1880.

Stark, James H. *The Loyalists of Massachusetts and the Other Side of the American Revolution.* 2d ed. Clifton, N.J., 1972.

Sutherland, Arthur E. *The Law at Harvard: A History of Ideas and Men, 1817–1967.* Cambridge, Mass., 1967.

Sweet, William W. *Religion in the Development of American Culture, 1765–1840.* New York, 1952.

Taylor, Robert J. *Western Massachusetts in the Revolution.* Providence, 1954.

Thomas, Dorothy, comp. *Women Lawyers in the United States.* New York, 1957.

Tudor, William. *The Life of James Otis of Massachusetts.* Boston, 1823.

Warden, Gerald B. *Boston, 1689–1776.* Boston, 1970.

Warren, Charles. *A History of the American Bar.* 3d ed. New York, 1966.

———. *A History of Harvard Law School and of Early Legal Conditions in America.* 3 vols. New York, 1908.

———. *The Supreme Court in United States History.* 2d ed. 2 vols. Boston, 1926.

Washburn, George A. *Imperial Control of the Administration of Justice in the Thirteen American Colonies, 1684–1776.* New York, 1923.

Waters, John J. *The Otis Family in Provincial and Revolutionay Massachusetts.* Chapel Hill, 1968.

Waters, Thomas F. *Ipswich in the Massachusetts Colony.* 2 vols. Ipswich, 1917.

Welch, Richard E. *Theodore Sedgwick, Federalist: A Political Portrait.* Middletown, 1965.

Whittemore, Charles P. *A General of the Revolution: John Sullivan of New Hampshire.* New York, 1961.

Wikander, Lawrence E., et al., eds., *The Northampton Book . . . 1654–1954.* Northampton, 1954.

Willis, William. *A History of the Law, the Courts, and the Lawyers of Maine, from Its First Colonization to the Early Part of the Present Century.* Portland, 1863.

Zemsky, Robert. *Merchants, Farmers and River Gods: An Essay on Eighteenth Century American Politics.* Boston, 1971.

DIRECTORIES

Catalogue Universitatis Harvardiane, 1854. Cambridge, 1854.

Chapman, George T. *Sketches of the Alumni of Dartmouth College from 1771.* Cambridge, Mass. 1867.

The Connecticut Register. New London, 1820.

Dexter, Franklin. *Biographical Sketches of the Graduates of Yale College, 1701–1815.* 6 vols. New York, 1885-1911, New Haven, 1912.

———. *Biographical Notices of Graduates of Yale College.* New Haven, 1913.

Fleet, Thomas, and Fleet, John. *A Pocket Almanack.* Boston, 1780-1787.

———. *Fleet's Pocket Almanack . . . to Which Is Annexed the Massachusetts Register.* Boston, 1788-1800.

The Massachusetts Register and United States Calendar. Boston, 1801-1840.

Fletcher, Robert S., and Young, Malcolm D. *Amherst College: Biographical Record of the Graduates and Non-Graduates, 1821–1921.* Amherst, 1921.

Hall, Hubbard, ed. *General Catalogue of Bowdoin College and the Medical School of Maine, 1794–1912.* Brunswick, 1912.

Harvard University. *Catalogue of the Officers and Students of the University in Cambridge.* 20 vols. Cambridge, 1821-1840.

———. *Quinquennial Catalogue of the Officers and Graduates: 1636–1925.* Cambridge, 1925.

Maine Register and United States Callendar. Portland, 1820-1841.

Main, John, and Fleeming, Thomas. *Massachusetts Register.* Boston, 1767.

The New Hampshire Register. Concord, 1820.

The New York Annual Register. New York, 1840.

The Rhode Island Register. Providence, 1819.

Shipton, Clifford K., and Sibley, J. L. *Biographical Sketches of Those Who Attended Harvard College.* 17 vols. Boston, 1873-1975.

Vaughan, Mary D., ed., *Historical Catalogue of Brown University.* Providence, 1905.

Whitemore, William H. *The Massachusetts Civil List . . . 1630–1774.* Albany, 1870.

Index

ABOUT THE AUTHOR

Gerard W. Gawalt is an historical specialist at the Library of Congress. He has written articles for the *American Journal of Legal History* and the *Journal of Legal Education*, and is the editor of *Adventures of a Revolutionary Sea Captain: The Journal of Gideon Olmsted* and *Memoir of John Paul Jones.* He is assistant editor of *Letters of Delegates to Congress, 1774-1789.*